The Complete Career Makeover

NIC PATON

guardianbooks

Published by Guardian Books 2010

2 4 6 8 10 9 7 5 3 1

First published in Great Britain in 2010 by
Guardian Books
Kings Place, 90 York Way
London N1 9GU

www.guardianbooks.co.uk

A CIP catalogue record for this book is available from the British Library

ISBN 978-0-85265-149-0

Designed and typeset by www.carrstudio.co.uk

Printed and bound in Great Britain by Clays Ltd, St Ives PLC

CONTENTS

PREFACE

Good Christmas break, was it? Or were there moments when you felt strangely despondent about the prospect of returning to work? It's well known that the time and space for reflection you get over a holiday can often be the trigger for reassessing your career. Celebrating a birthday with a clunking great zero on the end of it can have the same effect. It may be you're returning to a sea of newly cleared desks all hinting, none too subtly, that this is no longer the job or career for you; or it may be that you are the one who now has no job to go back to. Perhaps you simply have a nagging sense that there is more to life than this; that for all the time, effort, commuting and stress you have put into getting where you are today, it's not where you want to be or what you want to be doing. If so, and however you've arrived at the realisation, this book is for you.

The first thing to say if you're considering changing career is you're unlikely to be alone. A recession, unsurprisingly, encourages people to hunker down in their jobs, sit tight, hope for the best and wait for the storm to pass. We may not be out of the woods yet economically but, as things start to recover and confidence returns, so more and more people are going to be looking up over their computers to check out the world outside. Back in the autumn, research by HR consultancy Chiumento suggested that one in five employees was what it labelled a 'corporate prisoner', an employee simply sitting on their hands waiting for the first opportunity to jump ship once the economy improved. Similarly, a poll in September by recruitment firm Robert Half predicted that more than a third of workers intended to move jobs when the recession ended.

However, it cannot be ignored that for many people the decision to change career in the current climate is because they no longer have a job to leave. The past 18 months has seen the workplace take a hammering, with jobs being cut within all sectors and industries and across all parts of the country. Even the public sector, once a byword for job security, has not been immune from cuts, with the possibility of even worse to come as the pressure to balance the country's finances intensifies.

What this means is that there are not only thousands of people who now have little choice but to change and reassess their lives to earn a crust, but also that even for those of us who have come through this recession with our livelihoods unscathed, the jobs landscape may have changed forever. A book such as this has never been more relevant than it is today.

Too old to change?

Underlying these (hopefully) short-term recessionary trends, the ageing of the population is another key factor encouraging people to look at the ins and outs of changing career. According to the Office for National Statistics, by 2031 the population of England alone is set to have risen by nearly a fifth, to 60.4 million, with the number of people who will be at state retirement age rising by 58 per cent in the same period. The workplace thinktank The Work Foundation has also estimated that by 2050 the average age for an employee in the workplace will be 43 and people will have to wait until they are 68 years old before they will normally be able to pick up their carriage clock.

Improved healthcare and rising levels of affluence – despite the blip of the recession – mean people are living longer. Yet, with the country's pension provision and retirement saving in a mess, many people are being forced to work longer to fund their golden years. Last spring, for example, research by the National Endowment for Science, Technology and the Arts estimated that some 12 million people (or by its calculations about half the UK workforce) were putting nothing aside for their old age. So the idea of someone moving on to a second or even a third career throughout their (much longer) working life is no longer that unusual.

Frustration that you started out on the wrong foot can play its part in a desire to change career, too. The vocational qualifications body City & Guilds recently reported in a poll that nearly six out of 10 people felt the careers advice they got from school was unsatisfactory, with barely a fifth ending up in careers that had been recommended to them. How many of us, therefore – present 'lost generation' of school leavers struggling to find any work at all probably excepted – have essentially fallen into a job after leaving school, sixth form, college or university because it looked half decent, offered the prospect of reducing our debts and, most of all, simply because it was available? It's very easy then to wake up three, five, 10 years down the line with an expensive mortgage, loan repayments to meet, possibly a burgeoning family or caring responsibilities and find it's actually going to be much harder than you thought to leave behind the comfort blanket of a regular monthly cheque and change direction from that 'temporary' career choice you made all those years ago. The material benefits of a working life, the enjoyable social network of work friends you go out with in the evenings and the occasional promotion, pay rise or extra responsibility can all end up gradually diluting those aspirations and ambitions you initially set out with until you suddenly wonder, 'How did I get here?'.

How this book can help

A survey a little over a year ago for the Association of Colleges concluded that millions of people were already thinking about or planning to change their career, with the recession a key factor in their decision making. More than eight million people had already switched career in the previous three years, it calculated, with a further three million keen to follow their lead.

Which is where this book comes in. It isn't going to tell you which is the right career for you or, even, outline how specifically you should get there – that's up to you. What it will do, however, is show you the steps you need to be taking to make the transition a reality and to sustain your new working life. We'll look at the challenges of gaining a new qualification or skill and then, just as importantly, how to turn this training into a new career. Then we'll examine the central issues around turning your back on corporate life and offer advice on how to make a success of striking out on your own. As career changing is of course not solely about downshifting, we will also address the ins and outs of returning to corporate life after time out of the workplace, overcoming ageism and redundancy and how to recapture career momentum.

Changing career, changing direction and pursuing a long-held dream is something eminently attainable. Even if right now you feel stuck not so much in a rut as in a deep and slippery trench of a career, it can be done. You may question whether you can afford to change tack, or feel that in these uncertain times it is madness to leave the safety and security of the job you are in. You may be hesitant about spending a redundancy cheque on going back to college, starting again at the bottom of a new career ladder or gambling everything on setting up in business. However, once the seed of career change has germinated in your brain, once you've stuck your head above the parapet that has been your career and seen there might be green fields beyond, it's very hard to go back – and there's a lot to look forward to.

How to use this book

This book is divided into two main sections. The first section is focused on the ins and outs of retraining, so evening classes, vocational training, further education and higher education. We'll be looking at study at undergraduate level, for those taking their first tentative steps into a university environment, and at postgraduate level for those whose university days are perhaps now a somewhat distant memory.

Within this, there are chapters on how to go about identifying the right new career for you, working out what new skills and qualifications you are likely to need, how to find the right course and how to fund your studies. The practical challenges of juggling study with home, family or an existing career are examined, and we shall be taking a look at how the world of education and learning has changed from when you might have been in it last.

Once you are the proud possessor of your new qualification, you'll need to know how to make the transition from your previous paid employment – your comfortable, safe life where you had years of experience behind you – to the brave new world of your new career. This guide will show you how to build up work experience in your new field, rework your CV, shine in interviews and convince an employer that you have what it takes.

The second section of this book is focused on how to launch yourself out into the world of self-employment and be your own boss. This is something that many of us who have spent years feeling ground down by our own bosses yearn to do, but, particularly in the current economic climate, is not a decision to be taken lightly.

There are chapters covering what you need to think about before you set up in business and the practicalities and different options available when you do decide to take the plunge. We shall also examine a few possible alternatives, such as franchising, freelancing and contracting, that can still leave you being the boss but are perhaps not quite as full-blown as running your own independent enterprise or small business.

At the back you will find a resources section that gives details of a few useful websites and organisations where you can find out more.

What is clear from the accounts of the career changers whose stories you will read here is that changing direction is not something to be rushed into. It will probably not be easy and may require a significant financial commitment, either because you are spending money on gaining qualifications or establishing a business, or just because you are losing a previously lucrative income. It will also require a major emotional and time commitment, not only from you but also from your nearest and dearest. It will take perseverance and single-mindedness and there will probably be knock-backs and challenges along the way.

If changing your career was easy there would probably be little point in writing this book. But what comes through loud and clear from the career changers I have spoken to is how passionate and enthusiastic they are about their new careers, how they now look forward to their working day and don't for a minute regret what they have given up or sacrificed to make that change. You too can be one of those people. Good luck.

Nic Paton, January 2010

Introduction

CHANGE YOUR CAREER, YOUR LIFE, OR JUST YOUR JOB?

We all sometimes have bad days at work, days when we wonder why we bother or what it's all for. The start of a new year is also a natural point at which to sit back and re-evaluate. But the fact that it's cold and grey, dark by mid-afternoon and everyone is miserable and penniless after Christmas is not reason enough to change career, however much you feel you want to. The central message of this book is that changing your career is not something you should do on a whim; it should be the result of a series of carefully thought through steps and stages, each one taking you a little further along the new path you have set for yourself, a path that may not always go in a straight line.

If you're seriously thinking this year is going to be it, the year when you finally get on and take charge of where your life is going, the first thing to say is, congratulations – in a world where it is so easy to put decisions off and settle for second best, you've already leapt a major hurdle. It's also, however, the easy bit. In a moment we're going to plunge into the world of retraining and gaining the new qualifications and skills to set you on the path to your new career. But, before you even get to thinking about these sorts of practicalities, you need to spend a bit of time assessing where you are in your career right now, what you have achieved so far and what your current job can still offer you.

Given that this book is called *The Complete Career Makeover*, this may appear to be a rather curious place to start. Surely the fact you are reading this at all means you have already made the decision to change? Perhaps. It may well be that you are already clear on this in your own mind and are

1

adamant this is the new start you need. Nevertheless, one of the most important, and earliest, decisions you need to make is: do I need to change my career at all?

Don't jump too quickly

There may, superficially, be a lot that you feel is wrong with your current job, but if all you need to do is change job, that's a much less significant decision than deciding on a wholesale change of career. Nowadays people do change direction more frequently throughout their working lives; the idea of a job for life in one place or one industry has long gone. But a career change is not just for Christmas; we're not just talking about what you are going to be doing next, but possibly what it is you are going to be doing for the rest of your life.

So it's a question of sitting down and coolly and calmly blotting out the latest hurt or humiliation, going through what it is about your job that sticks in your throat and what elements of it still actually work for you. It may be there are parts of what you do that you still enjoy and all you really need to do is transfer into something that will let you focus on using those skills more effectively and rewardingly. It may be, too, that you're hacked off because you've not been given the responsibility you feel you deserve, or you've been landed with too much responsibility that you never wanted in the first place. In such situations it may be a question of evaluating a) whether the leadership or managerial role you want is ever going to materialise and whether, if not, you'd be better off doing a sideways or upwards move somewhere else or b) whether you can pull back from the managerial side of things without harming your career chances irreparably, perhaps by moving into another area within your organisation that feels more suitable for you.

Is it just a clash of personalities?

Similarly, if it's just the personalities that are wrong – that you hate your boss or feel like a fish out of water compared with how you felt in other offices or workplaces, it may simply be that you need to change that environment, move to another department or apply for a similar role somewhere else. If it's because you feel hard done by, perhaps because you feel you have been overlooked, either financially or in terms of your role or responsibility, it may be a case of needing to have a proper conversation with your manager about your ambitions and what the company can offer.

In these situations the key is to keep it constructive – make it clear you want to offer your firm more, even if means a change of role rather than a more senior one, and that you are still committed. And don't try the old 'if I don't get my way I'm going to walk' gambit unless you're prepared for your bluff to be called. Incidentally, if your overriding reason for wanting to change is a desire for more money, perhaps because you think you are worth more than you're being paid, then it is more than likely a new job rather than a new career that you should be after. Changing career will often involve retraining or going back a number of steps for the greater long-term good, or taking a gamble on self-employment – neither options that are likely to make you your fortune, or at least not straightaway, and so you may very well be more worse off materially than before you started.

Beware the grass appearing greener

As Charles Bethell-Fox, deputy managing director of recruitment firm Personnel Decisions International, makes clear, if you're unhappy with what you've got it's often human nature to see anything else as better. The danger is that you end up ignoring or overlooking the good points of your situation and only recognise what you had and have given up further down the line when it is too late.

'When people are in a particular situation, it is very easy for them to imagine that another situation will somehow be better than the one they are in. Typically, people will be acutely aware of the negative aspects of their current situation, along with the positive aspects of the alternative, future scenario they are thinking about, because that is often just how people are,' he says.

'People focus on the future because it is not what they are experiencing right now. But you have to be wary that your expectations may not match the reality. It is very easy to draw conclusions about your life and career that are one-sided.

'You may in fact find that all you need to do is to change your outlook and approach to your existing career, to do a sideways move to something or somewhere you enjoy more, than have to change your career completely. Then again, it may be that the more you find out about it, the more you are convinced this new career is for you,' he emphasises.

'Either way, what is important is that you do need to be aware of the fact that your brain can play tricks on you and make you think that something over the horizon is better for you than what you are currently doing. People make better choices when they are better informed,' Bethell-Fox adds.

It's the recession, stupid

In the current climate there may be wider economic issues to take into account as well. If there have been a large number of redundancies where you work it could be that you simply need to start working through the contingencies as quickly as you can in case it's you next. If you suspect your employer is in financial difficulties, or even that the career prospects for the industry you have committed yourself to have changed irrevocably as a result of the downturn and recession then, clearly, you need to be taking a long, hard look at your career path and likely next steps.

Whatever the context for your decision making, the key thing to be bearing in mind here is that handing in your notice is going to be a major, major decision. Even if you subsequently change your mind during your notice period, you may not be able to reverse that decision and, even if you can, it may harm your longer term promotional prospects.

At a practical level, when handing in your notice, it makes sense to do so from a position of strength, so not immediately after you've just had a huge row with your boss, as it'll look like a fit of pique, or impulsively when you have nothing else lined up. This is why the more forward planning you can do from the safety of your existing employment (though being wary that forward planning does not become an excuse for prevarication and delay) is a good idea. Whether it is ensuring you have a place on whatever course it is you want to go on, the nugget of your business plan in place or, at the very least, your next step mapped out, it's going to be a much more constructive conversation with your manager. They may even end up enviously wishing you well.

Some other practical points to bear in mind include deciding whether it makes sense to have used up any holiday entitlement before you hand in your notice. This will ensure you don't lose what is rightfully yours to take, plus, because you will be there right to the final hurrah, may help to smooth any tensions caused by your leaving (though whether you or they will care by that stage is a moot point).

Careful planning of when you hand in your notice should also, of course, allow you to work through some of the financial implications of what you are about to do. So, for example, it should give you more time to build up savings to tide you over or ensure you have whatever study funding you need already in place. Of course, if it's redundancy that has brought you to this book, you are unlikely to have the luxury of being able to choose the timing of your notice or the chance of planning it all out that carefully in advance – unless you have been offered a significant financial cushion, that is.

The self-audit

Assuming you've come to the conclusion that it is not the job or the personalities alone that are wrong, that it is actually your line of work itself that is the problem, then you may well be right in believing what you need is a change of career. So, given that you don't want to repeat the mistakes you made before and that, by reaching this conclusion you've now opened up a whole new world of possibilities, how do you decide what is the right sort of new career for you?

Faced with the vastness of a question like this – akin in a way to 'What do I want to be when I grow up?' – it makes sense to go back to basics. A great place to start is by doing what you can call a self-audit, though soul-searching pretty much sums it up too. So, has there been something you've always hankered to do and – assuming it's not become a fighter pilot, Prime Minister, Prima Ballerina or open the batting for England – is it something you might be able to achieve, realistically, at this point in your life?

If you have a hobby you are passionate about outside of work, assessing whether that has the potential somehow to become a career can make sense. But a couple of cautionary points should be made here. It is very easy to think a hobby can make you an income, yet often the reality of turning something that might easily make you a few pennies into something that provides a sustainable monthly wage can be much more challenging. Also, do you enjoy it precisely because it is a hobby that you can lose yourself in when you come home? Therefore, if it becomes the job you do all day every day, will you risk losing what was most valuable or enjoyable about it?

A good, simple and very practical exercise you can do here is to write down what it is you enjoy doing and what it is you don't want to do – this might be as wide as 'working outside' or 'not working in an office' to narrower desires or dislikes, such as working with disadvantaged people or wanting to be beside the sea, or whatever it might be. You may want to think about other basic things such as whether you want to work full-time or part-time, for yourself or for someone else, or, possibly, to start off working for someone else with the longer term aim of striking out on your own. This 'what I like/don't like' exercise may not in itself provide the full answer, but what it will do, especially if you do it a number of times each time narrowing it down, is get you thinking about things in a logical, structured way that will allow you to cross off some things and open up your thoughts to new suggestions.

Ask your audience

While doing this it makes sense to have a few heart-to-heart discussions with friends or close family, who may have long seen a talent latent in you that you have not spotted, or simply have ideas you may not have thought of. But you do need to be wary of starting this sort of conversation with someone who is simply going to try and scare you off, urge you not to take the risk or pour cold water on your ideas. Of course you don't want to gamble your future or your health on some hare-brained idea, but all we're doing at the moment is widening and narrowing options, nothing else, so let your imagination rip and then gradually bring it back to reality.

Unfortunately, unless you are independently wealthy or very, very lucky, reality – the mundane, practical day-to-day considerations of our everyday lives – does need to come into play. Will you, for example, have a family or elderly relatives to support during the career-changing process, and if so how much income can you afford to lose if you need to retrain or go back various career stages? Will you need (or want) to relocate or downshift and, if so, what, again, is this likely to mean for your children or partner? How will it affect your finances if you need to sell or buy a property, particularly a business premises? How long, realistically, can you give the career-changing process?

While one of the key messages of this book is that it is never too late to start, you may need to think carefully about how it is going to work if you are looking to enter a profession with a set-in-stone retirement age, especially if you are already near that age and will need to spend time retraining to get there. You may, of course, still be able to make it work, and you won't want to self-select yourself out just because of your age, but if you are likely to come up against an age barrier, whether implicit (perhaps because it is predominantly a 'young' industry though never actually stated out loud) or explicit, it is something you need to be thinking about.

It also makes sense to try and plot out at least an estimated timeframe for what you want to have achieved and where you want to be within a certain period. You may not stick to it and things can always change, but if you map out, say, a five-year plan for getting from A to B it can certainly help to focus the mind and bring any financial or family issues into much sharper relief.

Picking yourself up after redundancy

The blow of redundancy can fall in different ways. It is, of course, a financial blow, because the security of a regular wage is suddenly snatched away from you. But it can also be a harsh psychological blow, especially if you are the sort of person who has never been out of work before, has always been in demand, been the breadwinner, and has never claimed a benefit in their life. So much of our day-to-day life, often our very identity, is wrapped up in our work and the hours we spend there that to lose it, even if you know you are not the only one in the current climate going through this, can be deeply traumatic. It can take time to recover, time you often don't feel you have if debts and other pressures begin to crowd in.

If you're fortunate, your redundancy will have brought with it a cheque big enough to give you a bit of a breathing space and, if you're even luckier, access to what is called an outplacement service. There is often some confusion about what outplacement services are and do. There can be an assumption that their primary role is to parachute you as quickly as possible into a replacement job, ideally one vaguely commensurate with your skills and ability. Or, to the more cynical among us, they can appear to be a bit of a sop, something nice but relatively ineffectual provided by the employer to lessen public anger and, more importantly, head off any potential tribunal or court cases over the redundancy process. The reality, as ever, is probably somewhere in between.

Yes, a minority of employers do provide outplacement services with more of an eye on their public reputation than because of any sense of benevolence towards the workforce they are shedding. Yet at the same time, outplacement services can be a very useful resource for the newly redundant, particularly in helping them look at new careers and directions in life, and if it's offered it should definitely be something you consider taking up. But don't expect even the best outplacement service to be able to conjure you up a new job or career instantly. This is particularly pertinent when companies have been cutting jobs across the board as many have been for the past 18 months to two years, says Stuart Lindenfield, head of transition services at Reed Consulting.

'What an outplacement service can do is to help people take control of their careers,' he stresses. 'It may be that they are not going to be able to find something identical, especially if the product their company has been making is no longer in demand or there are just not the jobs out there. So it can be more complex. For someone older, for example, it might be just about prompting them not automatically to consider retirement or semi-retirement but to look at what they can still do.

'For many workers, when they are made redundant, the impulse is to get another job, any job, as quickly as possible. But you often have to work through the whole process of having lost your job – if you are not in the right place psychologically you are not going to come across well in a new job interview,' he adds.

'So it is not necessarily all about the speed at which you find your next job, for some people it is more about determining the right role or even the right career for them in the future,' he explains.

A good outplacement firm should be able to offer workers help on the psychological shock of redundancy, with many agencies running special workshops designed to help former employees think positively about the future and build up 'resilience'. On top of this, it should be able to help you look more widely at your options and how to access training, as well as offering practical help on things such as CVs.

Of course, none of this will be much help if you are simply out on your ear with just a month's salary in your pocket. In that scenario, clearly, finding paid employment as fast as you can will be the priority. Nevertheless, if you can, do try to use your redundancy as a reality check, as a moment to re-evaluate what it is you are doing, where your career is going and in what direction your future lies.

Even if you spend the next year doing whatever pays because you have to, try to carve out the time and space to think through some of the questions we have outlined above and not just fall back into any old job just because it is there. Having a career is about far more than that.

Part One

RETRAINING

FIRST STEPS TO A NEW YOU

It'll still be early days, but hopefully at this point you should have an idea of the basic job, vocation or career you want to move into. Coastguard, plumber, librarian, dog walker, teacher, pub landlord – whatever it may be, you've at least got the kernel of an idea to play with. What you need to do now is find out what this new career is really like, how you get into it, what qualifications you will need for entry and, most crucially of all, how you in particular are going to get there.

The internet is a good place to start. The graduate careers service Prospects **www.prospects.ac.uk**, for example, while nominally aimed at graduates and school leavers, has on its website a wealth of information about different types of jobs and careers, including basic descriptions of many industries and the types of roles within them. The site GradPlus **www.gradplus.com** offers similar information, as do many of the general online recruitment websites out there, including the *Guardian*'s **http://careers.guardian.co.uk**. The training body City & Guilds also has a comprehensive database of careers, at **www.cityandguilds.com/18495.html**. So use them. One of the great things about spending time looking at these sorts of profiles is that, even if you have a specific industry or career in mind, it may be you discover roles and jobs within it that you have not thought of.

Research, research, research

To pick an example pretty much at random, if you have come to the conclusion you'd like to become a graphic designer, a quick trawl on Prospects will show you it's a role that requires skills such as working to a brief, creative flair, up-to-date technical knowledge of industry software and good time and cost management. It outlines the various day-to-day

MAKING THE CHANGE

THE EXPERT'S VIEW

Corinne Mills is career management spokesperson for recruitment website Monster.co.uk and managing director of careers coaching firm Personal Career Management.

If you've been sitting comfortably in a career for a few years and then suddenly find you are once again out in the jobs market, either because you have deliberately chosen to change direction or it has been forced on you by redundancy, it can be a daunting experience.

There is now so much information and advice available online to people thinking of changing their career that it can be both a blessing and a curse. It's a blessing because there are a huge number of resources you can turn to and reams of information you can download and read. But it's a curse because you need to distil it down, find what's right for you and make sure what you have found has come from a credible source.

The jobs market has also become incredibly competitive, particularly in the current economic climate. Because jobs tend to be so widely advertised there are likely to be many more people applying for every job, so it is even more important to find ways to differentiate yourself from the crowd and, particularly, to get ahead by networking.

The first thing you need to do if you are thinking of changing career is to start seriously researching your new career. It's easy to get excited and impatient at the prospect of changing direction if you are bored or frustrated, but you have to do the legwork first. In many ways there has never been a better time for career changers – people are re-evaluating their careers, having to change direction because of redundancy or simply having to work longer, often in new careers, to fund their retirement. There are also more options and outlets for adult training than ever before.

Think about what isn't working in your current role

As well as looking hard at what your new career will entail and demand, you also need to take a long look at what it is you don't like about your current work or career.

What you want to avoid is jumping into something that simply ends up replicating the situation you were in before. So it may be, when you think about it, that the job you are doing is actually fine but you just have a horrible boss. But if it's the actual nature of the work that you are doing that is getting you down, that it just does not engage you, it may indeed be time to look for something else.

The other thing to bear in mind is that you may not need to change direction dramatically. People often assume career changing is about moving to something completely different – and for some people it is. But you may not need to throw the baby out with the bathwater, and it may be that all you need is a subtle change. It may be, for example, that the change you need to make is simply to highlight an aspect of your existing job that you particularly enjoy, but perhaps in a different environment. The advantage of this is that it is generally much easier to do and you are less likely to have to take a salary cut, which probably will be the case if you need to start again from scratch.

It's also worth looking at whether it's your career or you that is at issue. This can be hard, and may involve some self-analysis, but if you are consistently falling out with your managers or colleagues it may not be that the job is wrong but that you need to become your own boss and start your own business. Or you may need to look at your interpersonal skills or whether there is some other underlying issue that is causing you unhappiness.

A job for life?

To be honest, the whole idea of the 'psychological contract' with your employer – of having a job for life – probably disappeared about 10 to 15 years ago, and I don't think many people are under any illusion, particularly in the current recession when huge swathes of people have been losing their jobs, that there are any 'safe' careers anymore. Even the banks, once seen as some of the safest and most secure professions anywhere, have lost that reputation. In this environment, the idea of a 'portfolio career', where you do different jobs and carve out different careers over a lifetime, or the notion of moving into a second or third career, or even self-employment is no more risky, and maybe even safer, nowadays than having one permanent job.

What employers look for from career changers is clear evidence not only that you have acquired the relevant new skills but that you have also got some experience under your belt. So don't just concentrate on retraining, look at what practical experience – and it may even need to be voluntary initially – you can get. Speak to people who are in the profession you are aiming for and get as much help and advice as you can. Even if you are only nearly qualified and the right job comes up, being able to say you have got some experience too shows you need to be taken seriously and is a very powerful argument for why someone should take you on.

If you can show you have thought your new career through carefully, have researched it well, have taken constructive and logical steps to get there and done all you can to pick up relevant experience along the way, you will get there.

activities you are likely to be doing, such as drawing up a design to deadline and within budget, interpreting what a client wants yet thinking creatively, making presentations to clients, working with a range of media and software, accurately proofreading designs and so on.

You can get an idea of the sort of salary you can expect in this career, opportunities for career progression, typical hours, where in the country most agencies tend to be based and the potential for self-employment in the industry. Even more importantly from the career-change perspective, these sites will normally outline the sorts of skills and qualifications you are likely to need. So, continuing with the graphic design example, Prospects suggests a degree or Higher National Diploma-level qualification in an area such as graphic design, illustration, 3-D design, fine art, visual art, photography, film or television or communication design.

It also cautions that getting on to such a course is rare without completing a foundation course or a BTEC – and, don't despair, we're going to explain some of these more common education acronyms in the next chapter. The website goes on to suggest useful organisations to contact, in this case the Chartered Society of Designers and the International Society of Typographic Designers, as well as recommending other linked careers, such as animator, illustrator, web designer and so on.

Or how about getting away from the mouse and flickering screen and out into the great outdoors – the ambition of many a career changer – to become a nature conservation officer? Using this same process it's clear that without a relevant degree, ideally in an earth science such as ecology, geography, planning or sustainable development, you may well struggle to break into this profession. Candidates with Higher National Diplomas do sometimes get in, but graduate-level qualifications are better and sometimes even postgraduate master's qualifications are seen as a minimum requirement, points out Prospects. And all for a whopping starting salary of £12,000 to £14,000.

If you can't find an overview or job profile online it's worth trying to identify your target industry's relevant society or association – most sectors will have at least one – which should be able to help you out with relevant information and advice on qualifications for entry and common routes in.

Don't ignore what you already have

While the chances are that you will need to acquire a new qualification of some sort to make headway or just learn the ropes in your chosen career, it's important not to discount the skills and qualifications you will already have. Much as you carried out a self-audit of what you wanted and did not want to do, it's a good idea to carry out a 'skills audit' of what qualifications, attributes and qualities you will need to make the transition to your new life. The aim here is to pin down a) what you've already got b) what you don't have that you will need to acquire and c) how best to plug those gaps.

Within this, don't limit yourself to your formal, professional or academic qualifications. It may be, for instance, you have good interpersonal skills that will be useful in almost any environment, or that you're good with your hands or in technical areas such as computing. You may be very logical and analytical when it comes to dealing with problems or challenges. Perhaps, too, you have got foreign language skills, presentation skills, research or analytical skills that you may not have been using in your current job. The important thing is that you need to be looking not so much at your job title but the work you have been doing to do that job. Don't forget, either, that a now apparently irrelevant professional qualification from your previous career might nevertheless have given you some useful generic, transferable skills that could be applicable, even in just an informal way, to your new career.

Once you have identified your skills gaps, the next step is to work out how you are going to fill them. This might mean acquiring, as we have seen, some extra formal education, perhaps a vocational, undergraduate or postgraduate qualification, all of which we shall be looking at in more depth in the following chapters. It may be they are the sorts of skills you

MAKING THE CHANGE

From advertising to furniture making

Once a senior London advertising executive, Nick Gutfreund, 48, now runs a business designing and making fine furniture **www.NGfinefurniture.com**, based in Sheldon in the Blackdown Hills, Devon.

The catalyst for me was that my wife, Marie-Claire, and I had for a number of years been trying to have children but it hadn't worked and so I simply started to think 'What am I doing this all for?' I enjoyed my work well enough and knew I was good at it but I'd be leaving the house at 7am and sometimes not getting back until 11pm and I just started to re-evaluate what was important to me. Although I was in advertising I had never been a 'creative', I had been a 'suit' helping other people to fulfil their creativity, yet I had always loved making and creating things. So I felt I wanted something more fulfilling in that arena.

One night we sat down and had a long talk about life, what I was doing and what I wanted. I had come up with three options: photography, cooking and woodwork. I quickly discounted photography as being too close to my old world. While I loved cooking I didn't want to end up doing production-line cooking and I was worried that I would repeat myself and find myself slaving away at something I wasn't really enjoying; I wanted to keep it as a hobby. But with woodwork and creating fine furniture I knew it was probably something I could do and make a success of, as well as being something completely different from what I'd been doing before. I'd often made things for the house that seemed quite good, but I had never been trained. So by the end of the evening — well, several evenings and a whole load of research — we had come to the big decision that I needed to go back to college and retrain as a cabinetmaker and furniture designer.

Lots of people either said 'God, you're brave' or 'You're completely mad', and of course I knew it could all have gone wrong. We also had to accept we were no longer going to have the type of life, financially, that we had had before. Our quality of life was going to improve but materially it was not going to be the same, so we knew there would need to be an adjustment of our expectations. Before, we would not have thought twice about spending £200 on a meal out during the week – we would have felt we deserved it – or thousands on a holiday. But within days of coming back you'd feel just as drained and stressed as before you left.

Making the leap

I always think if you are going to do something this big and radical you have to make sure you are giving it as much chance of success as possible. I could have just rushed off and tried to start up a workshop but it wouldn't have worked, so I accepted I needed to go back to basics. I knew I needed to get a solid foundation and a specialist qualification if I was going to become anything more than just a cabinetmaker and be able to keep the wife and family.

After quite a bit of research I chose to do a City & Guilds course at the Building Crafts College in Stratford in London because I could do a NVQ level 2 foundation course in joinery, which would mean I could become a carpenter if I needed a fall-back, as well as a diploma in fine woodworking. The course ran over two years or six terms, although I managed to do it in five terms, completing it in August 2005.

After that it was a question of deciding how actually to make the transition. We were both keen to move back to the southwest – we are both originally from Bristol – in part for the quality of life, but also because setting up a workshop in London would have been prohibitively expensive. In a way, with something like this it doesn't matter where you are as long as you can travel to your clients, who can be anywhere in the country or even the world. So we literally picked out a nominal zone around the Devon, Somerset and Dorset borders that we reckoned would give us relatively easy access to both Bristol and London and their respective travel connections.

We hadn't planned to make the move until 2007 but in the interim we had adopted two girls, now aged six and eight, so we realised the sooner we were able to move the less upheaval and change it would be for them. There were of course also issues around what we could afford even after we had sold the London home, given that we would need a house and a workshop. Another factor that came into play was that after the course I had developed a mentoring relationship with a designer in Lingfield in Surrey, who invited us to come and look around. We decided at that point we would put our house on the market and simply see what happened. It sold for above the asking price within eight days.

One of the great things about having a mentor was that it meant I was able to set up, on a temporary, short-term basis, in his workshop and gain hands-on experience of how to run a workshop. You can get all the qualifications you like, but there is nothing like actual experience – and I really viewed it as an extension of my training. So I paid him £300 a month to rent some of his bench space and only had to provide my hand tools, which I already had, and could start getting the business established as well as bring in a little business for him. From my time in advertising and marketing I already had experience of dealing with clients and developing a workable brief, but in this line of work the delivery and end result are much more tangible.

The business is still relatively small – it's still only me – and the recession has made life a bit harder, but it is growing all the time. For example, I've recently completed my most prestigious commission – to make the Captain's table for the Royal Navy's newest destroyer *HMS Daring*.

Take your time

My best advice? Don't run before you can walk. Do the legwork and get qualified, then get some experience, perhaps through a mentor. Also, don't look too far ahead because otherwise you can get swamped by the enormity of it all. Take it in bite-sized chunks. Financially, if you can, keep some money back as a contingency fund for the unexpected – don't plan it right down to the last penny. And don't expect to be able to go back to college and then come out and straight away earn what you were making before. I am probably never going to get rich making furniture but that was, and is, not the point. I now have a very good, and definitely much better, quality of life. I get to spend loads of time with the children as well as a lot more time with Marie-Claire.

What's more, at the end of the day I have something to show for my work, something tangible that you can see and touch. When I get up in the morning now I look forward to work. I just love to walk into that workshop and create things.

can gain through on-the-job learning and, if so, you will need to look at how that's going to work in reality. You might need to work as an apprentice or under the mentorship of someone else for a few years while you learn your new trade, for example. It may also be a good idea to assess what skills and qualifications are vital to get under your belt right now, against what's important to acquire over time or once you're actually working in your new career.

Ask for professional help

As well as sounding out relevant industry associations or bodies, you may find it helpful to go and chat to a careers coach or adviser, particularly if there is one you can access for free. You may be able to find one through a local college, or try the government's Careers Advice Service, which can be found on the Directgov site, at **http://careersadvice.direct.gov.uk/**. If you're happy to spend a bit of money on this process there are also many professional careers coaches out there, but it is advisable to ensure they are reputable, with, for example, accreditation by the Association of Career Firms or the International Coach Federation. Prices will vary and it's a good idea to get a quote in advance so you know what it is likely to cost. Many coaches will offer an introductory session for free, after which you can probably expect to pay around £40–£50 for a 45-minute session, with some firms charging per appointment and others offering one to six-month packages where you get an agreed number of sessions for a fixed price.

The big advantage of using career coaches is that they will be able to look much more rationally at what you have done and your ambitions and come up with suggestions you might never have thought of yourself. They may also be able to offer a range of assessment tests to help you use more than your gut instinct to judge how you, say, relate to people, solve problems or what sort of person you are. On top of this they are likely to be able to assess your CV and what gaps you need to fill as well as give advice on marketing yourself, applying for jobs and being effective in interviews.

Help after redundancy

In the immediate aftermath of a redundancy, one place you may be able to access help and advice is Jobcentre Plus. Perhaps unsurprisingly, the service, provided by the Department for Work and Pensions, has been under severe pressure during the recession as the jobless total has continued to rise. This, in turn, has led to criticisms of its ability to help out-of-work

MAKING THE CHANGE

Olwyn Burgess is client services director at HR consultancy and careers specialist Chiumento.

It may sound obvious but it is worth spelling it out – if you're serious about changing direction or changing your career you need to spend quite a bit of time exploring what it is you really want to do. A lot of people, once they are in work, push to the back of their consciousness what it is they really want from their lives.

It might be redundancy that forces you to re-evaluate, family reasons, hitting a certain age or simply a realisation that the sector you have been working in is no longer going to work for you as a mode of employment. Whatever the reason, you need to, on paper, think both about what it is you grumble about in your work and what it is that makes you happy.

Look at the big picture

You also need to look at the other aspects of your life, how your social and personal or family life matches your work, how you see yourself and what work means to you in terms of identity and fulfilment, as well as money. You need to think about what you want from work but also what you don't want from it – what are the things you don't like about your work: is it the commute, the office environment, your boss or colleagues or the actual job that you do? It can be a good idea to ask yourself, if you were able to wake up and go off and do any job what would it be and how would it feel? Conversely, what would be your worst nightmare?

There are various exercises you can do, too. You can map out a lifeline for yourself, plotting out the highs and lows in your life and looking at when you have been happiest, what were you doing and, similarly, with the lows, whether there are any trends. So many people persevere in jobs where they are unhappy just because they get a bit stuck or because it offers a secure wage and they cannot see any alternative. But if you're not fulfilled, your self-esteem can end up being gradually eroded.

You can also work out what we call a wheel of life, where you apportion how you currently spend your time and can see how much you spend at work, how much on yourself, how much with your family and children and so on. Often it is only when people see it mapped out visually before them that they realise just how much of a treadmill they have been on. People almost always say they want to increase the amount of time they spend with friends and family and decrease what they spend at work. We get a lot of people coming to us who have been made redundant or have lost their job who, at first, say it is the end of the world and what are they going to do for money? But once they've been helped into something new they often wonder what was stopping them from making the change years earlier.

The best changes take time

Having said that, you do need to recognise that changing your career may not happen overnight. It may take longer than you think and you may have to take a pay cut, sometimes just for a few years but sometimes permanently. So you need to talk to your family and plan it very carefully. If you have been a high earner earning a six-figure salary, say, and are suddenly going to be downshifting or risking money on something you have always wanted to do, then that is inevitably going to affect your partner and any children you may have. You'll need their support and you have to consult them every step of the way.

You also need to look carefully and realistically at what sort of person you are. Are you, for example, a very collaborative person who thrives on the company of other people and works well in a team? If so, becoming self-employed from home, while a dream for many people, could end up being a very lonely existence. Similarly, when you are running your own business you may need to go out and sell or promote yourself and all the decisions and many of the jobs, however menial, can end up back with you, so you need to be the sort of person who thrives on that kind of pressure.

If you think you need new skills or retraining you cannot do too much research. So look at the colleges and courses around you, speak to tutors and admissions staff and (ideally) other students about what it's really like. Any learning or networking events and seminars that you can attend where you can speak to people who can advise you can often be helpful. You may, too, want to go a professional careers advice organisation – although it is a good idea to check whether they are members of the Association of Career Firms, which accredits the industry. There are also many self-help guides, organisations such as Jobcentre Plus and, of course, a lot of information on the internet.

Whatever choices you make, whether you simply change direction, accelerate your career or downshift, whether you end up earning more money or less, the result of successfully changing your career is that you are likely to be much better off emotionally and much happier. Ultimately, it is all about taking back control.

workers, particularly those who are more skilled or have been in managerial or professional roles. The *Observer* last year argued that many middle or high-income earners who had lost jobs were choosing not to visit their local Jobcentre because they did not believe they would be offered any relevant assistance or help.

Whatever the truth of this – which the DWP strongly refuted at the time – it helps to know that even if you are told you are not entitled to the full, means-tested jobseeker's allowance (perhaps because you have savings or a partner who is working), you may well still be entitled to the weekly contributory jobseeker's allowance. This is based on your National Insurance contribution record and is paid for a maximum of six months from when you sign on.

You can also ask to be referred to one of the service's recruitment specialists. This was something rolled out by the government last year but which jobseekers often complain is not mentioned in conversations with benefits advisers. For older career changers, it's worth asking about programmes such as the New Deal 50 Plus, designed to help more experienced people retrain and get new jobs. If you have a specific retraining need in mind, perhaps a vocational course or an access to further or higher education course, it is also definitely worth sounding out what assistance Jobcentre Plus may be able to offer in regard to fees, funding or locating a course. Don't assume the answer will be no – if you don't ask you'll never know.

Test the water

Finally, one of the best ways to work out what skills you are likely to need, as well as helping you crack the question of whether this is something you are cut out for, is simply to try it out. Now, clearly, you are not going to be let loose in an operating theatre just because you have a passion to be a surgeon or, ditto, put in charge of a famine relief operation or a lifeboat in rough seas. But, as Personnel Decisions' Charles Bethell-Fox explains, spending a bit of time trying something out, perhaps by shadowing someone for a day, offering to do a bit of volunteering in the field or even just speaking to people involved in your target career can be invaluable.

'What you need to do, as well as thinking about what sort of new career you might want, is actively to investigate it. There is nothing like actually trying something out to learn about what it is like. You might think something is more fun, perhaps because you do it as a hobby or you did it while on holiday, but until you genuinely try it you really don't know,' he emphasises.

'What you have to do, then, is have some down-to-earth, gritty conversations about it with people who are already doing it. You need to find out what the downsides to this new life are, and how people tend to manage them, as well as the positive sides.

'You'll be surprised how often people are happy to speak about what they do and to be open and helpful. You may – and it's a great thing to do if you can – be able to use up a day's holiday shadowing someone already doing that sort of work or job.

'Or you might just be able to go and see them and have a proper chat. Use any networks or friends or contacts that you have in the area – or contact that industry's trade, professional or sector association, or even your local business confederation or chamber of commerce, and see if they can help.

'It is all about filling gaps in your knowledge and getting a realistic job preview of what it is you want to go and do and how, in reality, you will be spending your time in this new role,' he advises.

Part 1: Chapter Two

FURTHER EDUCATION

Sixth form and further education colleges educate an estimated three million people a year, with mature students (who will often be career changers) one of the fastest growing groups. So, the good news is that going back into education at this level as a way to change your career is a well-worn path and one that colleges are definitely geared towards. However, navigating your route through the world of learning, either within further (by which we generally mean at a level below or up to university) or higher (university-level) education, can often be a bit confusing. First there's the jargon – BTECs, OCR Nationals, NVQs, HNCs, HNDs, entry-level qualifications and so on. There is a vast array of 'stuff' out there to plough through and make decisions about. From the deeply obscure through to the specialist and vocational, there are a huge number of courses in almost any subject you can think of. And learning is now delivered in many different ways, including online, in flexible modules that you can pick and choose from, conventionally within a classroom setting, or in the workplace.

A good time to learn

The past few years have seen an explosion in the number of schools, colleges, universities and academies that deliver different courses, with nearly 500 further education colleges and institutions around the UK. Then there's the profound impact that the internet has had on learning, meaning people can now learn from home or anywhere they can boot up their laptop. Further education (FE) colleges award half of all vocational qualifications and provide nearly half of the entrants to higher education and university, while nearly 200,000 people a year study higher education-level qualifications in an FE setting, according to the Association of Colleges.

What this all means is that, as we saw in the last chapter, it might well be clear that you are going to need an extra qualification or two to get you on the path to changing your career, but it may not be as simple as simply turning up at college *x* or enrolling on course *y*. There are important decisions you will need to make about where you should be studying, what level of course you should be doing (and whether or how you will then need to progress on to further study), what you should expect to be paying for the privilege and what funding support may be available.

Whatever level you need to study at to change your career, it should be stressed from the off that a guide such as this is not going to be a substitute for actually picking up the phone or physically going in and speaking to training providers, tutors, learning support and admissions staff. But what we can do is to remove some of the jargon and intimidating mystique that can often surround adult and mature education, and hopefully in the process help set you more clearly on the path to your new career.

Probably the best way to dip your toes into the murky waters of retraining, and before we get to the specifics of further education itself, is simply to go back to basics and take a bit of a canter through what all these different qualifications actually are and mean. After all, you may know you now need to gain, say, an NVQ or HND, but what does this actually mean or involve? What sort of skills will it give you, how long will it take to do, what will it cost and what sort of entry requirements are you likely to have to demonstrate?

Incidentally, for those who want to know more in this area, two pretty comprehensive resources out there when it comes to explaining all this are the government's Directgov website **www.direct.gov.uk/en/Education AndLearning/AdultLearning/index.htm** and the website of the Qualifications and Curriculum Authority **www.qca.org.uk**. Connexions Direct, though nominally for 13–19 year-olds, is also good **www.connexions-direct.com/index.cfm?pid=10**. It's also a good idea to check out the website of the relevant sector skills council for your chosen career, as these will normally be able to supply you with lots of useful information on the sort of qualification you need to be gaining as well as relevant education and training providers. A good place to start here is the Alliance of Sector Skills Councils at **www.sscalliance.org/**.

Entry-level qualifications

These are basic qualifications that sit at the bottom of what is called the National Qualifications Framework. To digress for a moment, the framework is essentially the template that schools and colleges in England, Wales and Northern Ireland (in Scotland it's called the Scottish Credit and Qualifications Framework) use to work out at what level a qualification should be recognised.

The framework, therefore, will bunch together qualifications that tend to place similar demands on you as a learner, rating them from 'entry' to level eight, with a course that is the equivalent to an A-level, for example, a level three, and one awarded at a level two as equivalent to a good GCSE. While we're on the topic, when we're talking about further education programmes what we normally mean is courses up to level three, from where you progress on to higher education. While FE colleges are primarily focused on the 16–19 (ie pre-university) age range, they also, as we have seen, now cater extensively to the needs of mature and adult learners, as well as often offering higher education-level courses.

Anyhow, entry-level courses are courses, often awarded as 'certificates' or 'awards', that can help you build up your basic skills, knowledge and confidence in areas such as English, science or maths or more vocational subjects such as retail, computer literacy or hairdressing. They come in three levels, one to three (though all still rated as level one on the National Qualifications Framework), and will normally be a stepping stone to a qualification such as a GCSE or NVQ or BTEC (of which more momentarily).

They are usually structured in units or modules, giving you some flexibility in how quickly you do them, with each unit assessed separately. While it will vary from college to college, they might commonly run for two hours once a week for a 30-week period and may take between one or two years to complete. Many further education colleges will often offer them for free, working on the assumption that they will lead you on to further study.

NVQs

National Vocational Qualifications (or in Scotland SVQs) are, as their name suggests, vocational or work-related qualifications focused on specific skills and knowledge needed to do a particular job effectively and to show, simply, that you are competent in that area.

So, if you want to retrain in, say, arboriculture (or tree care), you might look to get a level two NVQ (to recap, equivalent to a GCSE) and then move on to Higher National Diploma in something such as countryside management, or a level three NVQ in tree care. Essentially, they are nationally recognised occupational standards that show you are qualified. You can do them up to a level five, with assessment normally through on-the-job appraisal and training.

How long you take doing your NVQ will inevitably vary, but it will commonly take about a year to complete a level one or two NVQ and around two years for a level three. They are normally offered through further education colleges, often split between study days in the college and days 'in the field'. The cost, again, will differ and can range from free or a few hundred pounds to four figures. As an aside, you might also from time to time hear or come across the phrase GNVQs, or General National Vocational Qualifications – if you do, ignore it, because these more general introductory courses were phased out between 2005 and 2007.

GCSEs, AS and A-Levels

Perhaps some of the best known qualifications around, so we will not dwell overly on these. Suffice to say these are qualifications normally gained at age 16 or 18, though if you missed out or flunked them first time around, it is more than possible to go back and do them again.

They normally take two to three years to complete full-time, but longer of course part-time. AS levels are what are known as Advanced Subsidiary- (as opposed to Advanced) level qualifications and tend to focus on more traditional study skills. There are also now a range of more vocational A-levels, called GCEs, though currently only in 10 subject areas. Again, you are likely to be able to access such courses through a local further education college or a provider such as learndirect, of which more at the end of this chapter.

BTECs and OCR Nationals

BTEC qualifications and OCR Nationals are work-related qualifications, with subject areas ranging from art and design or business right through to public services, science and sport. BTECs go up as far as level seven on the National Qualifications Framework and OCR Nationals range from levels one to three. These courses will often be designed around a particular industry and will normally be delivered through a mix of theory, practice and work experience.

Sometimes you will be awarded what is called a 'technical certificate' or 'BTEC national diploma' on completion of your qualification, with assessment normally done by your teacher, trainer or an external examiner. These courses can be studied full-time or part-time, again normally through a further education college. They are often used as a stepping stone to a Higher National Diploma or Certificate. Fees, again, will vary, but should normally be in the hundreds rather than the thousands of pounds.

MAKING THE CHANGE

CASE STUDY: From the City to the classroom

Former investment banker Kevin Watson, 46, was made redundant in the last great City shake-out, after the dotcom bubble burst at the turn of the millennium. He has since re-made his career and become a physics teacher and head of year at Watford Grammar School for Boys.

When I left university in 1986 it was just at the point that the City was massively expanding and investment banks were paying more than anyone else, so it seemed like a great career to go into. I joined NatWest in 1987 and then moved into corporate finance, working for a number of banks such as JP Morgan and Dresdner Kleinwort.

Then in 2000 I was headhunted by Bear Stearns with a guaranteed three-year package. But it was at the same time as the bottom fell out of the market, and suddenly there was much less business being done.

To be honest, when the redundancy came in 2003 it was almost a relief because I had a very good idea it was going to happen sooner rather than later. It was clear they were going to make some redundancies and, to an extent, it is just the nature of the business. We could all see the writing on the wall and I, for one, was very happy to move on, although I was naturally concerned about what I was going to do as the next stage of my life.

At the time I was coming up to my 40th birthday and a lot of people in investment banking will tell you that you should leave by the time you hit that milestone. I had made enough money to pay off my mortgage and I had not been foolish with my money or had high expenses to maintain.

A lifestyle change

I also had three children who I had barely seen growing up because I had been working such long hours. Typically I would have been leaving the house at 6.45am and not getting home until 9.30pm. If I wasn't then travelling off somewhere on business at the weekend I was simply really tired and did not want to do much with them. So it wasn't hard to come to the view that it was now time to move on from investment banking.

Initially I thought I might still stay in financial services – I flirted with the idea of going into venture capitalism. I didn't rush making a decision, and was lucky in that I had a generous redundancy package and so had the financial space to consider my options. In fact the idea of changing to teaching did not come to me until about eight months after I had been made redundant.

It had always been something that I had been interested in, but the big stumbling block had always been the money. Compared to what I had been earning it was going to be much less. So, from the income side I really had to just discount it and recognise that there was simply not going to be as much money coming in as there had been.

But what was important was to think about what I really wanted from life, what really mattered to me. I knew I wanted to see more of my children and spend more time with my family and, once I had started on this track, I realised I got an awful lot of satisfaction out of teaching.

Rather than do a Postgraduate Certificate in Education, I opted to join the Training & Development Agency for Schools Graduate Teacher Programme, **www.tda.gov.uk/ Recruit/thetrainingprocess/typesofcourse/employmentbased/gtp.aspx** a one-year programme where you get on-the-job training in a school and a salary (anywhere from around £15,000), and which is specifically aimed at encouraging people who have been working in other areas to come into teaching. I did my training at Clement Danes School in Chorleywood and then moved to Watford Boys after two years.

New challenges in the classroom

It was hard work and you have to learn on your feet in the classroom. Anyone who has ever been into a classroom will realise very quickly that it is not an easy option. It is enormously challenging. Some of my banking experience in terms of pitching to potential clients or making presentations has certainly come in useful, as have the time management and organisation skills, listening and being able to negotiate.

You have to be prepared to start at the bottom. As a newly qualified teacher you will be treated as the lowest of the low, particularly by the kids, and walking into that classroom for the first time can teach you a huge dose of humility. But if you stick with it and adjust your lifestyle, it is a fantastic option. You have to be able to impose your will on the children while also making it an interesting and enjoyable lesson.

What I used to enjoy about investment banking, other than the money and lifestyle, was the intellectual cut and thrust, the challenge of working with some of the brightest individuals in their field and succeeding. And, in a way, teaching is quite similar. It is very difficult to teach a good lesson and come away from it knowing that people have enjoyed and really learnt something, that something has been achieved.

Every day is different and it can be challenging and exhausting, but it is hugely rewarding. For me, it is the only job that gets better with each passing year and I know it will tick all the right boxes for me until I retire.

Apprenticeships

Apprenticeships are usually aimed at younger workers and school leavers, last a year to two years and tend to be offered in sectors such as accountancy, construction, engineering and manufacturing – though there are many others. The idea is that you learn on the job, get paid a living wage (well, at least £80 a week) while also being trained to an NVQ level two or three.

Functional Skills and Skills for Life

Functional skills are new, practical qualifications due to launch this year that will be offered in English, maths, and information and communications technology (ICT). They will be available to anyone aged over 14 and will be woven into the training you get when you are doing apprenticeships, diplomas or GCSEs, though you will also be able to take them as stand-alone qualifications. They will replace the Skills for Life qualifications (though people will still be able to start such courses until at least August 2010) which are designed to improve people's basic reading, writing, numeracy and ICT skills. The functional skills qualifications are being offered at entry level and levels one, two and three on the National Qualifications Framework.

HNCs and HNDs

Higher National Certificates and Higher National Diplomas are work-related vocational higher education qualifications and are offered through higher education institutions and universities as well as through further education colleges.

HNCs normally take a year to complete full-time or two years part-time and HNDs two years full-time and longer part-time. They rate as level five qualifications on the National Qualifications Framework and will normally be assessed through assignments, projects and practical tasks. Most require that you have at least an A-level or equivalent qualification for admission.

At this level you can also get Diplomas of Higher Education, which are accredited professional qualifications, in areas such as accounting, construction, engineering or nursing or various sciences, technologies or design.

You may also be able to convert any of these qualifications into a full-blown bachelor's degree, with HNCs often allowing you to gain entry to the second year of a degree and HNDs sometimes even allowing you to fast track straight to the third year.

If this wasn't enough, there is something called a Certificate of Higher Education, which is broadly equivalent to an HNC but will tend to be for an academic rather than a vocational qualification. To complicate matters, you can also get undergraduate and postgraduate diplomas, often aimed at mature students who want to take part of a degree part-time, and possibly then in time progress on to the full degree qualification.

Diplomas

Not to be confused with undergraduate, postgraduate and higher education diplomas (even though they will all often be referred to simply as diplomas), diplomas are a relatively new qualification for 14–19 year olds, and so are unlikely to be hugely applicable for career changers.

Nevertheless, what they offer is a combination of academic learning within this age group and more practical, hands-on vocational training ¬ with subjects currently offered including construction and the built environment, engineering, information technology, 'society, health and development' and 'creative and media'. The intention is to have 17 of these in place by 2013 and they can be combined with GCSEs or A-levels.

Access to further and higher education courses

If you left school before doing A-levels but now reckon you need to get a further or higher education qualification under your belt to change your career, one answer may be to do an Access to Further or Higher Education Certificate or Diploma. Access to Further Education courses allow people to improve on their GCSEs so that they can move on to A-levels or diploma level courses, and may in turn lead to an Access to HE course.

Courses are normally taught through a combination of written projects and presentations and will look at things such as managing your learning, ICT, developing research skills, improving writing, punctuation and grammar, improving your learning in maths and science, and so on.

Access to HE courses are typically one-year courses where you will be studying for around 16 hours a week (though you are likely to be expected to add to this outside the formal study hours). They teach you all about studying at this level and the sort of work you are likely to be undertaking at university, and you'll gradually be building up credits as you go along.

Many universities and FE colleges offer these courses, and the fees are normally in the region of £500–£600, but costs will probably vary from college to college, with Access to FE courses normally coming out cheaper.

The Quality Assurance Agency for Higher Education, incidentally, has a good guide to access courses at **www.accesstohe.ac.uk**,while in Scotland there is the Scottish Wider Access Programme, **www.scottishwider access.org**.

Access courses are accepted by most universities and colleges as equivalent to a level three qualification (ie A-level).

There are no national minimum entry requirements to get on an access course, though it is likely you will need to have GCSEs at grade C or equivalent in subjects such as English, maths and/or a science. The criteria for an Access to HE diploma is often five GCSEs at grade C or equivalent, though, it is worth checking what exactly your local college requires as there may be some flexibility.

Colleges may look at your work experience or 'life skills' alongside your academic qualifications, as the emphasis is likely to be very much on encouraging you to make that potentially life-changing step back into education.

Foundation degrees

Unlike 'normal' bachelor's degrees, foundation degrees are designed and delivered in partnership with employers, and so will have a much more vocational feel to them. They are also sometimes described as 'intermediate-level' degrees, in that academically they are the equivalent of the first two years of a bachelor's degree and so will often lead on to conversion to a bachelor's degree and higher education more generally, or straight to a job in the relevant field.

Perhaps the biggest difference between foundation and bachelor's degrees is their emphasis on work-based learning, with learning often taking place on employers' premises. They can be taken through either further and higher education colleges and universities, with courses normally offered through a combination of part-time, full-time, modular, distance learning or online-based learning. Foundation degrees will usually take two years to complete full-time.

There are normally no set entry requirements and courses tend to be assessed in different ways, often through a mix of exams and coursework as well as assessment of your work in the workplace. You may also be required to submit a dissertation at the end of your course. Fees will vary and may be charged on a modular basis meaning, in other words, you pay per module as you study, with £200 per module (part-time) or around £3,000 per academic year (full-time) a good rule of thumb. Foundation degrees are a popular option at FE level, with FE colleges awarding more than half of all such degrees.

Bachelor's degrees

Also known as a 'first' degree, bachelor's degrees are what you go off to do at university for three or four years, although some courses (such as medicine) will take considerably longer, and it is possible to do such degrees part-time or flexibly. It is also possible to do degrees primarily within the FE setting, and which are then accredited by a higher education institution.

We'll be looking at the whole university experience in much more detail in the next chapter, but you will normally choose to do either a Bachelor of Arts (BA) or a Bachelor of Science (BSc) degree, though there are others, such as Bachelor of Medicine (MB) or Bachelor of Engineering (BEng).

You will attain either an ordinary or unclassified degree or, at the higher level, an honours degree, rated either as a first, upper second (2:1), lower second (2:2), third, pass or fail.

MAKING THE CHANGE

Leaving the salon and starting over

While many people yearn to duck out of corporate life and start their own business, Julie Wilderspin, 52, has gone the other way. After 10 years running her own hairdressing salon, she's now working as a travel insurance adviser with Freedom Insurance in Cambridge, having retrained through learndirect.

I'd always been adamant that I would stop hairdressing when I hit 50. By that point I had been running the salon for the best part of a decade and had simply had enough of all the paperwork and having to make all the decisions all the time. While I knew I was pretty versatile and good with people – you have to be as a hairdresser – I had absolutely no clue what I would do instead. Even once I'd sold the shop, which meant I had money in the bank to live off, I was still unsure.

I did a receptionist job for a few weeks and then my daughter suggested I retrain. She pointed me in the direction of a course learning Pitman shorthand and, from there, to my local learndirect centre. When I left school I had gone straight into a hairdressing apprenticeship so, apart from hairdressing, there was zilch on my CV. In fact I had never even had a CV. So my learndirect adviser suggested I initially do a GCSE in maths and one in literacy. Although I had managed the accounts for the salon, I'd always been self-taught, so for me it was a big step. When I opened the first book for the maths course it was on fractions and I nearly burst out crying!

But both the courses and the general advice I got from learndirect were very non-judgmental and the tutors were great; it was all about building up your confidence and thinking about what you could do. For example, I knew that after working in the salon for so many years I would probably find an office environment quite stifling, so I wanted to do something that still involved contact with the general public. And with the courses you could take as long or as short a time as you liked – I did mine in about three to four months, accessing the coursework completely from home. But I also liked the fact you could go into the learndirect centre and use it as a base for your studying. I used to visit the centre up to four days a week.

I completed the courses in December 2006 and so then it was a question of finding a job. The centre put me in touch with various firms that were looking for people. I ended up going for three interviews; one as a receptionist, one working in a garage and one at Freedom Insurance, which I knew almost straightaway was the one I wanted to go for. I did find it hard to be in an interview situation, and to sell yourself and your skills, but I certainly never came across any ageism during any of the interviews, which was great.

Using existing skills in a new way

While you can never really know why someone takes you on, I think what sold me to them was the fact that I am a pretty self-confident, outgoing person and that I saw it as an opportunity to learn and develop. It was clear that I could handle people well and, from my time in the salon and my general life experience, that I could deal with sensitive situations. But the fact I had done the courses and had the new qualifications also helped.

There have been things I have had to get used to in this job. In the salon I was always speaking to people face-to-face, so I got used to reading people's faces. Now I'm mostly speaking to people over the phone, which took a little bit of adjustment. It's also a change in that I am no longer in charge, no longer the top sausage. Having said that, I'm now doing a job where it's not hanging over me all the time. When I was running the salon I was a one-man band and if I wanted to take a holiday it was really difficult, but now it's just a question of booking it in. So I've absolutely no regrets.

The major thing for me is that, although I am no longer working for myself, I feel much more in control of my life. It was my decision to sell the business, my decision to go back and get some qualifications and my decision to take this job. The best advice I could give is simply to listen to what people are telling you, whether it is your family or professionals such as at learndirect. And with the studying, even if you fail you can go back and do it again and again and again. It's also good to know that there are other people out there like you, that you are not the only person who feels on the wrong track, and also that there are people out there whose job it is to try and help you.

It's worth being aware that in Scotland degrees can take a year longer to complete. Some universities in Scotland also have what are called 'designated degrees', the first two years of which are the same as an honours degree but in the third cover a wider variety of subjects, but in less depth.

To get on a degree course you will need to go through the University and College Admissions Service, of which much more in the next chapter, and you will be assessed through a mixture of coursework, exams and possibly a dissertation. Since the introduction of tuition fees in 1998, students in England, Wales and Northern Ireland have had to pay (as of 2009) up to £3,225 per year, though fees can vary, while students already living in Scotland pay no fees whatsoever. Again, finance and financing are going to be covered in more detail in later chapters.

Postgraduate study

Once you've completed a degree and graduated you can go on to postgraduate study, which means progressing to a master's degree such as Master of Arts (MA), Master of Science (MSc), Master of Philosophy (MPhil) or Master of Business Administration (MBA), though there are many other courses at this level.

You can also do postgraduate certificates (such as the popular Postgraduate Certificate in Education if you want to go into teaching) and diplomas and even go on to do a PhD or doctorate, usually for those interested in a career in academia.

Diplomas and certificates tend to take nine months to a year to complete, with master's qualifications a year to two years full-time or longer part-time. The main difference between these and undergraduate degrees is that they will be less taught, although there will still be a teaching element within 'taught master's. There will be more of an emphasis on independent study and research, with the whole point of a doctorate degree being that you are carrying out an original piece of research, normally over a minimum of three years, and you will almost always be required to submit a dissertation at the end of the course.

You will usually have to approach and apply directly to the university where you want to study, and funding, as there is little if any state or student loan support at this level, can often be an issue. Fees for such courses will vary considerably, with MBAs often running into the tens of thousands of pounds and other master's courses normally around the £4–5,000 mark when being studied full-time – though some may be higher.

Where to study

Whatever subject, and whatever level of course, you decide is right for you and will help you to change career, the next challenge is to decide where to do it and how to study. No one course, university or FE college will be the same and all will offer different pros and cons. But there are nevertheless a number of questions you should be looking to answer before making your choice.

Unlike school leavers, for whom distance or location is unlikely to be that much of an issue, for most career changers one of the primary considerations is going to be physical location. Of course, you may be able to do your course online or by distance learning, which will mean it won't matter where your tutor is. However, the vast majority of FE-level courses will require you, at least part of the time, to be there physically, whether you're studying in a classroom, studio, shopfloor, workplace or another location.

Key questions you will need to weigh up are likely to include the benefits of going for a course that is more local versus one further away that is, perhaps, better suited to your needs. Within this, of course, family and personal issues – the children's schooling, your partner's work, your work (if you are juggling work with study) and so on – will need to come into play.

If you are going to have a long commute to get to your college it's worth thinking long and hard about how this is likely to affect your study – you might think, for example, that you will be able to study on the train there and back, but what happens if you can rarely get a seat? Also, a long commute is inevitably going to make studying harder and you more tired, particularly if you have early or late classes, and it may also mean you miss out on any social events or guest speakers who come to visit.

Then, too, you need to be absolutely sure the course you are choosing is right for you. It's worth being aware that it may well be in the interest of the university or college to attract you to a particular course, though, to be fair, most are not going to try and entice you on to a course that is palpably not suitable for you. Ultimately, it is going to be your time, effort and money that is being put into the course and so you need to be sure it is what you really want.

Speak to people

It is important therefore to speak to the tutors, admissions or learning support staff and the college careers advisers about whether it is right for you, given where you want to be or go with it once you have completed it. It can be worth, for example, asking what other mature students have gone on to do or whether anyone who has done your course has gone into your chosen new career. Read up about it, look at similar courses nearby (even if they are harder to get to) and see if you can speak to current or ex-students about the course and how it worked for them – there may also be online chat forums that you can get access to.

Associations, institutions or sector skills councils related to your field may be worth sounding out as to which courses are best recognised and most likely to help you to get a foot in the door. It's unlikely to be as important at this level as when you get to university, but it may well be worth evaluating the sort of study facilities there are, so what the library's like or how much material is likely to be available online (as that is obviously going to mean you may be able to spend less time physically in the library).

How will it be taught?

It is important within all this to look at the methods of teaching. If it's going to be done through seminars and lectures, when will they be held? If it is in the evening or at weekends that may be good for juggling work and study but not so good for juggling study and childcare. Or how frequently will you physically need to be there? If the course is going to be delivered online, what sort of communication and contact will there be with the tutors and others on the course? What sort of computer connection or internet speed will you need to have, particularly if you are going to be required to be downloading big documents or films?

Will there be residential courses that you might need to attend, or the occasional face-to-face meeting with a tutor or classmates? How will the course be assessed? Who will you be able to go to for help or advice or if you feel you are running into difficulties? What will you be required to buy in the way of materials, tools or equipment, and will this be included in the fee and, if not, will there be any financial help or support available? What about general financial options or support?

In a way these are all pretty commonsense questions, but important ones nevertheless. Essentially what you need to be getting a clear view about is what actually is going to be expected of you over the coming weeks, months and years – studying for a new qualification is hard enough without unexpected surprises along the way.

At a more pastoral level, it's a good idea to look at what sort of mature student support the college offers, particularly around things such as returning to studying and essay writing, as these are the most common things that mature students find intimidating at first. Many FE colleges have specialist mature student or learning support officers, or sometimes even a dedicated office for the needs of mature students.

It also makes sense to take a good look at the application process for your course. For some courses it is likely simply to be a case of registering, paying your fee and turning up. For others, you might be required to show recent exam certificates and there might be an interview or assessment. All colleges will publish free prospectuses (many of them are now available online too) with information about their facilities and their courses. They will also usually run open days – normally publicised in the local paper or on the college website – where it is possible to go along and see what is on offer, meet tutors and other staff and ask questions or discuss any issues.

Relearning how to learn

Everyone adjusts to the reality of retraining and returning to study in different ways, and everyone will have different ways of learning, some of which you may only discover as you progress through your course.

It may be, for instance, that the best way for you to work is to block out set days or set times of day that you will dedicate to studying. Or it may be that you find you work best by, or have no other option but to be, slotting in time here and there during the day around your work or family.

Whatever works for you, the one certainty is that it will take commitment and perseverance, and this is something those around you, whether friends, family or work colleagues, are going to have to recognise. But the satisfaction and reward of finally getting that qualification can be immense – not to mention the potential for meeting new people and simply widening your horizons that returning to study brings.

What organisations can help?

If you have a particular career or course in mind it may well be a good idea to sound out City & Guilds **www.cityandguilds.com** or LearnDirect **www.learndirect.co.uk** and, in Scotland, LearnDirectScotland **www.learn directscotland.com**. City & Guilds – the only awarding body in the UK solely dedicated to vocational learning – estimates it has 2,500 people enrolling for its qualifications every day and 1,800 a day completing them.

City & Guilds has a database of 500 qualifications in 28 different industry areas, as well as offering potential career changers access to a tool called iPortfolio that claims to be able to match your personality and ambitions

MAKING THE CHANGE

From cleaning toilets to PhD studies

After leaving school at 16 and working in a variety of menial jobs followed by time out from the workplace as a single mother, Hazel Thompson, 42, went back to college and is now doing a PhD at the University of Bangor that she hopes will lead to a career in academia.

You name it, I've done it – office work, cleaning toilets, working in a chippy, on the line in a crockery factory. At school I had wanted to go on and do A-levels but at the time it simply wasn't an option, I had to get out there and start earning money. Then, after about twelve or thirteen years, by which time I was working as a secretary, I had my daughter Milly and, after taking my maternity leave, decided I didn't want to go back to work. I just wanted to be selfish and spend time with her.

That was great, absolutely fantastic, but once she'd begun school I started to get really frustrated – there's only so much cleaning around the house you can do. So I was looking through the paper thinking what was I going to do – I had been out of the workplace for five years by this point – and all the job adverts were saying you needed NVQs. I didn't even know what an NVQ was but it was clear I'd need one if I ever wanted to get back into work, so I approached my local college, Llandrillo College, to do an NVQ in administration.

Beating your demons

It was while I was there that I got chatting to someone who told me about access to further education and higher education courses, something that, again, I had had no idea existed. I didn't even have a GCSE in maths and I couldn't remember how to write an essay. So it was all very scary, but I enrolled on the GCSE programme at the college and found I loved it.

Finally getting that piece of paper, which had always been a thorn in my side, was such a good feeling, almost better than when I got my degree. One of the best things about these courses was that they were all free because, as a mum on benefits, there was no way I would have been able to afford to do them myself.

I did the access course and was constantly surprised that the marks I was getting back seemed to be really good – I was sure they were meant for someone else! And then, to top it all, I won a scholarship to Bangor to study Theology. I'd seen the scholarship advertised on a noticeboard at the college and just sat the exam – what I hadn't realised, and it was just as well, was that there was only one scholarship awarded for that course. I was awarded £1,500 over three years, which I put towards buying books. I had to get a student loan as well, which was really scary as I had never been in debt before, apart from having a mortgage, and I started a job at the weekends, working with adults with learning difficulties.

The whole notion of university was intimidating, too. I turned up to four open days and, for three of them, was unable to walk through the door. I just felt I was a complete idiot and was being ridiculous imagining I could go there. But when I did it, they were all really welcoming and friendly.

As well as the work, a real challenge was that I live in Prestatyn, which is an hour's drive away from Bangor, and I had to travel there four days a week, sometimes for 9am lectures. So I had to set up a complicated support network for Milly, but luckily my partner is very supportive. I had made a number of friends on the access course and was able to car share with a few people. My latest lecture was 6pm, which meant I wouldn't be finishing until 7pm and then still had to drive home. So I used a lot of good friends to pick up Milly after school and look after her until I got home.

When I first started university I imagined I'd be spending three years sitting in a corner of the library not speaking to anyone because I'd have nothing in common with them, but it hasn't been like that at all – though university is what you make of it. People will make time for you, even if it is just to go for a coffee or a chat. I've now started a monthly coffee morning for postgraduate students in our department, for example. You just need to get involved as much as you can, not just with the social activities but with the people on your course.

Helping family to understand

It's also very easy to fall into the trap of trying to lead two separate lives, one your family and one your university. I found this happening at first but I took Milly into university and let her spend the day there, one day every semester, to see what I did and where I was spending most of my time. It meant she could put faces to the names of the staff and students I was talking about all the time, she also came to some lectures, which helped her realise why my mobile was sometimes turned off! She also got to appreciate how long the journey was and why I had to leave so early and sometimes got home late. I did the same with my partner.

I think this really helped because it stopped them from feeling excluded from what became (and still is) a large part of my life. In the end we used to get 'family' invitations to events — when I went on nights out my partner was always included and I sometimes have students visiting me or staying at the house.

After I completed the degree with first-class honours in 2008, the department suggested I go on and do a master's degree and apply for Arts & Humanities Research Council funding in their annual competition. I, again not realising how competitive these things were — there were only 15 awarded at master's level — simply filled in the application, wrote a proposal and forgot about it. I nearly passed out when I found I had actually won the funding. But it was fantastic because it paid my master's fee and gave me a maintenance grant, although I had to give up my weekend work. If I hadn't got it, my plan had been to carry on working — the department had offered to reduce my fee with a £500 scholarship and Bangor had said that I could pay in quarterly instalments, which would have made it easier. But having the funding made a huge difference.

I've now gone on to do a PhD which, again, isn't cheap, but the fact I can now lecture on some of the first year undergraduate modules certainly helps. I find lecturing at this level hugely enjoyable, although it was very nerve wracking at first, and it is what I'd love to continue doing. Of course I could end up back stacking shelves, but if I can this is what I'm going to pursue.

The thing to remember is not to be intimidated by it. Academia does have its own language and many of the academics have never known anything else and so can be quite otherworldly. The other thing you need to recognise is that you have to be prepared to let things go. You cannot do everything. I've always got piles of ironing around the house, my windows don't get cleaned as often as they used to and the garden is a jungle. My partner and I now do the food shopping once a month instead of once a week and I'm considering doing the shopping over the internet to save even more time.

When you're doing a 9–5 job you can come in, sit down and watch the telly. But I get back, spend my time with Milly and put her to bed, and then it'll be sorting out her uniform and lunch for the next day and then, around 9–10pm, I'll sit down and start to study again. So it is hard. Letting go of the house and garden chores took a long time to sink in – at the start I used to try and do everything, but you just can't. You also need to have a partner who is willing to be ignored when deadlines or exams are pending. We have gone days without touching base, so it can take its toll.

But it is all worth it. Many of the women on my access course ended up pulling out because of the disruption it caused to their marriages, so I feel I have been very lucky. You feel guilty and selfish, particularly because you can feel you are not being a good mother, even though Milly doesn't mind. In fact she loves it, she loves the fact that I am studying like she is. You have to stop beating yourself up and just get on with it.

to your perfect job. The vast majority of City & Guilds courses are NVQs, with it awarding more than half of all NVQs given out in the UK, though some of its courses and qualifications are at a higher level. It also has close links with organisations such as the Engineering Council, the Hospitality Awarding Body, the Construction Industry Training Board and the Institute for Leadership and Management.

Learndirect, meanwhile, was set up in 1998 as an e-teaching organisation (so predominantly, though not solely, distance and online learning-based) aimed at providing over-16s with education, with the aim that its courses can be completed alongside a day job. It runs centres around the country offering help, advice and access to training, ranging from entry-level certificates in maths and English through to university-level qualifications.

Train to Gain **www.traintogain.gov.uk**, tends to act more as an education broker (through BusinessLink), helping employers access training for their employees, so it may be of less relevance for career changers – unless you have a very amenable employer of course! Many colleges and universities also have a Centre for Lifelong Learning that will run courses specifically aimed at more mature learners.

There are also a multitude of private providers out there, often specialising in a particular areas, such as healthcare, accountancy or teaching, though it is worth ensuring that their courses are properly accredited by a body such as the Qualifications and Curriculum Authority, or listed on the National Database of Accredited Qualifications **www. accreditedqualifications.org.uk**. Again, sector skills councils can also be a helpful resource here.

It is a good idea to check whether the qualification is recognised by an examination board such as AQA, OCR, Edexcel, WJEC (formerly the Welsh Joint Examination Committee), Northern Ireland's CCEA (Council for the Curriculum, Examinations & Assessment) or an awarding body such as City & Guilds. Alternatively, it may be that the qualification has been accredited by whichever institute, association or federation oversees the sector you want to go into, but that is worth checking out. These bodies will normally also be a good port of call for general advice and guidance about the best route to take, qualification to gain or most well-thought-of colleges or training deliverers.

Jobcentre Plus, too, may be able to help in providing at the very least a steer on training, and its personal advisers should be able to put you in contact with local colleges and training schemes as well as give you an overview of what is available in your area, how to apply and what sort of financial help there might be.

Most of all, however, the person who is most going to help you get on and get your vocational training is *you*. When it comes to retraining, at this level or at university, as a mature student, the onus is going to be on you to make that first enquiry, email or call, to research the right course provider and college and to have worked out that if you do course *x* it is likely to lead to scenario *y* and, ultimately, the career you're dreaming of.

Key points:

- There are many different qualifications that you can choose from
- Don't be afraid to speak to colleges, tutors, careers and learning support staff about what and where is the best option for you
- Recognise that your commitment to study will affect your family and friends as well as you
- Think about how far you will have to travel, how the course will be assessed, how well it is recognised in your chosen field and where you want it to take you

HIGHER EDUCATION

In describing how she turned up to four university open days and was unable to walk through the door for three of them because she was feeling 'a complete idiot' and 'ridiculous' for even imagining she could go there, Bangor PhD student Hazel Thompson, whose story we heard in the last chapter, illustrated very clearly the sense of intimidation many people can feel about higher education.

It may be you need to go to university for the first time after many years in the workplace, or it may be a question of returning to university after five, 10, 20 years away. Either way, for the career changer the prospect of becoming a university student can be a daunting one. Whether it's the thought of ploughing through reading lists, writing essays or dissertations, sitting exams, having to lead a debate in a seminar, being surrounded by youngsters or just the dread of being saddled with a hefty student debt, going to university is, at all levels, a big deal. It'll be a serious commitment of time, money and effort but, if you make the most of it, the opportunities that university education can provide are immense.

Whatever age you go, or return, to university it will change you. It will open new horizons, possibly lead you in completely different directions, generate new friendships and give you a new, or at the very least a changed, perspective on life, the universe and everything. At a practical level the resources that universities can offer are vast. They can include pure learning or research, careers advice and access to employers, the support of alumni (ex-graduates), networking opportunities, physical facilities and support around things such as starting up a business. Of course, you can get some of this from further education colleges too, but at university and higher education level there is just that much more of it.

Coming in as a mature student

What's more, for the career changer, when it comes to giving you direction, or helping you to change direction, universities are past masters. While the predominant 'market' for universities remains the school leaver, the days when that was all they catered for are long gone. Yes, that demographic is still very important and you should expect to be surrounded by fresh-faced young'uns at every turn. But these days virtually all universities are geared towards mature students, including the international students that they are keen to attract as a source of additional income.

In fact, it is estimated that 60 per cent of undergraduates in the UK are over 21 and, while many undergraduates do go straight on to post-graduate courses these days, just as many go out into the world of work and then come back as mature students. The recession has, if anything, exacerbated this trend, with the past year seeing universities reporting a surge in applications from older people applying to do degrees.

For simplicity, this chapter is split thematically rather than between undergraduate and postgraduate. In a moment we shall look at choosing the right course and university, including what you should be thinking about when you apply for a course. We'll then look at the practicalities of applying for courses at undergraduate and postgraduate level as a mature student and take in the realities and challenges of modern university life, and how universities have changed over the past couple of decades in how they teach students. We'll also cover where you can go to for advice and support, both to get you started and during your time at university. Finally, we will be taking a close look at the workings of the Open University, because of its status as one of the key resources for career changers who want to juggle learning and 'bettering themselves' alongside their career and families.

Choosing the right course and university

The first point to emphasise here is that you may not even need to go to a university to get a higher education qualification. Despite the vast expansion of the sector over the past decades, higher education provision is still patchy in some areas, particularly some rural ones. What you can get is further education colleges that can teach all or most of a degree, with the qualification simply being validated and then awarded by a university.

What also sometimes can happen is that a university will franchise the first year of study to an FE college, with students then transferring to the main university campus. As we also saw in the previous chapter, doing a Higher National Diploma or Certificate or a foundation degree can fast track you on to a full-blown undergraduate degree. In practice, in these circumstances, the likelihood is that you will simply progress seamlessly from your FE college to the relevant HE institution and complete your degree that way.

If you are starting from fresh as a career changer, however, perhaps after completing some A-levels, an access course or simply picking up and moving on from your existing school qualifications, choosing the right course and university is likely to be quite a challenging task. And with all the time and money you are likely to invest at stake, it is an important one.

It is estimated that around a fifth of students who drop out of higher education each year do so because they did not choose the right subject to study or university to study at. There is now such a vast array of subjects and institutions that making your mind up can be harder than ever.

In many respects, the factors likely to be governing your decision are going to be pretty similar to those we outlined for further education courses. Course content versus location is likely to be a key issue, as is length of commute, family, work and personal issues. While the specifics of the course are clearly going to be important, the wider reputation of the university is also worth considering – the *Guardian's University Guide* or *Postgraduate Guide* can offer useful information there. You may also want to research employment prospects after graduation, whether in terms of the university's record in getting people into placements and how well it is regarded, or simply its links with employers. It's also worth looking into whether it is either a hub itself or located near a hub for the industry or sector that you have in mind.

Assess closely what type of degree is being offered and whether it suits your needs. So, for example, will you only be able to do it full-time, or is there an option to do it part-time or on a flexible, modular basis or through distance learning? Similarly, it is increasingly common to mix and match subjects to create a combined degree and you may wish to consider that. Be careful, though, that you don't end up diluting what it is you were setting out to study or you could end up with a degree that is looked on less favourably, because it is less specialist, by the industry or sector you are aspiring to enter.

At postgraduate level there is often less face-to-face contact between tutor and student, but the tutor-student relationship can become a very important one, particularly during any later research-based phases of your qualification. So you may want to take a close look at the background

MAKING THE CHANGE

From security guard to environment manager

After years of feeling held back in his career aspirations by his lack of schooling, Spencer Thomas, 38, went back to college and did a degree through the Open University. The former shop worker and security guard is now an environment manager with airports operator BAA.

I didn't enjoy school or studying and left at 16 with just two CSEs and one O-Level. It didn't matter too much at first and I got a job with WH Smith and rose to the position of news manager. But gradually I began to get frustrated at my lack of formal education and got the sense it was holding me back. For any management or more senior roles you always needed either to have a degree or to have worked a much longer term of service.

Eventually I moved to a store at Heathrow Airport from which I decided to go and work for BAA, where I became a security guard. But, again, while I kept trying to make the transition into more senior roles, my lack of a degree kept coming up as a barrier. I was getting really frustrated and by 2002 I knew I just had to do something about it, so I decided to give adult education a try. I knew that if I wanted to gain seniority and earn more money I needed to have a degree and I was determined this was something that was not going to beat me.

Opening up to OU

I'd been noticing advertisements for the Open University for a couple of years and thought it was worth a go. What attracted me was that there was an array of courses to choose from and you were not bound by any one particular subject. The courses are modular and you just build up credits as you go along. Also you can do it as fast or as slowly as you want and it is virtually all done by distance learning, so it is easier to fit in around work. Initially I did a three-month 'taster' course on an introduction to social sciences, which was a steep learning curve, but the grades I got back were quite good and I hadn't found it that difficult, so I reckoned I would be capable of going on and doing a degree.

As well as the degree I chose a number of courses that would give me extra qualifications along the way. For example I did what is called a DD100 in social sciences followed by a certificate in social sciences. About halfway through I also achieved a diploma in systemic thinking.

Moving on to the higher level courses was quite challenging, particularly things such as learning how to write essays. The standard at OU is high and learning to write in an academic style was completely different to anything I had done at school – it was like learning a new language. But the sense of achievement when you got your coursework back and had got a good mark was enormous.

It was also at about the halfway point that I made the decision to switch from a general degree to a named honours degree, in Environmental Studies. I simply decided it would be more credible to have a degree that people could recognise and it would have more value.

The good thing, again, about the OU is that it was really simple to change like that.

Working while you study

Managing study alongside work is hard. Being a security guard and working nights and shifts, I was able to use my downtime to study, as well as my time off. But I think I was constantly reading books, and even took them on holiday with me. When you are ill or tired and the deadlines are creeping up on you it can sometimes get you down. About three years in I did get to a point where I nearly gave up but, having got so far, I knew I would regret it if I stopped. Because it is such a commitment you really do need to have the support of your partner or family. We'd be sitting down in the evening and my wife would be trying to speak to me and I'd have my head in a book, so she had to be very tolerant.

When it came to funding my degree, as it was a first degree I was able to get a student loan but otherwise I've just funded it all myself as I went along, which has been hard. I created a special account for my degree money and simply paid in a certain amount a month. When it came to communicating with other students, at the beginning

I got involved with quite a few offline groups because my computer connection was not great, but as it's gone on there has been more discussion and communication online. The tutors have also all been really accessible and helpful. Each course I did had a residential session but I could never get the time off to attend any of them, which I think is the case with a lot of OU students.

Where your studies can take you

I completed my final course in October 2008 and graduated in May 2009. In a way it felt strange – yes there was a sense of massive elation that I finally had an honours degree but there was also a feeling of 'What am I going to do now?' I actually secured a place on the BAA management development programme while I was doing the degree, and then in April 2008 was appointed airside environment manager. I'm sure the fact I was at that point three-quarters of the way through the degree made a big difference.

Doing something like this is a huge commitment. There will be times when it will feel too hard and there will be tough days. But you shouldn't put it off just because it is difficult to do. If you stick with it and are committed to it, it is completely achievable. But you do need to have your family with you all the way, not only because of the commitment in time and money but because it will change you as a person, in the best way possible. It changes you fundamentally, how you think about things and how you see things, so you have to make sure you take them with you.

I'm happy with what I'm doing right now but at some point I'd like possibly to start my own business and set up an environmental consultancy. And I might even consider going on to do a master's or PhD, though what my wife would say about that I'm not sure!

and research interests of your potential tutors, and whether they match your own interests. You may not be intending to go on to do a PhD, but if you were to change your mind halfway through would it be the sort of department you might want to do it through? Similarly, what sort of library and research facilities are there – if it is a world-renowned research centre in your particular field, that's inevitably going to sway you. Although we will be looking at scholarships, bursaries and other funding in the next chapter, if there is funding on offer, at whatever level, it clearly makes sense to give that university or course serious consideration.

Will there be support?

It is worth investigating the sort of mature student support networks that the university has – there may be specific mature student facilities, a postgraduate guild or association, or it may be that the university has particular good childcare facilities or is well equipped to cater for people with disabilities or other special needs. The charitable organisation the Daycare Trust **www.daycaretrust.org.uk** is a good port of a call on childcare provision in higher education, as is Skill **www.skill.org.uk**, the National Bureau for Students with Disabilities, for special needs provision.

It's probably going to be of lesser importance, but should certainly be part of the thinking process, but how will the university fit in with your interests and lifestyle? If you're a mad-keen sailor, for example, it makes sense to check out whether the university has a sailing club. Your university's student union may also have a mature student body or association that will help you with making friends and contacts.

As with FE colleges, every university publishes an extensive prospectus and will hold regular open days at undergraduate and postgraduate level. Tutors, admissions tutors and support staff are normally happy to help. The University and Colleges Admissions Service (UCAS) also offers what its calls 'The Stamford Test', a short questionnaire designed to help students match their interests and abilities to possible higher education subjects.

How to apply

As a mature student at undergraduate level, and unlike school leavers – virtually all of whom will go apply to university through UCAS – you may be able to apply directly to a specific course or university. Admissions requirements can vary, so make enquiries with the institution you are interested in.

It's likely that you'll still have to go through UCAS but the point is it is worth being aware that some universities will, at the very least, consider direct applications from people with a background in the 'university of life' or extensive workplace experience to draw upon. This is particularly the case if you are looking to study part-time, as there may be a whole different local admissions system for part-time applicants. Often making an appointment with an admissions' tutor will help to make things much clearer, as well as giving you an initial feel for the university, its facilities and atmosphere. Checking out a university in person before applying is always a sensible idea.

In terms of timeframe, while the vast majority of applications take place just before and after the A-level summer rush, for mature student career changers there is often more flexibility – you are less likely to be constrained by exams and term times in the same way as school leavers. Nevertheless, don't leave it too late to approach or apply to a university or you risk having to defer for a year.

Whether or not you are applying through UCAS, you will need to provide evidence of your ability to study at graduate or postgraduate level, or evidence of relevant experience. This might be A-levels, an access course or a CV listing your educational achievements (which may be more vocational and professional) and employment history. Even if your qualifications are old, such as O-levels or CSEs, they will be taken into account.

The UCAS application

If you are required to apply through UCAS, it's worth going carefully through the advice and support sections on its website **www.ucas.ac.uk** and taking your time about it. You will have to complete a range of sections, including registration, personal details, the course or courses you are choosing, your education and employment background, a 'personal statement', references and a declaration that all the information you have given is correct. Much of this is self-explanatory, but it's worth highlighting a few areas of note.

When it comes to your choice of course you will need to indicate whether you intend to live at home (the more likely option for most mature students) or in student accommodation, and whether you're applying to join the next available course or deferring entry for a year. For references, what's normally required is a reference from a tutor, careers adviser (perhaps from an FE college if you are making the transition from there) or another professional, which could feasibly be a previous employer or senior colleague if you have been out of education for many years. The university will be looking for information that shows what you are like and your suitability for the relevant course. Your application won't be processed without the full details of your referee and the text of their reference.

Your personal statement

The personal statement is a crucial part of the UCAS application form and it's something that many students, both school leavers and mature students, often find challenging. It is designed to give you a chance to explain to the university why you are applying for the course and why they should take you on as a student there.

This is something that should be thought through carefully, and will probably require quite a few drafts to get right – bear in mind it may also be the basis for an interview later on. There are no hard and fast rules here but it makes sense to outline why you are choosing the course, particularly if it's something you have not studied before, and why you want to go to university. You may also want to give details of your work background – don't simply repeat the employment history section of the application, focus in on why it is relevant now or why it will be relevant to your future career. If you can, ask someone you trust to read your statement through as well as getting people's ideas and feedback about what you should put in.

As well as perfecting the content, it's imperative that you get the grammar and spelling right and that it is clearly presented. The personal statement can be up to 4,000 characters long or 47 lines of text, and you cannot use italics, bold or underlining or symbols such as accents. If you are typing it direct into the application it is advisable to draft it offline first. If you're working online save your statement regularly as the application will time-out after 35 minutes of inactivity.

Personal statement dos and don'ts

On its website UCAS provides a useful list of dos and don'ts for filling in the personal statement. These are:

Do

✓ Create a list of your ideas before attempting to write the real thing.

✓ Expect to produce several drafts before being totally happy.

✓ Ask people you trust for their feedback.

✓ Check university and college prospectuses, websites and entry profiles as they usually tell you the criteria and qualities that they want their students to demonstrate.

✓ Use your best English/Welsh.

✓ Convey your enthusiasm – if you show your interest in the course, it may help you get a place.

Don't

✗ Let spelling and grammatical errors spoil your statement.

✗ Feel that you need to use elaborate language. If you try too hard to impress with long words that you are not confident using, the focus of your writing may be lost.

✗ Say too much about things that are not relevant – if you think that you are starting to, take a break and come back to your statement when you feel more focused.

✗ Rely on a spellchecker as it will not pick up everything – proofread as many times as possible.

✗ Leave it to the last minute – your statement will seem rushed and important information could be left out.

✗ Expect to be able to write your personal statement whilst watching TV or surfing the internet – this is your future, so make the most of the opportunity to succeed.

✗ Lie – if you exaggerate you may get caught out at interview when asked to elaborate on an interesting achievement.

On that last point, be aware applications may well be checked by the service's 'Similarity Detection' process. This is used primarily to catch out potential students who have simply cribbed (or even bought) personal statements off the internet.

Once you've pinged the application off, it is sent to the university and they will decide whether or not to make you an offer. You can normally track the progress of your application online.

The interview and the offer

The university may ask you to come for an interview, which will often mean a discussion with a tutor or an admissions tutor. You are likely to be asked, again, why you want to apply for the course (probably not too hard a one to answer for the average career changer), your ambitions during and after it, your background and why you think you will make a good student.

What the institution will really want to gauge is whether you will be a committed and dedicated student, serious about investing your time, effort and money in their course. The average career-changing mature student should have an advantage here. You will almost certainly have more life experiences to draw on than any school leaver and, assuming you are completely focused on where you want to get to, these questions will already have gone through your head many times

It's normally less of an issue for mature students, who will often already have their A-levels or access qualifications under their belts, but sometimes you will get a conditional offer based on your predicted grades, with each grade worth a certain number of points. More commonly, mature students will get an unconditional offer, though you may still be asked to provide proof of any qualifications you have said you have.

Finally, at undergraduate level there is a system known as clearing, which is essentially a national pool that you enter if you have not been accepted on to your first choice of course but still hope to land a place somewhere. This tends to be more applicable to school leavers but could nevertheless be an option for you.

Applying for postgraduate courses

When it comes to applying for a postgraduate course – and we pre-dominantly mean a master's here, as people commonly progress relatively seamlessly on to a PhD from there – the system is very different, largely because there is no central UCAS-style admissions system.

Much as it will be up to you to make the running during your study as a postgraduate student, so will you be expected to get off your hind legs and approach the university or department directly, speak to tutors and so on. Normally it will simply be a case of downloading an application form directly from the university. In some instances, such as with postgraduate teaching courses, you may need to apply through a specific admissions service for that profession, in this case the Graduate Teacher Training Registry **www.gttr.ac.uk**.

Time-wise, as most courses start around early October, you should normally be looking to apply at the end of the previous year or the start of the year in which the course starts, though it is quite possible to cut it finer. Most universities accept applications for postgraduate courses on a rolling basis and so will not have an official closing date – but if you apply too late you may be asked to defer for a year.

On the application form you will be asked to outline your academic background and subsequent career, show evidence of your degree qualification and, if you have one, a course transcript from your undergraduate tutor about what you did during your degree.

For some financial, business or maths-heavy master's courses, such as a Master of Business Administration (MBA), you might be asked to do a few

MAKING THE CHANGE

CASE STUDY: Moving on with an MBA

Former engineer Simon Ling, 33, has just completed an MBA through Nottingham University Business School and is using the school's business start-up facilities to help get a new business idea off the ground.

I was sponsored through university by BAE Systems and joined them straight after graduating in 1999. I quickly moved out of pure engineering roles to more business analyst, strategic roles but, by the end of 2006, I could see the writing on the wall. There was a lot of restructuring going on within the business and shifting about and, while I was being offered lots of different things, none of them really appealed so I decided to take voluntary redundancy.

If I'm being honest, I'd had itchy feet for a while and already felt I'd stayed there too long. What had kept me from moving had been the fear of losing my job and not having any money, so in that sense the timing of the offer of redundancy was great because it forced my hand and also gave me enough of a financial cushion to spend some time really thinking about what it was I wanted to do next.

I had two basic ideas. I had already applied for an emigration visa to the US because I have family over there and had worked there before and really liked it. The other idea was that I wanted to do an MBA, whether here or in the US, it did not particularly matter.

The first thing I did was to take a complete break and spend six months renovating my flat and selling it. But it did mean that, for the first time since my early twenties, I found myself moving back in with my parents, which was probably a bit of a challenge for all of us!

Choosing an MBA

The visa application fell through at the start of 2008 so the MBA was the next best option. My experience up to then had always been quite practical and what I wanted was to get a more formal business education. I felt I had hit a ceiling in my career as an engineer and that an MBA would potentially help me to move into other industries.

I looked at a number of full-time MBAs at different business schools, particularly London Business School and Lancaster University Management School, as well as Nottingham. Previously I'd sat in on a number of modules at Lancaster to see how they worked and what they were like. But what I liked about Nottingham was that they had different types of MBAs, including one in entrepreneurship. I also liked the careers service there when I spoke to them.

Using the money from the sale of my flat to fund the course, I started on the full-time MBA in September 2008, initially on the general MBA but then I quickly switched to the entrepreneurship one. I realised that what had been frustrating me about work was less the work itself and more the fact that I had been having to toe the line and fit in all the time.

Starting a business was not something that had really crossed my mind when I started on the course but after speaking to people on the MBA and talking to people on the entrepreneurship course I realised that was much more the direction I wanted to go in.

Going back to study was challenging at first. It is a complete change. But one of the great things about an MBA is that you are surrounded by a completely different, often international, group of people who all have a huge range of experiences to draw on.

Relearning how to write in an academic way was probably the hardest bit. I'd got used to writing reports for business and strategy documents and so on, but it is a completely different way of writing and thinking.

It's been very intense, which has not been a huge problem for me as I don't have any family or outside work commitments, but for some of the others, particularly some of the international students with children, it has been hard. There was one student on my MBA from Japan who was learning in his second language and his wife had just had their first child, so I don't know how he did it.

Another great thing about a course like this is the speakers that they get in and the careers advice and support that you get, which can be anything from rewriting your CV to discussions about whether you should go on and do a doctorate. It gives you a great confidence boost.

While I was doing the course I started to develop an idea for a business. It's early days and it hasn't got a name yet but the basic idea is to offer online business advice and various tools to stimulate entrepreneurial behaviour; so how to get licences for intellectual property and patents, how to link with universities and to be more effective around business planning and financial modelling and so on.

Giving your business a head start

I've been able to use the university's enterprise laboratory, the UNIEI lab, to start getting it up and running. What it does is that it provides business support for entrepreneurs who are, or have been, studying at the university, whether at undergraduate or postgraduate level. They provide you with a desk, a business address, a phone service, marketing and assistance from people in industry. It has been a hugely useful resource because it gives you a professional front straightaway, with people who can answer the phone for you and so on.

Changing your career is a very scary decision to make because of the uncertainty. For me it was about getting something into my head that I was willing to commit to – in my case doing an MBA and seeing where it led. So it was about facing that uncertainty and being willing to take that first step. If you don't take that first step, nothing is going to happen. Also, don't assume you will follow the path you have mapped out. When I first started, I expected I'd be moving into another corporate role, just something a bit more strategic. But within a month I realised that what I really wanted was to try something completely new and different.

numerical tests, just to show that you will be able to handle this side of the course. Don't worry, though, if your undergraduate degree is back in the mists of time, as that will be taken into account.

Research proposals

If you are applying for a research-based master's (known as an MRes) you will probably be asked to write a research proposal outlining the area you want to investigate, how you intend to go about it and what sources of information you intend to use. For a taught master's you will normally be asked to complete a supporting statement as part of your application.

Much as with the UCAS personal statement, this is often the most challenging part of the application and is not something to be rushed. What you want to be getting across is why you feel passionate about studying the subject, why you feel you would make a good postgraduate student and any particular interests that might be able to be converted into research at a future date. You are not expected to be an expert on the area that you want to study – that's why you are doing the course after all – but you should be showing evidence that you have the potential to carry out independent research. Again, don't cut-and-paste or plagiarise, as more likely than not it'll get spotted.

As with an undergraduate application, you'll need to supply references. These will normally be from two people, commonly tutors (or 'academic referees') who have supervised your work at undergraduate level. If that's not an option, perhaps because your first degree was many years ago and you no longer have access to its academic referees, there is the option of supplying professional referees, although these will still need to be as relevant as possible to the course you are applying for.

The postgraduate interview

Once you have submitted the application, chances are that you will be called in for an interview, though it's by no means always the case. The style and tone of this will vary from institution to institution but you will normally be asked about your reasons for choosing the course or particular department, your motivations for studying at postgraduate level and why you feel you will make a good postgraduate student.

You may, too, be asked about your career or work experiences, what you hope the qualification will do for you and about your studies at undergraduate level. What can help here is getting clear in your head exactly why it is you are applying and what you want to get from the course, where you want it to take you and whether the research interests of some of the staff overlap with yours, or what you think might be yours.

The interview – and this will be as applicable for undergraduate inter-views too – is also a good opportunity for you to find out things such as how the course is run and taught, what tutor or supervisory arrangements are in place, whether there are any changes to the programme being planned or any new courses introduced and what sort of research you will be expected to carry out.

Similarly, the interview can be a great opportunity to discuss issues around finance and financial support, particularly the possibility of accessing any grants, bursaries, scholarships or awards. Once accepted, you will normally be offered a provisional place until you have paid a non-refundable deposit, usually a percentage of the course fees that has to be paid prior to starting the course, often at the latest eight weeks before.

The life of a mature student

If you're doing an undergraduate degree what you can expect is a fairly structured week of lectures, talks and seminars, normally led by a tutor and lecturer, interspersed with regular essays or projects and often topped off each year by exams and then, commonly, in the final year by a dissertation.

When it comes to scoring your degree it will vary from university to university and course to course but often what happens is that exams and coursework become progressively more important as you progress through the course, both to give you a chance to find your feet in the early months and as a way of ensuring that if you make a howler early on you still have a chance to recover your grade.

But it also means the pressure inevitably builds over the years you are there. The pace of the work – despite the stereotype of students spending their days hanging around the bar – will normally be quite intense, even at the beginning, and the key is to try not to fall behind.

For mature students, whether at undergraduate or postgraduate level and especially if you're not used to this type of working, it is a good idea to investigate taking part in some study skills sessions, which most universities run. These tend to be geared more towards international students who need to adjust to the British way of study, but they can be equally helpful for British mature students.

These sessions will tend to be run in the first week of the term, and may include how to use the library effectively, essay writing, effective academic reading and critical thinking. There may also be advice on pitfalls to avoid, such as ensuring you are using references properly and steering clear of plagiarism.

Before the academic year starts in the autumn, many universities will run 'visit days' where mature students can come and meet current mature students and discuss their experiences of university life. You might even be able to spend a day shadowing a current undergraduate student, including attending a lecture or visiting the library.

Many universities will run a mature student 'orientation programme' right at the start of the year, including things such as a campus tour, talks on funding support, childcare and study skills and how to log on to the university IT network. This will also usually include opportunities to meet current mature students and a social event in the evening. Academically, one of the challenges many people find with university is that, even though the study at undergraduate level is fairly structured, it's still going to be up to you to pace yourself, to get on with the work and do a lot of unguided work and this can take some getting used to.

This is even more the case at postgraduate level. Whether you are studying full- or part-time, flexibly or remotely for a master's, you will probably be expected to do a series of core and optional modules, each of them accruing you points, followed by a dissertation of around 20,000 words.

The best way to get a proper feel for what you are going to be doing is simply to go on to your relevant department website and follow the links through until you get to the one entitled 'programme structure'. There are no hard and fast rules as to how courses will be structured, but a common approach is to devote the first and second terms to a mix of core and optional modules or have one term devoted solely to core modules and one to optional. Then the third term (normally from about May onwards) and the summer will tend to be devoted to the dissertation, which will usually be expected to be submitted by the end of September.

For part-time students, what commonly happens is that the core and optional taught modules will be completed during the first year and then the dissertation during the second. A variation on this might be an initial term of modules in the second year followed by the dissertation.

Don't become isolated

The biggest difference between undergraduate and postgraduate study will be the fact there is less hand-holding and the range of subjects and modules you will study will tend to be much narrower. The relationship you have with your tutor, which at undergraduate level is still pretty much a teacher-pupil relationship, will probably be more equal, with the tutor or supervisor's role likely to be more about support and guidance rather than formal teaching. There will probably be less contact time, smaller study or seminar groups and it may well be that you will be required to make presentations or lead the debate within a seminar rather than the tutor taking the lead. You will also normally be taught about research methods and some of the problems and practices around academic research.

More widely, in terms of throwing yourself into university life, one of the problems mature students sometimes complain about – and this can be particularly the case with postgraduate mature students – is isolation.

Because you may be juggling family or work pressures and perhaps physically visiting the university only infrequently, you may be less likely to feel a part of university life. Similarly, if a lot of your work is being done through distance or online learning it is easy to become academically isolated or feel adrift in your studies. You may assume everyone but you knows what they are doing, or feel demotivated if you are struggling to achieve the marks you want to.

Remember, though, university requires significant adjustment for everyone, even those progressing straight there from sixth form college. Also, remember there are people you can go and speak to, primarily your tutor but also often mature student support officers or student welfare officers.

There is also the issue of getting back what you put in. It's a cliché, of course, to say university is what you make it but, time and again, when you speak to mature students that's the message you get back. Yes, you may be older than those you are studying with but if you throw yourself into this new life rather than being stand-offish you are much more likely to get a lot back. You may find younger students actively value the life experiences or different perceptions you can bring to discussion or, say, the time management or work-related skills you have built up in your former career.

Social life

Socially, universities are normally awash with clubs and societies as well as an array of social, sporting and recreational facilities. You should be able to find out about a lot of these during the 'Freshers' week', the first week of the autumn term, plus the mature student support officers should be able to guide you.

The university Students' Union is a good first port of call to find out what is going on and simply meet people. There may, too, be a postgraduate guild or organisation of a similar name, often with its own building or premises, that can be a useful place to hang out and meet people. The student charity Uniaid, incidentally, has an online game on its website **www.uniaid.org.uk** that allows you to go through a term as a virtual student and so get a handle on what life as a student might be like. What's more, being a student, you should be entitled to discounts on travel and many other facilities and there may well be a range of offers for local shops, clubs and other organisations.

Particularly in that first, hectic Freshers' week it can all seem a bit of a blur, but there are many people who can help you find your footing. Beyond your academic department or faculty, there will normally be student wellbeing advisers, mature student support officers, learning support officers, disability officers, accommodation officers, student finance officers, student union officials and so on. If you start to find it is all getting too much, all universities now have counselling and mental health support services, too.

The main message here is, if, for whatever reason, it's not working for you, support is available. Changing your career through retraining may have its challenges but it should be a positive, enjoyable experience too.

How universities have changed

If you're returning to university with fond memories of how things were in your undergraduate days, you'll probably be in for a bit of a shock, as universities and higher education have changed a lot over the past couple of decades. First, the expansion of the sector has led to there being a much more diverse population, including, as we have seen, many more international students as well as many more people studying part-time and more vocationally-focused courses.

Then there is the whole area of technology. Gone (mostly) are the days when you were expected to submit your essays in pen and ink and you came out of a lecture hall with a big inky stain up your hand and writer's cramp. Now lecturers sometimes complain of looking up over a sea of luminous laptop screens rather than faces, although many faculties and departments do still frown on the use of laptops in lectures or seminars.

There will also probably be much more online (or intranet-based) learning than you remember – with online discussion forums and postings, tutor notes and essays being submitted online. The library is much more likely to be open 24 hours a day, and there may be more online learning facilities, for example for reserving or ordering books.

Some universities are even experimenting with the use of podcasts and vodcasts (the same as podcasts but with pictures), video streaming technology and wikis – webpages that can be updated and changed by its users.

From the mature student's perspective, one of the great advantages of all this technology is that it may well mean you do not need to be on campus so frequently. Now that there are resources, or even whole texts, that you can download or read online or other online resources that you

MAKING THE CHANGE

Emma Jeggo is senior student development and support assistant in the University of Sheffield's Student Services Department

We have mature students who have come back to university in their mid-20s, and others who are in their 70s, so it is a very diverse population of students, who will all want different things from their study.

The thing I find most mature students struggle with is fitting their study in around their family lives, work or other commitments. When you are 18 and have an essay deadline you can just shut yourself away in your room for three days or work until 3am or whatever to get it done, but as a mature student you are likely to have other commitments and pressures on your time.

Having said that, I also find that mature students are often hugely positive, determined and diligent, because they have really decided this is what they want to do and have made that commitment. They often end up doing really well, certainly as well as and often better than the younger students.

One of the other things mature students often complain about is feeling isolated. If you are one of only a few mature students on a course you may feel isolated socially, especially if you cannot spend all your time at the university or go to social events in the evenings. But at the same time, it is what you make of it. The younger students will often really value the experience and knowledge you have, so if you are prepared to throw yourself into it, you will normally get a lot back.

Adapting to a new learning landscape

Universities have changed a lot since the days when you just turned up, went to a lecture or seminar and that was it. Now there is much more online learning and tutors will be frequently posting and making notes available online, so it's no longer the end of the world is you miss a lecture, because you can normally still access it online.

At Sheffield, for example, we have a resource called MOLE, or My Online Learning Environment, where you can submit assignments, download course information, look up modules and lecture notes, access admission and exam dates, chat on forums and so on, without physically having to be at the university. But it is a resource that is really in addition to the face-to-face contact you need to have and maintain with your department. Each department also has a mature student tutor who is available for anyone who has problems or needs help or advice. There are mature student talks at open days and an 'offer holder' event prior to students starting their course, along with a named contact for pre-entry enquiries. For example, at Sheffield I am the named mature student contact while students are on their course and so I organise a welcome day and evening a few weeks before the start of term to help people familiarise themselves with their new surroundings and meet other new and current mature students. These welcome events are followed up by a series of social events in Freshers' week, and ongoing events throughout the year.

A lot of mature students choose to study locally, which is very understandable, but you do need to think carefully about what this is going to means in terms of commuting to the university. If you are having to spend two hours a day or more travelling on top of your studies that can add a lot of stress. And if you have to be at lectures by 9am you can end up working very long days.

Getting help – from essays to employability

Mature students can also access various study skills programmes on things such as essay writing or revision and exams. We have an English Language Teaching Centre that, while predominantly for our international students, can be used by any student. You can get advice, for example, on how to write something in a more 'academic' style. For a lot of students, not just mature students, how universities teach and the whole learning process of being at university can be a challenge. There can be very different academic expectations at university.

If you're using your studies as a stepping stone to changing your career, it is a good idea to speak to the university careers service as early as you can. It can even be a good idea to speak to them before you start the course to find out what sorts of jobs there might be at the end of it. They will normally have statistics on the number of people who have gone on to jobs from a certain course, what sorts of jobs they have gone into and so on.

For example, we get a lot of people who are keen on archaeology. But you have to recognise there are not that many jobs likely to be available at the end of it and what there are, are generally not paid that well. That's of course not a reason not to go for it if it is what you really, really want to do, but speaking to a careers adviser will help you understand better what you are getting yourself into.

Money matters

Most university websites will include a lot of information about funding and finance, so it is worth spending time researching this. You do have to recognise that for a second degree you are unlikely to get a student loan, so for many mature students funding can be a real issue.

Since the introduction of fees there is much more general funding support available and there may be bursaries or scholarships that you can apply for. If as a student you experience unexpected or higher than average costs there may be support available through the Access to Learning Fund **www.direct.gov.uk/en/EducationAnd Learning/UniversityAndHigherEducation/StudentFinance/Extrahelp/DG_171615**. So there is money out there but you need to speak to the individual university about it. Often the student finance office (rather than the finance department, which will deal with the university's finances) is the best place to start.

The most important thing to remember about going back to college or university is that you will not be alone, so take all the support and help that is available. Use mentors, study skills sessions, careers and tutor advice and support officers. Secondly, remember it is up to you. It is easy to get isolated and end up thinking negatively about the whole experience, but if you can make a point of meeting a few people early on, even just regularly to have a coffee, it can make a big difference. Universities can help you get where you want to go, but it will be up to you to get there.

can access from the comfort of your home the studying experience has become more flexible and less stressful. It is exactly this online and home-based flexibility around learning that can tempt career changers to turn to the Open University for their undergraduate and postgraduate qualifications, an option that we shall now look at more closely.

The Open University

Founded by Harold Wilson's government in 1969, the Open University, or the OU as it is more popularly known, is the UK's only university dedicated to distance learning. It has no campus and, before the rise of the internet, was best known for its late-night lectures on TV by academics with perhaps the most curious assortment of ties and hairstyles anywhere in the world.

Its focus on distance learning means that, while it does run short residential and weekend courses that can supplement coursework, the vast majority of the study is carried out remotely, online, by post, through DVDs and so on. The beauty of this is that it means you can juggle study much more easily with home and work life and you can be anywhere and anytime (in a hotel room with your laptop, say) and still feasibly be studying.

This makes the OU a hugely popular option for people trying to boost their CV or carve out a new niche, but who can't or don't want to give up the day job or live on or commute to a campus. You can take as long as you like to gain your qualification or study really intensively to gain it more quickly.

The university currently has around 150,000 undergraduate and 30,000 postgraduate students on its books, of all ages, backgrounds and abilities, though this could well increase on the back of government plans set out last year that the OU should start to work with other universities to develop digital versions of other degrees. Nearly all its students learn part-time and it is estimated 70 per cent of its undergraduate students are combining study with full-time employment, with a third studying for a qualification despite having entry qualifications at a lower level to those normally demanded by UK universities. It is also a perfect means of learning for people who are less mobile or unable to venture out of their home that easily, and the university has 10,000 students with disabilities.

The OU way of learning

So, how does it work? The OU uses a method of delivery called supported open learning, which means you are required to do the majority of your learning and reading in your own time, including writing assignments and online tutorials – so an ability to self-motivate is essential. You will be supported by a tutor, who will set, mark and appraise your work and provide feedback and be at the end of an email should they be needed. Tutors may also sometimes arrange phone, online or even face-to-face tutorials.

The university, which has its headquarters in Milton Keynes, operates a network of 13 regional centres, where many of the residential or day school events are held, and has an extensive online library that you can draw upon, including newspapers, periodicals, journals, extracts from primary sources and so on. Beyond this, once you are registered and paid up, you will be sent (or be able to download) a range of printed course materials, set books, audio and video cassettes, DVDs, CD-Roms and, for more scientific courses, home experiment kits. Course materials are also available in alternative formats for students who have disabilities.

Open admissions

Another attraction about the university is its policy of 'open' admissions. By this it means there are no set entry requirements for joining a course – although you do have to be over 16 (apart from in exceptional circumstances) and, if you are studying full-time elsewhere, you will need to get written permission from that institution agreeing for you to take the OU course.

So it's just a question of choosing your course, registering (which you can either do online or by phone), paying your fee and off you go. What this means in practice is that it's perfectly possible simply to dip in and out of courses that take your fancy and learn for learning's sake. It also means you can test the water of an interest first and then decide a) whether study is for you and b) whether it is something you want to pursue at a more serious and dedicated level.

However, while it may technically be possible to go for absolutely any course at any level, it does not necessarily mean that you should. OU courses are set at different levels ranging from those appropriate to people who have never studied, to those at postgraduate level.

The university makes it very clear that it is your responsibility to choose the right course for you. Going straight for a postgraduate course may seem attractive but if you've never studied at higher education level you will inevitably struggle, probably fail and simply end up wasting your money and everyone's time. Be realistic and pick your course wisely.

The points system

Courses are graded by level and by points. So, if you want to do, say, a history undergraduate degree you will get a choice of level one to level three optional and compulsory courses, the majority being worth 60 points each but some worth less, with students 'strongly advised' to take level ones before progressing to level twos and so on.

Some courses will be more generalist, such as, say, sticking with history, an overview of the medieval to the modern world from 1400 to 1900 (a level two course) or more specialist, such as Empire 1492 to 1975 (a level three course).

To get an honours degree you'll need to build up a total of 360 points while a taught postgraduate master's is 180 points. Alternatively you can gain what's called an Open degree with 300 points, which is a flexible degree unique to the OU where you mix and match the courses you want to do – the learning for learning's sake we touched on earlier – and build up what is, in effect, a general degree.

One thing you do need to be careful about, however, is ensuring that if you want to get, say, a full honours degree in a specific subject, you build up the right points from the right courses. It is quite easy to choose a course that you assume will count towards your degree only to find later on that it hasn't and that, unless you are happy coming out the other end with a more generic honours degree, you may end up doing more courses than you intended.

While the OU's website is certainly useful when it comes to planning out what courses and modules you should be doing, it makes sense to speak to your regional adviser – who you will be assigned as soon as you register for any course – just to make absolutely sure that if you take a certain course it is going to count in the way that you want it to. Foundation degrees require 240 points, diplomas 120 points and certificates 60 points. You can also choose to do as many or as few courses as you like at any one time, though the more courses you do, obviously, the more challenging it will be.

If you are juggling a day job it probably makes sense not to attempt to do more than one or two courses at a time, depending on their level. This can of course mean it takes much longer to get your degree, sometimes as long as six years or more compared with the conventional three, but it's important to consider what you can feasibly manage alongside your other day-to-day pressures. It's worth being aware, too, that there are some courses with a time limit on them – for example, the OU's MBA must be completed within eight years.

How courses are assessed

Courses will normally be assessed through a combination of written, tutor-marked assignments (TMAs) and examinations. The examinations will normally take place in a venue local to you, such as a local further education college. On some courses there may also be more substantial projects or a dissertation to complete.

Much as in a 'normal' university, your course, which will usually last for between six and nine months, will follow a set schedule, with assignments needing to be submitted by a deadline, though it is sometimes possible to ask for an extension if you have a good reason.

Studying from home

One of the challenges of such learning is ensuring you don't become isolated. While you won't have the automatic contact with other students that a classroom setting brings, it is now possible to communicate (or grumble!) with other students through the university's various chatrooms and forums.

There is a conferencing facility called FirstClass and the university runs an Open University Students' Association. The OU's website has a pretty good support section offering advice on some of the skills you will need to study effectively, how to do assignments, exams and so on. There is also an OU careers advisory service that you can access.

Key points

- Look at location, the specifics of your course and facilities
- Speak to admissions staff, tutors and support officers for advice
- Consider attending an open day, going on a mature student orientation day and doing some pre-course study skills sessions
- Universities, and university life, have changed considerably in recent years, with more diverse courses and increased use of technology
- Be prepared to throw yourself into the experience and you will probably get back what you put in

Part 1: Chapter Four

FINANCE AND FUNDING

The average debt racked up by a full-time undergraduate student in their three or four years at university is estimated now to be £15,700, and rising. Even for those who are able to continue working while studying, whether by doing a vocational course in the evenings, studying part-time or flexibly or just by burning the candle at both ends, the costs for a mature student can be a serious issue. As well as paying for course fees, books and materials you may also have to budget for 'incidentals' such as childcare or travel – though the word of course does not do justice to their importance.

The key message, therefore, in this chapter is that doing the legwork can often pay dividends. Accessing and applying for funding can feel bureaucratic, demoralising and time-consuming but there is a wealth of state and other support targeting the mature student, including relatively cheap student-oriented finance from the banks and 'free' money in the shape of bursaries, grants and scholarships.

The difficulty, much of the time, is knowing who to ask and what is out there. But don't just assume you're not going to be entitled to *something*, because if you pipe up and ask you may well be pleasantly surprised.

Finance and funding at the FE level

The first thing to recognise as a mature student at this level is that, unlike those going straight on from school, you are in all probability going to be stung for fees. One possible exception is if you live and are studying in Scotland, though even then this is not guaranteed (see below). The fees will, of course, vary according to the institution and length or scope of the course that you are doing. They could be anywhere from a few hundred pounds for an NVQ, including the registration and tuition fee, through to the thousands for more substantial courses, such as BTECs, HNDs or HNCs.

Many career changers plan their move for some time and therefore are more able to save up and self-fund but, if that is not possible – perhaps because you are on a low income or not earning at all – there are sources of funding support you can turn to. FE and HE colleges also go out of their way to attract mature students and will often have discretionary funding support packages in place. The bad news is that there is a lot of competition for these and, if you're going to have to fall back on the state for support, it is all means-tested and, quite rightly, geared towards those on lower incomes.

One source of support in England worth looking into if you're on a relatively low income (at time of writing up to £19,513 if you're single or £30,810 for a combined income) is an Adult Learning Grant. This will pay out up to £30 a week during term time if you are doing a full-time level 2 or level 3 qualification (so, if you recall, the equivalent of GCSE or A-level).

You must also be studying at a college funded by the Learning & Skills Council. Unfortunately, if you're already claiming jobseeker's allowance you won't be eligible, though you still may be even if you are working full-time. The payment tapers depending on how much you are earning so, for example, you only get the full £30 a week if you are earning below £11,810 and if you are making above £15,406 (but still below the £19,513 threshold) it goes down to £10 a week. Payments are made directly into your bank account, and will normally be paid out for two years or, at most, three years. You can apply through the Directgov website. You may also hear talk of the Education Maintenance Allowance, which pays up to £30 a week (again means-tested) but, as it's only for 16–17 year olds studying full-time, it is not really relevant for career changers.

If you're studying full-time at a sixth form in England, perhaps if you are retaking A-levels or taking them for the first time so you can change direction, you may also be eligible for the sixth form College Childcare Scheme. This is for any parent aged over 20 and is worth up to £160 a week per child (£175 in London) though, again, is means-tested. It can be used for fees towards childcare costs or the cost of any extra journeys between home and an Ofsted-registered childcare provider. To be eligible for the full whack your household income has to have been less than £30,502 in the previous tax year, tapering off to between £32 and £35 a week outside and inside London respectively, for households bringing in up to £50,501. It is also possible to get this benefit if you are studying part-time, though the figure will be reduced accordingly.

On top of this, there is the government's Free Childcare for Training and Learning for Work scheme, aimed at out-of-work parents who have a partner in work and are looking to retrain or study for new skills. It can provide up to £175 per child per week to help with childcare costs. It too is means-tested and only available to those with a household income of £20,000 or less a year.

Many colleges have what are called Discretionary Support Funds to help people on low incomes or in financial hardship with things such as childcare, accommodation, course-related equipment and travel costs. The amounts will vary so the thing to do is speak to your college student support or welfare officer. It's worth being aware that these used to be called Learner Support Funds, Access Funds or Hardship Funds so, if you hear someone referring to those, what they mean is Discretionary Support Funds.

Career changers aged 50 or over may also be able to access a Fifty Plus In-work training grant, which you can apply for through Jobcentre Plus. These are grants for if you are trying to gain a new trade or industry qualification, learning computer skills and so on, and will give you up to £1,500 towards any work-related training, whether provided by an employer, local college or other provider. They can be used for tuition fees, books, exams and registration fees and any other course-related costs. To qualify you have to be currently working (though self-employed counts), have previously claimed from a range of benefits including Jobseeker's Allowance, Incapacity Benefit, Employment and Support Allowance and Income Support (Directgov has a full list) continuously for 26 weeks. You need to be no longer receiving benefits and still within 52 weeks of stopping your claim, and you will need to have been aged over 50 when you terminated your claim.

City & Guilds offers a number of what it calls 'access bursaries' to those aged 16 or over and living in the UK and studying for one of its qualifications. These can be used to help with course fees, living costs, childcare or travel or equipment and materials. You should expect to be interviewed as to why you think you deserve this kind of support.

Professional and Career Development Loans

Another source of funding is the Career Development Loan or, as they have recently been renamed, Professional and Career Development Loans. This is essentially a special loan that can be gained through a number of high-street banks (currently Barclays, the Co-operative Bank and Royal Bank of Scotland) but arranged through the Learning and Skills Council, that allows you to borrow between £300 and £8,000 to help you fund between two and three years' worth of learning.

The LSC pays the interest on your loan while you are studying, so you will normally only be expected to start picking up the tab a month after you complete your training. You will, of course, pay interest on the loan but you can make repayments over an agreed period at a fixed rate. These loans tend to be particularly popular with cash-strapped postgraduate students, but are just as applicable for people doing lower-level courses (though not foundation courses that are intended to lead on to an undergraduate degree). The Learning & Skills Council has more information on these at **http://pcdl.lsc.gov.uk/**.

The situation in Scotland, Wales and Northern Ireland

Since devolution, if you are studying full-time in Scotland for a non-advanced course, such as a Scottish Vocational Qualification, you may not have to pay tuition fees. This doesn't happen automatically though, and you will have to apply for a fee waiver so that your eligibility can be determined (this is normally based on your residency in Scotland). If you are studying part-time or doing a distance learning course you may still have to pay tuition fees, much as in England, but if you are on a low income or on benefits you may be exempted. The key, as ever, is to check with the individual college concerned.

If you are on an income of £18,000 a year or less you may also be eligible for a Scottish Individual Learning Account through ILA Scotland **www.ilascotland.org.uk** that will fund you up to £200 a year towards the cost of retraining. For those wanting to study part-time for a higher-level qualification there is also the possibility of accessing a £500 ILA.

Wales also offers such Individual Learning Accounts, as well as the Assembly Learning Grant from the Welsh Assembly, that provides extra support for Welsh-domiciled students from low-income families who are pursuing an FE or HE course, to a maximum (in 2009/10) of £2,906. In Northern Ireland, where back in 2007 its 16 FE colleges were merged to create six area-based FE colleges, there are also a range of bursaries and access funds available through the various colleges.

Finance and funding at undergraduate level

Whenever the phrase 'student debt' is mentioned, what we're normally referring to is undergraduate study. And it is true, mostly because the length of study is so much longer than for most other sorts of study (except feasibly a PhD), that it is undergraduates who tend to be under the most financial pressure. Though say that to a room full of postgraduates and the atmosphere is likely to turn distinctly frosty.

However, there are millions of pounds of financial aid available at undergraduate level, a large proportion of it 'free' money that does not have to be repaid, as well as support in the form of student loans.

What will it all cost?

First, though, what does studying at this level tend to cost? There will, as ever, be variations but what you will normally be looking at are annual tuition fees of around £3,000 – in 2010 these are £3,290 in England, Wales and Northern Ireland and around £1,775 in Scotland (for non-Scottish residents).

So, assuming basic living costs of, say, £10,000 for nine months in London, as estimated recently by the London School of Economics – and, in fact, probably pretty conservative for most mature students with a mortgage to pay and family to keep – it is easy to see how things can rapidly start to escalate. Fees for courses such as HNDs or HNCs will normally be slightly lower.

Getting a loan

While this level of debt can be daunting for those who have never been in the red, what is important to be aware of is that there is structured financial help and support out there. Your first port of call should probably be the Student Loans Company **www.slc.co.uk** which administers all government-funded student loans and grants to students throughout the UK. Incidentally, it also has some good basic information about student finance on its website, as do UCAS and Directgov.

Along with bursaries, which we shall come to in a moment, student loans and grants are the main source of funding support for full-time undergraduates. All students who are eligible for a loan can get one to cover the cost of their higher education course tuition fees in full, as well as what is known as a 'maintenance loan' which is designed to help with the cost of accommodation and other living costs, although this is means-tested. You do not need to start paying back student loans until after you've left your course and are earning more than £15,000.

Once you hit this threshold you'll start paying 9 per cent of whatever you earn over £15,000, though payments will stop if you subsequently

MAKING THE CHANGE

Like so many, Abbie Smith, 31, fell into a career, in her case in charity fundraising, after leaving university, only to realise a few years down the line that it was not what she wanted to do. After going back to college and doing an MA, she is now working as a production assistant at media company TwoFour in Plymouth.

After my degree, in business studies at Plymouth University, I landed a job doing fundraising at my local hospital, which then led to various moves until I was appointed head of fundraising for a hospice in Cornwall. In a way I'm still not entirely sure why it went wrong, but it did. The environment was not particularly friendly and it was all very insular. One problem, I think, was that, despite the fact I was 27 and had seven or eight years' experience under my belt I looked quite young, so some of the people there clearly did not think I was up to the job. So, in 2005, when I was offered voluntary redundancy, I decided to take it. It had been a pretty prestigious job but I was completely disenchanted. By that point I had come to the conclusion I had taken fundraising as a career as far as it was going to go. The problem was I had no idea what else I wanted to do, or what to do next.

A chance to take stock

What the redundancy money gave me was some breathing space. I went off travelling for a few months, to places such as Singapore, New Zealand, Fiji and the US, just to get some time to think about what it was I really wanted to do. It's very rare once you've started employment that you get a chance to take three months out just to take stock of your life, but it was definitely worth it. I gradually began to realise that what I'd always liked best about my career had been the more creative elements, particularly sorting out TV productions.

I was in New York looking at a few jobs online when I saw an advert for an assistant for a film festival in Cornwall and, more out of hope than any sense that I might actually get it, I applied. But I did get it, which was great because it really showed me it was the sort of area I wanted to work in – but I realised that what I was missing was the technical skills. I had lots of general production and organisational skills, but I had no idea about things such as shooting film or editing or actually operating cameras.

But I knew it would be a big commitment to go back to college. When you've been in employment and started earning money it is much harder to go back. You have a mortgage, you're probably running a car, and it's just even the lifestyle of having money and going out with friends who are also working. So it is something you have to think about really hard. While people I spoke to said it was possible to move into TV production without doing a course, a qualification could give you an advantage.

I had identified the MA in TV production at University College Falmouth as the course I probably wanted to do and so started off cautiously by emailing the director of the course asking whether we could meet, simply so I could sound her out on whether it was a good investment. I turned up just expecting to have a chat and a coffee but there were people there with their portfolios having interviews. When she offered me a place straightaway, it was a complete shock.

Making ends meet

The next hurdle was the cost of it all. It was a one-year course and the fees alone were around £4,000. I decided the best thing to do was to take out a Professional and Career Development Loan, which I did through Barclays. I got an £8,000 loan that covered 80 per cent of the course fees (the maximum amount allowed) and then the rest went towards living and other expenses. I read about them on the Learning and Skills Council's website and then found out which banks offered them, spoke to a few friends about them and looked to see which had the lowest interest rate.

Once I had chosen which lender I was going to go to it was simply a question of applying through the website, having a conversation with them over the phone, filling out a number of forms, showing proof of my mortgage, and then getting the money paid into my account.

In retrospect the biggest mistake I made was that I went for a loan with a short repayment period, thinking that when I had finished I would be able to roll it into a normal bank loan. But I haven't been able to do that because of the credit crunch and so have ended up having to make quite high payments on it. But the upside is that I am repaying it more quickly. More generally, the student funding office at the university was very helpful in offering advice on things such as hardship loans and other funding sources, so it is definitely worth going to see them. I was also eligible for a Disabled Students' Allowance because I had dyslexia, which helped me to get a lot of useful equipment to help me on the course.

Stepping stones to the right job

One of the great things about going back to study, apart from getting the qualification, is the potential it gives you for networking and meeting new contacts. For example, I got my current job because I went to talk to TwoFour as part of my dissertation. In fact, although I only graduated from the course in September 2008, I was offered the job here the month before, so I really feel as though I fell on my feet.

When it comes to finding a job in a new field what you have to do is sell your new skills but also sell your existing strengths. You shouldn't disregard your previous experience just because perhaps it's not precisely relevant to the job description. I drew on a lot of the strengths I had built up over the years in fundraising, for example showing that I knew how to function effectively in a working environment, unlike perhaps someone fresh out of university.

When you switch career later in life you are going to have to invest a lot of time, energy and probably money in doing it, so you really need to be sure it is the right move for you. You cannot just chop and change around and go back. So if you have a new career in mind what's a good idea, if you can, is to get some experience of it while you are still in your old career. It might mean that you take a week or fortnight's holiday to do some unpaid work-shadowing rather than jetting off somewhere hot, but it will be worth it in the long run. Also, try and talk to as many people who are in that industry about what it is really like, how you get in, what employers look for and your prospects.

It has been a hard slog, and financially it has been really difficult, but I am so glad I've done it. For me it was definitely the right decision to make. Each year you delay doing it someone else is coming up and getting a job in 'your' career. You'll need to do the leg work and take the time to research it properly, then, once you're doing it, you just have to embrace it and talk to everyone, get as much advice and take every opportunity that comes your way.

fall back below that mark. Another good bit of news is that if you're due to start paying back your loan from April 2012, you will have the option of taking a repayment break for up to five years.

It is worth being aware that there are some age restrictions, with tuition fee loans only available to the under-60s in England and Wales or the under-50s in Scotland, though you can still get one if you are aged 50–54 and planning to work after your course.

While the tuition loan will cover the full cost of your fees, there are maximum limits on maintenance loans, as well as entitlement being decided on the basis of your income or that of your partner (or, and admittedly this is likely to be less relevant to the average career changer, that of your parents).

For example, this year, according to the government, London-based students could get a maximum maintenance loan of £6,928, with those outside London getting up to £4,950. But do be aware that the final academic year of a course is viewed as having fewer weeks than previous years (because previous years include the need for financial assistance during the summer holidays) so any loan you get will be lower in your final year.

In Scotland, assuming you meet the residency criteria, the maximum fees that will be paid for you will be £4,625 a year for a standard 30-week course. However, if your family income is over around £55,550 a year you will only receive £915 a year.

Access to Learning fund and grants

Students (either undergraduate or postgraduate) from disadvantaged backgrounds or experiencing financial hardship may be entitled to help from the government's Access to Learning fund, which you apply for through the student services department at your university. Awards tend to range from £100 to around £3,500, though they cannot be used to pay for tuition fees. One of the good things from the career changer point of view is that mature students are considered one of the priority groups by universities and colleges for access to this funding.

The next important source of funding is grants; around a third of new students are eligible for full Maintenance Grants or Special Support Grants and around another third are eligible for a partial grant.

These grants are for students from low-income households (up to a family income of £25,000) and are worth up to £2,906 in the 2010 academic year, though you can only get Special Support Grants if you already receive

Income Support or another means-tested benefit, such as housing benefit. You can apply for this support up to nine months after the start of the academic year. The threshold for a partial Maintenance Grant is a family income of £50,020.

If you are studying part-time and are on a low income you may be entitled to a Part-Time Fee Grant or Course Grant. The fee grant will help with tuition fees and the course grant is designed to help with books, course materials and travel expenses. What you get will be based on how 'intensive' your course is; in other words how long it takes to complete compared with an equivalent full-time course. The maximum for this is around £1,470.

If you normally live in Wales and are studying at a higher education institution there, you will also be entitled to a Fee Grant of up to £1,940, which does not have to be repaid. This is available irrespective of family income, and is paid directly to your place of study. There is also, as mentioned above, the Assembly Learning Grant, with the grant replacing the Maintenance Loan up to a value of £1,288.

Parents' Learning Allowance and Childcare Grant

Other grants that may be of particular interest to mature students and so well worth investigating include the Childcare Grant and Parents' Learning Allowance though, again, these are both means-tested (or dependent on the cost of your childcare).

The Childcare Grant can cover up to 85 per cent of your childcare costs during term-times and holidays, up to a maximum of £148.75 a week if you have one child and £225 a week for two or more children. It is potentially available to full-time students with dependent children under 15 in registered or approved childcare (or under 17 if they have special needs). But be aware if you or your partner also get an element of Working Tax Credits you won't be able to get this.

The Parents' Learning Allowance can pay you between £50 to £1,508 to cover the cost of books, course materials or travel expenses, though what you get will be very much dependent on your household income. Then there is also the Adult Dependents' Grant that is available for full-time higher education students who have an adult who depends on them financially – perhaps a partner or elderly relative – though not, unfortunately, grown-up children, however 'dependent' they may sometimes seem! This is, once again, means-tested, but was worth up to £2,642 in 2009/10.

Where to find out more

The primary bodies you need to go to for more information are:

- in England, Student Finance England through Directgov at **www.direct.gov.uk/en/Dl1/Directories/UsefulContactsByCategory/ EducationAndLearningContacts/DG_172310**
- in Wales Student Finance Wales **www.studentfinancewales.co.uk**
- in Northern Ireland (you've guessed it) Student Finance Northern Ireland **www.studentfinanceni.co.uk** and,
- in Scotland, the Student Awards Agency for Scotland **www.student- support-saas.gov.uk**.

Another good way of finding out what universities are offering and whether you are likely to be eligible is to use the 'student finance calculator' that most of these bodies will have. The link to the English one is here: **www.studentfinance.direct.gov.uk/portal/page?_pageid=153, 4680089&_dad=portal&_schema=PORTAL**.

Bursaries and scholarships

The next tranche of funding comes from bursaries and scholarships. Bursaries will tend to be means-tested payments by universities that you can get on top of any student loans and grants and which, again, you don't have to pay back. It's worth knowing, too, that while most bursaries and scholarships will be in the form of hard cash some universities do offer part of their bursary in the form of a discounted service, for example discounted accommodation or entrance to sports facilities.

The main difference between bursaries and scholarships, incidentally, is that bursaries tend to refer to income-related awards while scholarships will usually be based on some other criteria, normally academic prowess. But it's also worth knowing that many universities use the terms interchangeably.

Bursaries

The thinking behind these bursaries is that universities that want to charge more than £1,285 in 2009/10 for a course (in other words pretty much all of them) now have to provide extra non-repayable bursaries to students who are receiving the full Maintenance Grant or Special Support Grant.

The other hugely important thing to know is that when you are completing your student finance part of the application form you should tick the box entitled 'consent to share' as this will allow the university to consider you for a bursary. This is because many universities and colleges use a bursaries administration service run by the Student Loans Company to assess and pay eligible bursaries and scholarships direct to you, meaning the information you supply in your student finance application form becomes critical.

In England, if you are getting a full Maintenance Grant or Support Grant and being charged the full tuition fee, you will be entitled to at least a £319 bursary a year, which is often called the 'Minimum Bursary'. But most universities and colleges will also give you a bursary if you're eligible for some of the Maintenance Grant or Special Support Grant, and some will give a bursary to everyone, regardless of household income, points out the Office for Fair Access, which works to promote fair access to higher education in England.

On average, a student who started in 2009 and received the full Maintenance Grant could have expected to receive a bursary of just over £900 a year, which is certainly not to be sniffed at.

If you are studying in Wales, you have to go through the Welsh National Bursary Scheme which is essentially the Welsh equivalent and pretty similar to the English scheme, with a minimum award of around the £319 mark, means-tested and based on your family income. The situation is pretty similar in Northern Ireland. In Scotland, though there is no bursary scheme equivalent there is a scheme called the Young Students' Bursary (for under 25s) where you are paid a bursary instead of part of the student loan, so it reduces the amount of the loan you need to take out. If you are eligible for this you may also be eligible to receive an additional loan of up to £605, again means-tested. In all the countries it is worth checking out whether you might be entitled to any funding or grants because of various specific needs.

In Scotland, for example, there are a range of supplementary grants for lone parents, those with dependents, those leaving care to go into higher education and those with disabilities. Similarly, in England, there are a range of adult dependents grants and childcare grants. If you are going into health or teaching, there are also a range of bursaries covering these two professions, with more information from the Training and Development Agency for Schools **www.tda.gov.uk** and, for the NHS Bursary, the NHS Business Services Authority **www.nhsstudentgrants.co.uk**.

Scholarships

When it comes to scholarships, it's really just a case of approaching the individual university student finance departments. You can often get scholarships for specific courses or subjects or you may even be able to pick up one that has been provided by a private organisation or institution or, again, it might be one based on specific financial need or hardship. Sometimes it can even be because you are from the local area, perhaps because the university is keen to attract local students.

The key with scholarships is not to discount yourself, as they can be worth a lot of money and there will often be many of them. To pick out a typical example, the University of Westminster offered a range of 'gold' and 'silver' scholarships in 2009, worth between £12,000 and £6,000 over three years to cover tuition fees.

These scholarships were open to any undergraduate to apply for and, while largely based on academic grades achieved, this was not the sole criterion. On top of this, the university offered a vast range of privately funded awards, such as through its Helena Kennedy Foundation, Terry Chalk Scholarship, Organ Scholarship or 'Care Leavers' scholarship, for example.

Why doing a second degree just got expensive

Westminster also had a scholarship offering funding for students studying for an 'Equivalent Level Qualification', known as an ELQ, or in lay terms doing a course that is at an equivalent or lower level than an existing qualification that a student already holds. Government changes to how these qualifications are funded, and so charged for, are potentially an important issue for career changers, who might well be going back to college to do a qualification such as, say, a second undergraduate degree, despite having graduated in a different subject some years back.

As of 2008/09 the government withdrew funding subsidies for all UK students studying for ELQs, meaning that universities would no longer receive any central funding for such students. This means, in turn, that universities will need to pass on this extra cost through higher tuition fees for those doing ELQs.

While some universities held their fees for 2008/09, by 2009/10 it is expected that most will by now be passing on the higher cost, meaning such students may have to pay much higher fees, perhaps around the £6,000 a year mark or at a level similar to that of international students.

But, again, it is worth checking with the college or university directly as there will often be exemptions for various courses and types of student.

Finally, while it will probably be a drop in the ocean, don't forget that students can often get some quite substantial day-to-day discounts on living expenses. If you join the National Union of Students you can get its NUS Extra discount card offering discounts on various shops and retailers, with more details available at **www.nus.org.uk/en/NUS-Extra**. There are also some specific websites, such as Student Discounts **www.studentdiscounts.co.uk** or Student Advantage **www.studentadvantage.com/discountcard** tailored to offering cheap deals for students.

Finance and funding at postgraduate level

With a one-year full-time master's now likely to set you back somewhere between £4,000 and £5,000 – with many costing much more, particularly MBAs – going the postgraduate route is not cheap. What's more, the biggest difference between funding at postgraduate and undergraduate level is that the Student Loans Company doesn't cater for postgraduates so, in effect, you are much more on your own financially.

However, when it comes to fees, it is worth recognising that if you are studying part-time you may well be able to pay half of the fee one year and half the next, helping to spread the financial burden. On some master's you can also pay on a modular, termly or pay-as-you-go basis and it may even be possible to pay monthly or quarterly, though it is probable the university might levy an extra fee for allowing you to do that. Either way, it's worth sounding out the student finance office as to what your options are likely to be.

As we touched on earlier, Professional and Career Development Loans are a popular funding route for postgraduates, though it can also be worth checking with your bank whether you might be eligible for a Professional Studies Loan. These are available through a number of banks for both undergraduate and postgraduate study in a range of 'professional' areas such as accountancy, engineering, law and medicine. Applicants can borrow up to £25,000, but will need to start making repayments within six months of the end of the course.

The role of research councils

There are also a number of government-funded Research Councils that support research, and so are one of the most important sources of funding of postgraduate students, funding an estimated 10,000 studentships a year between them.

There are seven grant-awarding councils, which can be found at Research Councils UK **www.rcuk.ac.uk**. Competition, inevitably, is desperately fierce, with the most common type of award at master's level being a one-year 'Advanced Course Studentship' that normally covers tuition fees, a Maintenance Grant and a contribution towards expenses such as travel and books.

It is possible to get some public or state-funded support for postgraduate study, though again it is hugely competitive and much sought after. The Students Awards Agency for Scotland **www.saas.gov.uk** has a Postgraduate Students' Allowances scheme available to Scottish-domiciled students planning to study in the UK.

Similarly, the Department for Employment and Learning in Northern Ireland **www.delni.gov.uk** offers some funding support at postgraduate level for Northern Ireland-domiciled students and UK and EU students who want to study in Northern Ireland. The European Social Fund **www.esf.gov.uk** also supports a number of vocational postgraduate courses in the UK.

More places to look for financial support

There are various private charities, foundations and trusts that award partial funding for postgraduate study. These range in size from the Wellcome Trust **www.wellcome.ac.uk**, which awards hundreds of studentships each year, to much smaller groups, such as the British Federation of Women Graduates **www.bfwg.org.uk**, which offers a small number of 'cost-of-living' bursaries for female postgraduates in the second year of a research degree.

Another option, though it is more likely to happen at PhD than master's level, is to try and pick up a bit of teaching work, perhaps as a Research or Teaching Assistant. And, much as at undergraduate level, pretty much all universities will offer a range of postgraduate bursaries and scholarships, ranging from full-fee studentships (often for research-based study) and Maintenance Grants, to a simple contribution to your study costs. As with the undergraduate options, it makes sense to trawl the university website and speak to your department or tutor and the student finance office.

What the vast majority of postgrads do is 'mix and match' their financial support as far as they can, combining self-payment with studentships,

MAKING THE CHANGE

CASE STUDY:
From building site to dog-grooming salon

Laid off in 2007 as the recession first started to make its presence felt, former builder Chris Cox, 25, now runs a busy dog-grooming business in Stourbridge, set up with the help of Jobcentre Plus.

I've always loved animals, particularly dogs, so being made redundant in a way made the decision for me. It wasn't an easy time because, as I was a contractor rather than being permanently employed, I didn't get any pay-off at all. So you do think, 'What am I going to do, how am I going to feed the family and pay the bills?'

I got the idea simply because one day I was looking on eBay and noticed an advert for a mobile dog-grooming van and thought it was a great idea. When I spoke about it to my New Deal adviser at Jobcentre Plus she was really helpful and encouraged me to look into it in more detail. I found a really good 30-day fast-track course on dog grooming in nearby Market Drayton but, at a cost of £3,000 I thought it would be beyond me to do it. So I was really surprised when my adviser said Jobcentre Plus would be prepared to pay for half of it and then my parents offered to pay for the other half. I signed on it at the start of December 2008, achieving a City & Guilds level two certificate. It was hard work but great fun and because it was something I knew I really wanted to do – and because I recognised this was probably the only way I was going to be able to support my family – I felt really driven to do well. I had also already started advertising the business on a small scale, and we were even beginning to get in potential clients, so I had to pass!

The course had a two-day segment at the end on running a business, which was very useful. But I've also had a lot of advice and support from Birmingham Chamber of Commerce, who I still speak to pretty regularly. They helped me to draw up a business plan and just really gave me a whole load of general advice. I am lucky in that I have been able to set up the business in my parents' garage and they were prepared to pay for all the equipment, so I haven't needed to get a bank loan. My dad also helps me with keeping on top of the accounts.

From concept to reality

We formally launched Bow Wow Dog Grooming in March last year and, while it's still only small financially, I've already got more than 70 regular clients, so it is going really well. It's very busy – I'm probably doing three to four dogs a day now. I do a lot of local advertising, particularly in a local listings magazine, which last time it came out brought in 120 clients.

It's important to develop a clear brand and identity quickly. I've made sure all the stationary is properly done, that the car matches the business cards and the advertisements match everything else, and so on. It has to look and feel professional straight away.

You need to think quite hard about how you are going to price the services you offer. I had a good look at what other similar businesses were charging and have pretty much pitched myself in the middle. I'm not the cheapest but I'm not the most expensive either. It really depends on who you think your likely customers are going to be and then trying to position it at the right level. I also try to think of it as not just a dog-grooming service but as a service for the customers, somewhere they can come for a chat or to relax and have a laugh.

Other than that, my only advice would be not to give up, even if you have been made redundant, and just to listen to what people tell you. I've been given so much useful advice and information and had so much support along the way, so you just have to gain as much knowledge as you can before you start.

scholarships, grants, bursaries, competitions and prizes and so on.

If you did your undergraduate degree at the same university it can be worthwhile checking out whether there are reduced postgraduate fees for alumni students. It's probably less relevant for career changers, but some postgraduates also manage to secure an element of sponsorship from their employers. As well as sites such as Directgov, there is the National Postgraduate Council **www.npc.org.uk**, a charity which promotes postgraduate education in the UK and has a lot of useful information on its site. Websites such as PS (Postgraduate Studentships) **www.postgraduate studentships.co.uk** also have a wealth of information about what can be accessed, where and when.

The Open University (again)

As we saw in the previous chapter, the OU works in different ways to other universities, and it revels in its difference when it comes to finance and funding too. The first big difference, as we touched on in the last chapter, is the way you can pay as you go, registering, signing up and paying for individual modules. What this means is that it is much easier to spread the financial burden when you study through the OU, depending of course on how much time you are intending to spend completing your qualification.

The OU's finance side is overseen by Open University Student Budget Accounts (OUSBA) and how it works is that when you register for a course, OUSBA will pay your full course fee and then give you the option of paying it back in two ways. You can either pay back the full course fee to OUSBA before the course starts, in which case you won't pay any interest on the 'loan', or you can pay it back in instalments. If you go this latter route you start repaying about a month after your course begins, making monthly payments over the duration of your course, but incurring interest (currently of around 8.5 per cent). If you change your mind once you have registered it is possible to get a refund – if you cancel before the course start date you will get back 100 per cent of your fee and if you cancel after the start but before you are a third of the way through you will get half your fees.

Course Grants and Fee Grants

When it comes to financial support, much as with more conventional degrees, if you are on a low income you may well be eligible for a Course Grant and/or a Fee Grant. A Course Grant is a non-repayable grant, a bit like a Maintenance Grant, to help with general support and study costs, while a Fee Grant, as its name suggests, is to help pay for course fees.

If you are not on benefits, there are different income thresholds for financial support depending on where you are in the country. In England and Northern Ireland, for example, you will need to have a household income below £16,510 to be eligible for a full Fee Grant and £24,915 for a partial one. A full Fee Grant here will be worth £805 for courses of 30 to 60 points and £1,210 for 90 points. A partial Fee Grant will be a minimum of £50. Students with a household income of up to £30,000 will also be eligible for some discretionary fee support of up to £200. When it comes to Course Grants, the threshold is a household income of below £24,915 for a full award and £27,505 for a partial award. A full Course Grant is worth £260, a partial Course Grant will be a minimum of £50.

In Wales, the household income threshold for fee grants is below £16,530 for a full award and £26,925 for a partial award. A full Fee Grant is worth £635 for 30–60 points of study, and £955 for 90 points, with a partial Fee Grant a minimum of £50. Those with a household income of up to £30,000 will also be eligible for some discretionary fee support. For Course Grants, household income needs to be below £24,925 for a full award, and £27,615 for a partial award, with a full Course Grant worth £1,075 and a partial one worth a minimum of £50.

In Scotland, if you have a household income of under £16,510 your course fees will be paid in full. Similarly to other courses in Scotland, if your personal income is £18,000 or less a year you can open an Individual Learning Account and claim up to £200 a year towards the course fee if you are studying for a course worth fewer than 60 points. If you are studying for more than this, you can still apply for £500 towards course fees.

Other OU financial support

There are also other financial support schemes to be aware of. OU students in England and Northern Ireland, for example, who are already receiving statutory support for their course fees, can apply for the university's Computer Purchase Scheme to help them buy a computer, something that can prove to be invaluable given that the OU is predominantly delivered online. To get this you need to contact the OU's Financial Support Office, which can be emailed at **financial-support@open.ac.uk** or by calling 01908 653411. Once you have registed for a course you will be able to get a grant of £260 to spend on a new laptop or PC. If you did not receive statutory support for your course fees, the OU suggests it may still be worth applying to the Access to Learning Fund (see above) after your course has started for support towards the cost of a computer as well any other study costs.

As we saw earlier, if you are studying for a second first degree or an equivalent higher education qualification to one that you already have, you will now be precluded from receiving a fee or course grant for further study if you are resident in England, Wales or Northern Ireland. Nevertheless, the OU does offer some discretionary funding for students who have a household income of less than £16,510. To be eligible you also need to be studying towards a foundation degree or topping up a foundation degree or other non-honours degree to honours level (and not already have an honours degree). Other criteria for eligibility include being in receipt of a Disabled Students' Allowance, of which more below, or being able to show that you have previously been awarded OU funding towards a second degree-level qualification, which you are still in the process of completing. Students in Scotland in this situation, and who are on certain benefits or have a household income of less than £16,090, may also qualify for their course fee to be paid in full.

If achieving your qualification is going to take longer than six years, the limit set for government-funded support in England, Wales and Northern Ireland, there is some other discretionary funding available that is worth asking about. This will normally take the form of additional fee or study cost support and will go up to a maximum of two years extra. At the other end of the scale, if you are studying for a course worth less than 30 points (some modules for example are worth as little as 10 points) you may be able to apply to the OU for some financial assistance – as courses this small will be outside the remit of the government's course fee grant scheme. Generally speaking, however, only students who are unemployed or on benefits are likely to be able to get any support at this level.

The OU, like many universities, also has a Financial Assistance Fund that provides financial support for students who are experiencing hardship. The money is provided from voluntary donations by the trustees of the university's development fund, with students able to apply for support towards living expenses and unfunded study costs. The amount of support will inevitably depend on individual applications and demand, with awards normally a minimum of £25 and a maximum of £200.

Every little helps?

Finally, at undergraduate level a somewhat quirky avenue for financial support for OU students, and one that has been remarkably unpublicised, is Tesco. This is not so much the delights of stacking shelves to fund your studies, but more about what you put in your trolley and using Clubcard points to pay for course modules.

Back in early 2007, the OU agreed a deal with the supermarket giant to allow its students to pay for all or part of any OU course by exchanging Clubcard vouchers. It works in much the same way as when you cash in your points at the checkout, except you (rather laboriously) have to send off for vouchers, which you then use to pay the OU.

The other advantage with using your Tesco points this way is that you get more 'cash' for your points than you do if you simply trade them in for groceries. Currently how it works is that for every £10 of Clubcard vouchers that you earn you get £40 towards an OU undergraduate course.

OU support at postgraduate level

At postgraduate level, your options are going to be more limited in much the same way as they will be at any university, with Professional and Career Development Loans again one of the main sources of funding.

However, if you are already an OU graduate, perhaps if you are simply progressing from an undergraduate to postgraduate qualification, you may be eligible for its Crowther Fund. This is a fund that was set up in tribute to the university's first chancellor and is part funded by The Open University Foundation, which itself supports disabled and disadvantaged students and runs a research facility. The fund, which is not means-tested, is designed mostly to help students carrying out formal research projects or build on study already completed.

While it's not set in stone, the maximum award is usually around £1,000, though the vast majority of awards will normally be in the hundreds of pounds range. The board that administers the fund will generally look for evidence of a plausible progression in a student's study, a clearly thought-out study plan and a good honours degree, with some consideration of whether you have come from a deprived background – though the organisation stresses it is not a hardship fund.

Some good news for readers of this book is that the fund says 'proposals which relate to a change of career are encouraged'. More information on this can be obtained by emailing **OU-Crowther-Fund@open.ac.uk**.

MAKING THE CHANGE

THE EXPERT'S VIEW

David Barrett is assistant director at the Office for Fair Access **www.offa.org.uk**, which helps promote and safeguard fair access to universities, mainly by monitoring and regulating higher tuition fees and university bursary packages for full-time undergraduate courses.

Universities have worked hard to improve access to higher education since the new student finance system was introduced in 2006, allowing universities to charge higher fees. Before then a lot of the access to funding through scholarships and bursaries had been rather ad hoc, but now all universities and colleges that want to charge higher fees for their full-time undergraduate courses have to give a minimum bursary to the poorest students and many offer bursaries far more widely.

The main message therefore for people who are thinking of going to university to do a first degree is that no one should be put off on financial grounds. There is a lot of support out there both in the form of government grants and loans, and non-repayable bursaries and scholarships from universities and colleges. People often assume that they will not qualify for support because they are not 'poor enough', but the income thresholds used to calculate support often extend further than people think. So, whoever you are and whatever your financial situation, it's important to check what may be available to you. Whether you are coming to higher education later in life or not, the main message is, yes, there are now fees but you should not be put off because there is also a lot of help and support out there.

So what exactly is available?

You can take out government loans to cover both your tuition fees and help with your living costs. Also, if your household income is below a certain level you will be eligible for the non-repayable state Maintenance Grant. You can find details of all the state support on the government website Directgov. Grants don't have to be paid back but loans do and some students worry about building up a debt. It's really important to remember that student loans are a low-risk investment rather than a commercial debt. If you take out a student loan to pay your fees, payment is deferred until after you have graduated and are earning above £15,000. From then, interest is charged at a low rate and if your income dips back below the £15,000 mark, your payments will cease until you're earning above this level again.

When it comes to bursaries and scholarships, this is non-repayable money paid by individual universities and colleges on top of any grants and loans you may get. The amount you receive can vary significantly from one university to another so it's important to check out what's on offer when you're researching where to study. Many universities and colleges will also give you a bursary if you're eligible for some of the Maintenance Grant and some give a bursary to all their students, regardless of household income. Universities and colleges are expected to pay a total of more than £300m to more than 300,000 students in 2009–10.

Surely these funds aren't for me?

We have found that not everyone who is eligible for a bursary is claiming one, so do make sure you are not one of those people. Most universities and colleges pay their bursaries automatically to you through the Students Loans Company, so it's important to make sure that, when you're filling out your form applying for student loans, you agree to share your financial information with your university or college. Some universities and colleges administer their own bursary payments, so look out for any instructions on how to claim bursaries and scholarships in any joining literature or welcome packs.

Don't assume that you won't be eligible for a bursary because you don't get the state Maintenance Grant. Funding support is not just for students from the poorest backgrounds (although poorer students do account for a large proportion of the support offered) and you may be able to get support even if your family income is as high as £50,000. Some bursaries are awarded on non-financial criteria, for example on whether you live locally or on the basis of the subject you are studying (particularly if it is one where there is a shortage of students) or your academic performance prior to coming to university. The value of a bursary can range from a few hundred pounds –

with a 'minimum bursary' being £319 a year – to around £4,000. So it is very important when you are researching a degree to look at both the fees and the possible support available.

If you decide to study part-time or at postgraduate level, the fee and support arrangements are different. Fees for these courses vary more and fees for postgraduate courses are payable upfront, or during the year you're studying, rather than being deferred. However, you may be able to pay in instalments which can make it easier to budget. As with undergraduate study, it is well worth spending a bit of time and effort checking out what's available in the way of support. It may be, for example, that you can get support or a discount if you have already done an undergraduate degree at that particular university, or if you are a local resident.

Most universities will include a lot of this sort of information on their websites but, particularly if you are studying part-time, you may have to dig a little deeper to find information on the part-time elements. The main thing is not to discount yourself or assume you are not eligible.

In short, whether you're hoping to study full-time or part-time, at undergraduate or postgraduate level, for a degree or another qualification such as a certificate of education, Higher National Diploma or foundation degree, it's worth looking into all the costs. Think about both the tuition fees you'll be asked to pay and the financial support you'll be eligible for. Don't assume that the same courses cost the same. They may well vary depending on where you're studying – especially for qualifications other than full-time undergraduate courses and in further education colleges. For general advice, websites such as DirectGov are useful, as is Student Finance England, but if you can't find what you are looking for, either here or on the individual university website, simply ring up the university or college student finance or support office and ask!

For research and PhD students, much as elsewhere, apart from self-funding there is the chance of gaining a research degree studentship which will pay your fees and, in some cases, a Maintenance Grant of up to £13,290 (in 2009/10). There is also a 'dependents fund' to help full-time students who have financial dependents.

Financial support for students with disabilities

The extra financial help that students with disabilities can normally get on top of the general student financial support package can, broadly, be broken down into three main elements: Disabled Students' Allowances, the Access to Learning Fund and Disability Living Allowance. Alongside this there may be entitlement to Employment and Support Allowance (which replaced Incapacity Benefit as of autumn 2008). It is also worth being aware of the fact that, just as for able-bodied students, there is no statutory funding for course fees for disabled students at postgraduate level.

Taking Disabled Students' Allowances first, these are grants to cover the extra costs that students with disabilities may face as a direct result of their disability. These could include things such as specialist equipment or computer software needed for studying, a non-medical helper, note-taker or reader, extra travel costs related to your disability or other expenses, such as tapes or Braille paper. These are not, you will be pleased to hear, means-tested and do not have to be repaid. To be eligible you have to be doing a full-time or part-time course of at least a year, with the condition on the part-time course being that it does not take more than twice as long to complete as the equivalent full-time course.

You will, of course, have to show evidence of your disability, such as an appropriate letter from your GP or other medical professional. If you have learning difficulties such as dyslexia you will need to provide evidence of a 'diagnostic assessment' from a psychologist or suitably qualified teacher. It's worth noting that, even if you have had one of these done in the past, it may need to be updated. If you are getting some other form of bursary or award, perhaps for postgraduate research, you may not qualify. How much you get will, inevitably, vary according to your individual needs and requirements and there are limits to how much you can receive.

The Access to Learning Fund, as we have seen, is primarily aimed at helping students facing financial hardship or from disadvantaged backgrounds, particularly mature students. Where it can help students with disabilities is in the fact that universities and college will decide how money from the fund is to be paid out locally, with students with disabilities another of the priority groups for support.

Disability Living Allowance, also known as DLA, is a tax-free benefit for under-65s who are physically or mentally disabled, need help with caring for themselves or have walking difficulties. It comes in two components, a care component for help looking after yourself and a mobility component for if you can't walk or need help getting around. The different components are paid at different rates and you may get one but not the other depending on your needs.

Skill, the National Bureau for Students with Disabilities **www.skill.org.uk**, publishes a range of free online booklets and has an information service and helpline that offers advice. There will also be help and support available from individual charities such as, say, the RNIB or RNID, if you have specific issues around visual or hearing impairment and study.

Key points

- There is a lot of support out there, so don't be afraid to ask
- Most universities now have to provide bursaries to students who are receiving full Maintenance Grant or Special Support Grant
- The funding situation various across the different countries of the UK
- You cannot get a student loan for postgraduate study, but there are still other sources of funding, including Professional and Career Development Loans

GETTING A JOB

If it wasn't for the fact that it would make the rest of this book look rather unbalanced, this chapter could probably be summed up in two words: 'work experience'. If you are seriously considering changing your career, and even if you've gone to all the trouble and hard graft of retraining and gaining a new qualification, without some sort of practical, hands-on experience of working in your new field (even if it's only experience gained as part of doing your qualification) there's a chance you will struggle.

With recruitment budgets being squeezed in all directions and newcomers likely to be up against both experienced candidates and newly qualified graduates desperate for any and every new position, the challenge of landing a job in a new career can be daunting.

The big danger for career changers is that, having made that first push and commitment to retrain, it is all too easy to scurry back to the comfort of your previous existence once you are out the other end. Or, perhaps you simply fail to push on and make that final transition because of completely understandable financial pressures.

Remember you're not starting from scratch

The other big hurdle as a career changer is that it is common to feel that you are starting again at the bottom, which can be demoralising. It is true that as a career changer you are venturing into new territory; that, after all is the whole point. But that does not mean everything that has gone before no longer counts or no longer has value. Quite the contrary in fact.

Applying for the first job in your new career may feel as strange as when you first came out of school, college or university but, remember, it's not the same. Even if you are completely changing tack and retraining in an area that appears to have absolutely no link to your previous career and life, you are still you and all those years of experience and working, while perhaps no longer as directly relevant as they might once have been, retain plenty of value.

You will have life skills that you can draw on: just the fact you're probably vaguely sensible, have consistently managed to get into work on time for many years or are able to talk professionally over the phone can be valuable. You may have useful and valuable people skills, or administration, team or time management skills.

Then there may be management and supervisory skills you can highlight from your previous career, or perhaps the fact you are a motivated self-starter (as illustrated simply by your being prepared to retrain). You might be able to draw on more specific skills, such as experience of running, chairing or planning meetings, technical accounting skills, communication, marketing and promotional expertise, sales skills, computer packages that you are au fait with and so on. Similarly, even if the job title you had before is no longer relevant, what you were actually doing in that job – managing projects, building customer and client relationships, overseeing budgets, regularly hitting targets, mentoring or coaching staff, say – may all still be just as relevant in your new field.

The point here is that, while there may be bits of your CV that may no longer count *as much*, there is now a floor below which your CV cannot go.

The challenge though, and what this chapter is going to address, is how to get to the point where these generic skills that you probably have in abundance from your previous career are the 'second sell' on your CV and in the interview.

You want ideally to be reaching a point where employers in your new field choose you because of what you can offer them as the new you, as well as because of all that wonderful baggage you can bring from your previous life. But how?

Develop a brass neck

The answer, as you might have guessed from the opening comments, lies mainly in work experience. The importance of gaining experience in your newly chosen field while retraining cannot be overstated. Many courses these days, particularly more vocational ones, will come with built-in placements, and you should definitely make as much as you can of these if you are offered them.

When you go on such a placement ask questions, speak to people, network, learn and generally put yourself forward as enthusiastically as you can – though don't be over-pushy or ambitious as it may come across as threatening. It's good, if you can, to develop a mentoring relationship with someone in your field, someone who is happy to guide, support and advise you and even perhaps put in a good word with the people they know.

The key is to not sit around and assume the career will come to you just because you have or are in the process of gaining a new qualification. Particularly as a career changer you have got to go out there and show you mean business. You have to prove this is not something you are flightily coming to before dancing off to another career; that this is an area you are serious about and therefore it makes eminent sense for an employer to take you on. The challenge is to give them enough good reasons not to turn you down in favour of someone straight out of college and coming to this as their first career.

So, how should you go about doing all this? As ever, there are no hard and fast rules but two great first points of contact while you are still at college or university are the careers service and, particularly at the higher education level, the alumni (ex-graduates) association.

A good careers department should have a lot of practical resources that you can use to give yourself an advantage when you finally step out into that jobs market. These may include CV workshops, internet access, job and career profiles, advice and coaching on interview techniques, and assistance on filling in job application forms.

The value of alumni

While we often think of alumni societies or associations as predominantly social organisations, many nowadays will also have a careers section or network, which may even be formally linked to the university careers service. It may be able to offer direct access to alumni who have gone off into your chosen field, who may, as we have seen, have the potential to become highly useful mentors or simply be able to act as valuable sounding boards. The university careers service will normally be able to point you in the direction of the alumni network, if it doesn't already have a pretty obvious presence on campus or within your college. Many of them also now have their own dedicated websites and online social networks.

Have a plan

Remember at the start of this book that plan you laid out for your career change? Well, this is the point where it really comes into its own. The key is to go into your retraining already thinking 'What is it I will be doing after this?' and, just as importantly, 'What do I need to be doing during

MAKING THE CHANGE

Setting up a graphic design agency

Former PA Pam McHale, 51, retrained as a graphic designer and succeeded in getting a job in her new field that, in turn, led to her launching her own graphic design agency based in Brackley, Northamptonshire

It was turning 40 that did it for me. As a child I'd wanted to go to art school but we were not well-off and my parents could not afford it, so when I left school at 16 I became a secretary and then became a PA, a job that I ended up doing, and enjoying well enough, for 24 years.

Initially I wasn't even thinking of changing my career, I just wanted to learn about art and imagined I might just take a sabbatical and then return to secretarial work. So in 1998 I decided to do an access to higher education course in Fine Art at North Oxfordshire College and School of Art.

My reasoning behind choosing an access course was that it was a way of reintroducing me to learning, which was something that, to be honest, I was a bit fearful about as at school I had not been particularly academic.

I also knew that if I was going to study it had to be near to my home, so I researched colleges within a 40-minute drive. I also talked to a lot of other people who had done similar courses to get their feedback and recommendations.

One of the great things about the access course was that it catered specifically for mature students, so it helped to build my confidence as well as being exciting and interesting. I was made to feel really welcome and the tutors were fantastic.

I found I was enjoying it so much that I decided to go on and do an art foundation course followed by a Higher National Diploma in graphic design, which I finally completed in 2002.

Initially I found it daunting, not only academically but also socially. The foundation and HND courses were with teenagers and I was old enough to be their mum! But they were generally a great bunch and, because I joined in, I was accepted quickly and simply treated as one of them. In fact, eight years on I count a number of them as close friends and we still meet regularly. The tutors were also careful who they put me with and I had a female tutor who was very sympathetic.

Putting training to work

The next challenge was whether I could get a job in this new career. I applied for a graphic designer's job at a local publishing company and was interviewed by two of the company directors.

Having the HND qualification and a portfolio of work was absolutely critical in helping me to secure the job, although the interpersonal skills I had developed over the years as a PA also helped.

The directors recognised that, because I had taken the trouble to go back to college and get an HND, I was serious about making this my career. And, for this sort of position, your portfolio speaks for itself.

I spent four years working at that company, in the process building up invaluable experience and contacts. But, while I enjoyed working there, it was a two-hour commute and I had a hankering to work for myself from home and so, in October 2006, I decided the next step was to set up my own company, No Limits Creative Services.

Counting down to launch

The first thing I did was sit down with my husband and talk it through because anything like this is going to take a lot of commitment, both financial and in terms of time, so you have to have the absolute support of your family. We looked closely at our financial situation and how the loss of a secure income might affect us but also how the new business might generate sales and find customers.

I drew up a business plan, looking at what I'd need to buy in terms of hardware and software plus things such as office furniture. Because it was going to be home-based and initially employ just me the overheads were not going to be that high but you still have to be realistic about what you are going to need. There was also quite a bit of work around deciding on a business name, setting up and registering the company and creating the website and corporate identity.

When it came to launching, I was fortunate in that I got some business from my previous employer, which helped. But most of it has just been down to networking and marketing myself. I keep a good customer database and a lot of work comes from word-of-mouth and client referrals. I get quite a bit of repeat business now but I also continue to do a lot of networking.

The business is still pretty small – last year it turned over around £15,000 – so I am in fact earning less than I did as a PA, but the money is not the point. I had to do it otherwise I would have regretted never having tried. I have much more job satisfaction, more flexibility and a better quality of life. I don't have to commute anywhere and within two years I have paid off all the initial investment costs of starting up the business.

For anyone thinking they need to change, I would say go for it. As a result of what I have achieved through going back to college, changing direction and now running my own business, I am a much more confident person and feel better able to handle challenges and changes, whatever they may be.

But you do need to prepare well, consult others, ensure you have the support of those closest to you and look at all your options before you take the plunge. You also need to treat it as a journey that will unfold as you go along. You may not know your final destination or have all the answers at the start.

Changing my career was not something that happened quickly or easily and at times over the past 10 years it has been scary and daunting. But it has also been hugely rewarding and fulfilling. I have finally managed to do what I have always wanted to do.

this course to ensure I can achieve my goal after it?'

So you need from the off to be actively targeting the organisations, associations or people who will be making the hiring decisions when you come out with your new qualification. If there is a particular journal or publication for your new trade or sector, it may be worth subscribing to it. If that's too expensive, find out where you can get hold of copies (it may be your local library takes it or, if you ask, that your careers service can get hold of copies. You could also try an organisation such as BusinessLink).

Regularly reading the relevant trade press will not only give you an insight into what sorts of jobs are out there, but also what the key industry issues are, and will be vital in the interview. You may also be able to access these specialist publications online, but it's increasingly likely you will have to register or subscribe to view them.

For the same reasons it is worth identifying which newspapers have sections devoted to your industry or sector – for example in the *Guardian* it's the media, PR, advertising and marketing on Mondays, education on Tuesdays, public sector on Wednesdays and IT and technology on Thursdays. Other newspapers are similar, though tend to run different sectors on different days to each other, to maximise their potential audience.

There may be specialist online jobs boards that you can sign up to, though be aware that some of the more generalist ones can have a bit of a scattergun-approach. You might also want to register with a specialist recruitment agency in your field, particularly if it's going to be a way of getting past the application pile and fast-tracked into an interview.

To ensure recruitment agencies don't waste your time it is worth being clear with them so they understand what you want from them, the sorts of jobs you want them to put you forward for and how (and how often) they should contact you. There can sometimes be a temptation to sign up to multiple recruitment agencies but, unless it's something where it is relatively common to spread yourself about (for instance if you are registering with them for work as a freelance contractor) this isn't always advisable. There is a risk that employers end up getting multiple applications via different agencies from 'you' for the same job, especially if the same agencies are all chasing a diminishing pool of jobs.

Get networking

Given the intense competition for almost all advertised jobs these days (and the fact that many may have been filled even before they make it to the newsstand or website) you need to spend as much time and effort as you can building up your networks and contacts in your chosen field. So, again, shamelessly use tutors, industrial placements, alumni, social networks and so forth. Think about approaching industry associations or organisations and asking if you can come in and have a chat about career prospects in your industry, or make speculative approaches about work experience or job opportunities to relevant companies. It may be that there is nothing available imminently but your get-up-and-go is likely to be noted favourably.

With cold calling and speculative letters or emails, the key is to keep your approach light. Make it clear you are not after something that is going to cost them time and money directly (though of course it will if they eventually hire you), that you appreciate they would be doing you a favour even by replying and that you are just really keen to help out in any way that you can. Flattery, politeness, cheerfulness and an eager interest in them will often get you far!

As part of your strategy aim to have more than one option or plan of attack. Obviously you don't want to dilute your ambition or ultimate goal but if you are, say, happy to try for a range of positions or roles in your chosen field, that will widen your chances considerably. So, if possible try to see beyond a single job title, location and organisation and stay open to other opportunities.

Another option is to target any careers or trade fairs that are specifically oriented to your target sector or industry. These may happen through your college or university, but if not it's worth searching online to see where and when these events are taking place. If there is an industry body or association for your area, it may well know and, indeed, may well hold networking and careers events itself.

Applying for your new job

Assuming you've now found the job you want to go for, the next challenge is applying for it. As this is a career-changing guide rather than just a careers guide, we're going to make an assumption that you are unlikely to be a complete novice when it comes to writing job applications and letters, drafting CVs and so forth.

You will probably have applied for different jobs in your previous career and have had some experience of interviews and, hopefully, some successes. But, as we've already seen, applying for jobs in an area where you have many years of experience and, probably, an inside track on the politics and what's going on is very different to applying for jobs where you (and it) are suddenly much more of a blank sheet. It may also have been many years since you last found yourself in a similar position. Having to put yourself about and market yourself in this way, particularly if the career change has been forced on you by redundancy, can be an intimidating prospect.

Your new career CV

First, then, the CV. Career guides often love to spend pages and pages reproducing sample CVs; in fact you can get whole books on how to write the perfect CV and how to present yourself in that all-important job application. And if it is standard CV templates that you are after there are a multitude out there online these days. Recruitment firm Monster, for example, has loads of sample CVs on its website: **www.monster.co.uk** and there are many others out there too. Most university and college careers services will have stock CVs that you can look at and learn from. There are also a vast number of consultancies that will, for a fee, provide you with coaching, advice and even write your CV for you.

The danger, however, with just copying an off-the-shelf CV is that your CV loses its personality. No one person's career is 'standard', just as what an employer looks for will not be standard. You may not need to go to the extent of drafting a completely different CV for every job application you make, but it's worth getting into the mindset or at the very least re-reading it through and, if necessary, tweaking or tailoring it before approaching each employer.

For more personalised advice the *Guardian's* extensive online careers portal, **www.careers.guardian.co.uk**, runs a CV clinic where you can submit your CV to be given the once over by selected experts – although you do have to be ready and willing to accept negative feedback along with the positive.

There are some useful rules you can follow when it comes to writing your CV. Most of the best CVs, or at least the ones that tend to get the furthest when it comes to job applications, are the ones that don't make a huge noise but just clearly, concisely and efficiently get on with the job of doing what they are supposed to do – showing an employer who you are, what you've done and what you can offer.

So, while it is more than possible to knock up a CV awash with hyperlinks, photos, wobbly fonts and even videos, it can be the equivalent of that dreaded 'wacky' CV you used to see printed on coloured or marbled paper. For the busy recruitment or HR person if it's not easy and quick to read it's much less likely to make the cut.

If you've been out of the jobs market for a while, the good news is that the basic CV rules haven't really changed that much. Keep it concise, ideally a maximum of two pages, and don't cram all the information together. Ensure it is logical, so perhaps a personal statement followed by your employment history and qualifications or, if it's a new qualification you are now more looking to sell, perhaps the other way around.

You may want to list some personal interests, but be aware that this can be seen as padding, so don't let it take space away from the more vital details such as work experience. Especially if they're recent and related to your new field, some references are normally a good idea. You will want to be outlining throughout, as we have seen, not only your past role and job titles but the key things you achieved or skills you gained. Take the time to make sure your CV is all spelt correctly and is grammatically sound.

Get your CV online

The days of laboriously sending off a paper CV are pretty much consigned to history, so whether you're loading it onto a jobs board or pinging off an email application, it's essential that your CV is computer-friendly.

Use a clear, standard font that isn't going to be mangled in someone else's computer, as well as a widely-used word processing package like Word, that the recipient will be able to open. Some careers experts recommend that you paste your CV into the body of your message, rather than sending it as an attachment. Doing this will save the recipient time because they won't have to open the attachment and means they won't have to worry about it containing viruses. It will also mean there's no chance of it being stripped out automatically, as some company email systems now do. Avoid weighing the document down with large photo or other files that will take time to download or could clog up the employer's computer. It can often be a good idea to include a reference number or a job-specific subject line in your email heading to ensure it gets through to the right place.

Tailor your CV for your new career

As we've touched on earlier, from the career changer's perspective, the key challenge when rewriting your CV for your brave new career is going to be how to weight it towards your new ambition. Ultimately there's probably going to be no getting around the fact that you are going to have less experience and less to 'sell' than you are used to, so the more work or job experience you can get in your new field while you are retraining the better.

It may be a question, rather than simply going straight into your (now less relevant) employment history that you downgrade that to further down your CV and instead focus in hard on your new skills and ambitions. Consider using your personal statement to outline what it is you will be offering people in your new career (keep it brief though, and expand on this in your covering letter) followed by your new qualifications and any new experience you have. Then you can go into your previous employment history editing it very carefully to highlight any skills that will still be valuable in your new field and then run on into your older academic achievements or professional qualifications.

A logical structure could look something like this:

First page:

- Name, contact details
- Personal statement, or straight into ...
- New qualification(s)/work experience in your new field
- New career/qualifications references

Second page:

- Older employment history, highlighting relevant competencies, and other professional qualifications
- Evidence of any other relevant experience, academic, professional or otherwise
- Older academic history
- Generic 'employability' references (but only if you don't have any references for your new career to call on)

So, to try and give a practical example, it might be that you have decided you want to give up the office rat race and become a librarian. To do this, you may have gone back to college and attained an NVQ in, say, information and library services.

This will normally have included some work placements where you will have been assessed and let's assume you've also managed to do some relevant voluntary work, perhaps at your local library or within a school library.

On your CV, therefore, you would obviously want your NVQ and all your relevant new work experience to be prominent, along with any other professional qualifications you have gained along the way, for example membership of the Library Association. You would also want to include any relevant references, such as a tutor or someone from the place where you volunteered.

Then, when it comes to your previous career, you would want to highlight any people or customer skills, problem-solving skills, organisational and data-handling skills, and any languages that might be a selling point if you are going to be dealing with a multicultural community, for example.

MAKING THE CHANGE

Howard Grosvenor is a chartered occupational psychologist and head of consultancy at psychometric assessment and aptitude testing firm SHL.

In the current climate, where there is increasing competition for roles and where people are more likely already to have good quality technical or professional qualifications for any position they are applying for, there is much more emphasis by employers on what personal and acquired skills you might also have. This is something that can be advantageous to people who are currently trying to change to a new career.

Yes, you need to have got the right qualifications and it helps to be able to demonstrate some work experience in your new field, but being able to show you also have experience of things such as planning and time management, team-working, leadership, project management, meeting deadlines or customer needs – skills that can be acquired in almost any job – can help a lot. So it is important not to discount what you learned in your previous career but perhaps look at it in a more general way and assess what transferable skills you have gained over the years that may still be relevant to your new career.

Keeping up-to-date

While it is important that your CV does not feel dated, it does not necessarily need to be filled with all the latest internet or graphic technology. Hyperlinks, for example, if they are relevant can be the icing on the cake, but employers are much more interested in what a CV is saying than in how attractive or sophisticated it might look. I remember one time we were sorting through 500 CVs for an engineer's position and there was a CV that was a truly impressive document, with lots of colour and pictures and even a bound cover. But it didn't make the first cut because it had not been tailored or pitched right for that particular job.

While there has been a lot of talk about how employers are using social networks to vet and recruit potential employees, in my experience they tend to be used more by head-hunters than actual employers. So, while it can be a good idea to maintain an internet presence, and is definitely wise to ensure you do not have anything embarrassing or potentially damaging about yourself out there online, it is not the be-all and end-all.

Another change of the past few years is the number of employers that now use online applications. What is good about these is that they level the playing field. If you get 500 CVs in for a job they will all be different. But if you have 500 people filling in the same online application it is much easier to compare and contrast them objectively. As with any application it is important to read carefully what is being asked of you and only provide relevant information. Some of the questions may be open-ended and looking for information about your skills and competencies and how you have dealt with certain situations.

Along with online applications, many employers nowadays use all sorts of screening tools that can come into play before you even make it to the interview. You may be asked to sit an online or multiple choice test, or there may be a phone interview. The key with all of these is to prepare and practise. It is no good trying to conduct a phone interview, or maybe do a timed online test, while sitting in a busy, noisy internet café where the connection might go down at any moment. Or if it's a numerical reasoning test don't start it and only then realise you've forgotten your calculator.

Preparing for interview

When it comes to interviews, because of all this extra screening beforehand many companies will now only do one interview. But it may be what is called a competency-based interview.

The best way to deal with this is simply to research the job you are applying for very closely and identify perhaps five or six areas that are likely to be the key competencies for that job. You then need to think about relevant instances in your life – and it could well be from your past career – and how you responded.

There has also been more of a move in recent years towards firms using psychometric testing during the hiring process. Again, practise is a good idea and it is possible to find places online that let you do trial psychometric tests. For example, at SHL we have a website, **www.shldirect.com** that lets anyone have a go. It may not change the result in whatever test you eventually do but at least it means the whole process, and the sort of questions you are likely to be asked, will be less of a surprise. You would be surprised how many people rush in to them never having done one before.

As to the future, I suspect there will be more what is called 'fidelity assessment' where you are given an actual task that you will be likely to have to perform in the job and assessed on how you do. So if you are being hired for a buyer's job it might be, for example, that you will be given a spreadsheet and asked to come up with a pricing strategy, or something like that. That sort of task can really tell employers how someone is likely to perform in the job. There has also in the past three or four years been a massive rise in 'situational judgment tests' where candidates are asked to choose what they think is the right option in response to a particular scenario, for example a customer complaint.

With this sort of testing and the pre-interview screening becoming more important, I expect that over time the face-to-face interview is likely to be something that has less value attached to it. It may well become shorter and more about simply finding out whether someone, who by then an employer will already know has all the right technical and professional skills to do the job, also has the right organisational values and will fit in well with the culture and outlook of that organisation.

The covering letter

The other critical part of the application process is, of course, the covering letter. Again here, for those returning to the jobs market after time away, the good news is that the rules by and large haven't changed that much.

You will still need to keep your letter clear and concise (no more than a single page) and get the spelling, punctuation and grammar right. Be sure to address it to the right person and, of course, the right company – that may sound odd but it's surprising how often job applicants get these last points wrong, much to the weary hilarity of HR and recruitment professionals.

Similarly, it needs to be a personal document that is clearly written by you, so steer well clear of jargon, clichés or any other material that looks like it has been taken from the internet. Try to keep your letter feeling human: just because it's formal and has a set purpose doesn't mean it has to slip into police-speak – and it goes without saying that using informal language or writing as you would socially is never going to give a good impression.

Your letter needs to show you have researched your industry and sector and, head on, you should explain clearly why it is you want now to come and work in this area. This is very important as a career changer.

A few dos and don'ts

The key is not to be overly negative ('because I hated my boss in my old career') or too vague ('I love working outdoors') or to pretend that the fact you've just spent 20 years working in a completely different field isn't an issue they are going to want to know about.

So be honest and explain, briefly and plausibly, why you are giving up what you were doing before and why it is you want to move to your new career. Let the employer know what you've done so far to get yourself along that path, how you think the job you are applying to is going to help you take the next step, and what you will be able to bring to it that others cannot.

Avoid having too many 'I's in the letter and be aware that formatting such as bullet points, underlining and italics can disrupt the flow of a good letter.

Keep your letter clearly structured. A good rule of thumb is single short paragraphs (ideally five lines and no more than seven) for each of the topics mentioned above. This, with an opening 'I am applying for' paragraph and a concluding 'I hope this will make me a suitable candidate for an interview' paragraph, would give you five paragraphs at most which should, if you keep it tight, fit on a single page.

A few other 'don'ts' these days include using manual typewriters and hand-writing your letter, unless of course it is specifically requested in the advertisement. Generally speaking, enclosing a photograph of yourself, unless you're going for an acting, modelling or other performance job, is unlikely to work in your favour – if they want to find out what you look like, they can always ask you to come for an interview.

Rise of the application form

Another thing to be aware of is that more and more employers are now using standard application forms rather than requesting CVs and covering letters. The thinking behind this from the employer's point of view is that it creates a more level playing field, both for the applicant and, more importantly, when it comes to screening out unsuitable applications.

Using forms reduces the time spent sifting through applications, and they can be used to set the selection criteria more rigidly. Predominantly nowadays these will tend to be online applications, though you can still get occasions when they thump through your letterbox. Intriguingly, too, while rigid forms used to be pretty much the preserve of the public sector, many more private and commercial employers are now going down this route. For anyone used to the CV and covering letter approach, these sorts of forms can be a bit of a shock and a challenge.

Common pitfalls when it comes to these application forms are not reading the questions properly or ignoring some sections because you assume they are irrelevant when, in fact, all the sections have to be filled in with at least something. Candidates often fall into the trap of cutting and pasting from previous applications because the question looks pretty similar, only to find out later that in fact it wasn't.

So, treat the application form with respect, even if some of it seems pretty pointless. And, just as with your conventional CV or letter, print off a hard copy and carefully proofread for grammar, spelling and meaning before pinging it across. Also, keep it succinct, even if the box you are typing into is extendable. On the other hand if you've deliberately been left a big space for an answer it's probably because it's for a question that the company deems important and your answer should reflect that. This could be, say, listing examples of where you have achieved certain things or demonstrated behaviours such as leadership or team-working.

These behaviours will often be described by employers as 'competencies' and have over the years become one of the most important parts of the modern job interview, the next stage of which we shall now turn to.

The job interview

If you have landed an interview for a job that is going to allow you to make that final leap into a new life, the stakes are going to be high and it is, inevitably, going to be a high-pressure situation.

What you have to remember and keep in your mind is that you've been here before and succeeded – you've landed jobs, maybe even ones that at the time you thought were 'dream jobs', you've sold yourself in an interview and impressed someone enough to be taken on permanently.

The difference now, of course, is that you will be out of your comfort zone (if it is ever really possible to describe interviews as comfortable). You may have landed your last few jobs through a friendly chat with someone you already knew well and it may be that it is some years since you've actually been on this side of the interview table.

The upside is that you will probably be surprised at how it all comes flooding back. Be sure to get the basics right – turn up early, dress the part, do your research, do lots of preparation for the sorts of questions you think you are likely to come up against, work out what you are going to say, appear confident and positive (even if you aren't) and have lots of questions to ask. With that done you should, at the very least, acquit yourself honourably and, hopefully, knock all those first-timers into second place.

Be honest about why you want a change

As with the covering letter and the CV, the fact you are looking to change career is very likely to be one issue that will come up at interview. Again, it's important to have a credible tale to tell, ideally the truth! So, be honest. Be clear and concise about your reasons for moving on – 'I'd felt I'd achieved everything I wanted to', 'I was good at my job but this is something that has been building up inside me for some time now', or 'I enjoyed my time and am proud of what I achieved but for me this is the next phase of my life' should probably cover it.

Your interviewers may, of course, want you to talk about some of those achievements, so you will need to tread a fine path between being positive and enthusiastic about what's now under the bridge and not overdoing it so they wonder why it is you are packing it all in. Equally, you'll need to be very clear about why it is you want to join your new profession, your short-term, medium-term and long-term goals and all the wonderful attributes and skills you will be able to bring to the job.

The panel interview

If you find yourself in a panel interview, something that is quite common particularly in the public sector, it can be an intimidating experience, as you will be being grilled by, as it sounds, a panel of people. The key here is to try and speak to all of the panel members and not spend your time fixedly gazing at just one of them. Try and give each person's question the same time and attention and don't be afraid to ask questions or initiate conversations. These sorts of interviews, because of the way they are structured, can often come across as more formal and impersonal so if there is a chance to make it more personal, perhaps if you are allowed to introduce yourself or shake hands with each individual panel member do so. But sometimes, if you're unlucky, the intention is to be deliberately intimidating simply to see how you handle it.

The competency-based interview

For anyone who has been out of the jobs market for a while one new thing you may well come across is what is called the competency-based interview, which is now very popular with employers in all sectors.

In 'normal' interviews, or what are called unstructured interviews, you can expect it to be pretty much a two-way conversation between you and the interviewer where they will simply be looking to find out a bit about you and whether you are a good fit for their organisation.

Competency-based interviews will be much more structured, with the questions designed to see whether you have particular skills or how you behave in or react to certain situations. Whatever answers you give are then likely to be matched and marked against pre-decided criteria, often listed as 'positive' or 'negative'.

The attraction of this sort of interview from the employer's point of view is that the whole process is more rigorous and systematic – you're never going to get someone hiring you on a hunch in a competency-based interview – and it will leave them much less open to complaints of unfairness, bias or discrimination. It'll vary, of course, but the sorts of skills an employer will be looking for may include adaptability, communication skills, creativity or innovation, delegation, flexibility, independence, being a team player and so on.

As the interviewee, the one word you need to keep repeating to yourself in a competency-based interview is 'evidence'. What the interviewers want to see are concrete examples of whatever traits or competencies they have identified as important for doing the job.

So, questions will often be phrased along the lines of 'Describe an example of ...' or 'How did you handle situation x, y or z?'. What you therefore need to have prepared are lots of real-life situations that will reflect on you positively. It might be an example of where you've taken the initiative (perhaps in leading a campaign or project or running a money-raising appeal for some worthy local cause), resolved conflicts (perhaps when too many people with too much time on their hands have got involved in said money-raising local cause) or, even, in how you responded to a setback or something that went wrong.

In this sort of scenario it may not be that sensible to dwell too much on things you've achieved in your course. Given that everyone else will probably have similar qualifications, going into great depth about how you researched and gathered material for a course project, say, is probably not going to cut it, unless you did something above and beyond the ordinary.

In a way, the sorts of answers you should be giving in a competency-based interview may not be too dissimilar to the sorts of stories you should, if you are on top of your game, be telling in an unstructured interview to illustrate a point about youself or something you have achieved. The difference in such stories and directed (as opposed to rambling) anecdotes will be the whole point rather than something incidental to all the feeling around you may be more likely to encounter in an unstructured interview. The key, as with any interview, is to prepare – have something up your sleeve and ready to drop in 'by chance'. Everyone will know it won't be, but that's all part of the game.

Reasoning tests

Particularly for very competitive jobs where employers are trying to screen out a whole tranche of people before they have to go through the more time-consuming process of face-to-face interviews, you can get numeric and verbal reasoning tests and/or a telephone interview. The tests, first of all, may be timed, which makes it imperative that you clear the decks and make sure you're not going to be disturbed while you are doing them.

The practicalities of doing them will be fairly straightforward, and it should simply be a case of following it through on the computer. It may also be possible to get sample tests to practise on, perhaps from the employer or, often, from a college or university careers service.

In telephone interviews, the sorts of questions and how these are structured will vary – with such interviews sometimes being relatively informal and sometimes more structured. As with any other interview, preparation is the key. Make sure you know when the call will be, that you are somewhere quiet where you will not be disturbed, and that the phone will be free.

It may be a good idea to take the call on a landline to lessen the chances of the signal being lost. If you've been asked to call them, make sure you do it at precisely the right time and check the day before that the dial-in details have not changed. It can make sense to have your CV and covering letter to hand and to have jotted down on a piece of paper some of the key messages you want to get across.

MAKING THE CHANGE

Melanie Flogdell is head of HR policy at energy giant Centrica, which employs 27,000 people in the UK and is a member of the Employers Forum on Age, which works to combat age discrimination in the workplace.

In a business of our size we, of course, employ workers of all ages, genders and ethnicities; our workforce is very diverse. But the changing demographic of the workplace, with more older workers and more people working for longer, is a huge issue for employers. The talent pool out there is increasingly being filled with older workers and people on their second or third career – we even now have apprentices who are aged over 50 – so what's important, and will become even more important in years to come, is hiring on ability and not age. It is about looking at what people, irrespective of their age, can bring to the table. We, for example, removed the age box from our application form a long time ago and we remove the age from people's CVs when they are being assessed.

A wealth of experience

What employers tend to like about older workers is that they will often have life experiences they can draw on and skills and behaviours that they have developed over many years. But what we have also found is that, contrary to the stereotype, older workers are often hugely willing to learn new things. They bring an added dimension to their role, a maturity if you will, and this is something younger workers can learn from them, while in turn older workers can learn from the younger generation.

There are still, of course, many preconceptions around older workers, that they will be stuck in their ways, will be harder to manage, get ill more, take more time off and cost more. But when you work with and employ older workers these myths just don't stack up. Older workers in our experience can be hugely loyal, committed and hard-working.

When it comes to the issue of younger managers managing older workers, it's simply up to the organisation to ensure it is training its managers correctly. Managing an older worker should be no more challenging than managing any other kind of worker, assuming you are focusing on that person's abilities and performance rather than their (or your) age, gender or ethnicity.

Skills to be proud of

Many years ago it might well have been the case that an employer would look askance at you if your CV showed you had moved around a bit. But that's generally not the case anymore. If anything, assuming there are not question marks or anomalies around the moves you have made, what this is likely to show to an employer is that you can be flexible and adapt to new environments, which is a real selling point.

For someone who is at an older age and looking to move into a new career, what it's all about is transferable skills. A high number of jobs, at their heart, involve the same sorts of skills, whether it is dealing with people, time management, working effectively as a team and so on. So it is about focusing on being able to demonstrate the positives about you, to be able to show your willingness and adaptability. Don't make assumptions about what you cannot do but look at what you can offer or learn. Look, too, at your specific skills and competencies and at what you have done that is transferable or where there are gaps that perhaps you need to fill with a new qualification or questions that an employer might ask about.

Sometimes, despite the laws now in place against it, you may still get age discrimination in the workplace, which is a real shame. If you're up against someone who has got a fixed mindset against you, ultimately it will be their loss. What you have to focus on is what you can offer, your positives, what you can learn or what you can bring to that workplace or team – it is all about showing willingness, being prepared to learn and being positive.

One of the most common questions you might get asked in a phone interview is that old chestnut, 'Tell me about yourself'. What they're not going to want here is for you simply to read out your CV (as they should have that in front of them too) but to get a feel for how you speak and communicate, your telephone manner and how confident you sound.

What you may want to do therefore is draft a brief outline of yourself and what you will say – don't write it out word for word as the temptation will then be to read it out but jot down some key points, milestones, achievements and so on about yourself.

Assessment centres

Another relative newcomer that is becoming increasingly popular is the assessment centre. These are where candidates are brought together in groups to carry out a series of intensive tasks designed to demonstrate particular competencies, do a load of interviews and possibly a presentation or two.

More often than not you get assessment centres being used for things such as whittling down the candidates for a popular graduate training programme (they are, for example, much loved in the City) which means, as a career changer, you may be less likely to come across them. But it's still a possibility.

The main thing to remember if you find yourself in an assessment centre situation is to be calm and positive, to put yourself forward but try not to come across as pushy or overly assertive and to remember you are likely to be under observation all the time, even in apparently informal 'down' times. Simply try and be yourself and let your natural attributes and abilities show through.

Psychometric tests

The other thing you might find yourself being asked to do in an assessment centre or, increasingly, in any interview situation these days, is the psychometric test. This is the final new kid on the block when it comes to modern-day job hunting.

These are also sometimes known as personality tests and the key things to remember are a) not to be scared of them and b) whatever anyone may say you cannot second guess them. As there are no 'correct' answers you also can't do a lot in the way of preparation for them and so it's really just a question of trying to answer them as honestly as you can.

Testing organisations such as SHL (see the case study on page 108) do offer sample tests online that are worth a try simply to give you a better idea of what to expect. Whether, of course, employers actually end up finding out anything worthwhile about you as a result of carrying out a psychometric test is an altogether more contentious matter.

Hiring in a virtual world

It may be by and large in the future, but it is worth being aware that more and more employers are embracing new Web 2.0 internet technologies when it comes to recruitment and hiring.

Some firms already, for example, have 'offices' and conduct interviews in the virtual reality world Second Life while for many employers the 'Holy Grail' of recruitment at the moment is to work out ways of finding, engaging and hiring people through social networking sites such as Facebook.

With increased employer attention on social networking sites it's common sense not to leave anything embarrassing or potentially damaging to your career publicly accessible. These sites are sometimes used to check up on candidates, though there is some debate within HR circles as to the merits of actually making hiring decisions on the basis of these checks.

Overcoming ageism

Ever since autumn 2006, age discrimination has been illegal in this country. What this means in practice is that firms cannot cite age in their job advertisements, cannot hire or fire on the basis of someone's age and cannot treat you unfairly simply because of your age. Cue hollow laughter all round.

This is because, whatever the statute book might say, speak to many older workers and you will probably find the reality is that age discrimination still very much exists in the workplace. It may now have to be much more covert and some of the more blatant discrimination may well have been stamped out by the laws, but for many older workers the truth is that once you are beyond a certain age, often 50, the jobs market can suddenly become a colder, less forgiving place.

All at once you're 'too experienced' for a multitude of roles, 'over-qualified' or just 'unlucky' this time around, passed over for promotion or shunted sideways into dead-end projects. Managers who are younger than you, and who may be doing the hiring, don't want to know or feel threatened by the thought of managing someone with more life experience than them.

It may be assumed (though probably never stated out loud) that you will be too expensive, that people believe you are simply coasting to retirement, that you will not be physically up to the job or not resilient enough or that you will be stuck in your ways and unprepared to learn or difficult to manage.

It's perhaps no wonder that so many older workers end up becoming self-employed, starting up their own businesses or moving into more mature worker-friendly areas such as franchising, as we shall see in some of the chapters in Part Two.

For example, a survey of nearly 400 people back in October 2008 by the Third Age and Employment Network, **www.taen.org.uk** which campaigns to help older workers, described old-age discrimination in the UK as being 'endemic', with four out of 10 over-50s complaining of being branded too experienced or over-qualified and nearly two thirds being told they were seen as too old. Just a tenth said they had never experienced age discrimination at work and, while half said they believed they had been discriminated against because of their age, the vast majority also shrugged their shoulders about it and pointed out that such discrimination was very hard ever to prove.

The saddest part of all this, of course, is that older workers by and large are often more committed, more loyal, better at dealing with customers and more prepared to embrace change and learning on the job precisely because of having to battle against such prejudices and preconceptions. They will also often act as informal mentors and guides for younger workers and bring a more experienced, cool-headed perspective to workplace issues. And, it should be pointed out, many more enlightened employers have indeed grasped this and go out of their way to hire older workers and retain the experience and knowledge that their older workers have.

It's their loss

So how do you overcome such entrenched ageism as a career changer? To be honest, if you're up against someone who is dead-set against you because of your age, though doing everything by the book legally, there is probably not going to be a huge amount you can do about it. And, to an extent, you need to think of it as their loss.

After all, even if you are mid-50s, that will still mean they will have potentially lost a good decade's worth of valuable input and graft from you, and probably much more. Would they have got that from a callow, ambitious graduate? You can never tell, but probably not.

The important point to recognise here is that it is not you that is at fault. Yes, constant knock-backs will inevitably be demoralising but if employers really don't want to take you on because of your age they will always be able to come up with excuses that allow them to get away with it.

That's not to say there are not things you can do to try and swing the pendulum back in your favour. There are practical things, such as not putting your age on your CV or not putting dates to your education (though they may well be able to work it out) and ensuring you have some recent qualifications under your belt to show you are still open to learning and new ideas.

Sell your skills

But there are also more intangible ways of presenting and carrying yourself that will give out the message, even subliminally, that you are someone who should not be being written off.

On your CV, in your application and at the interview you can, for example, focus on the transferable skills you have, skills that won't go out of date, so for example being good at communication or team-working or managing projects. You can emphasise your ability to learn and take on new ways of working – the fact of having a new qualification should be the key selling point here but you might also want to cite other examples of new things you have done, perhaps taking up a new hobby or blogging (as long as it's not work-related in a critical way) or showing you are up to speed with the latest technological changes in your industry and so on.

As well as showing you are willing to learn new skills, you might want to make the point you are happy to pass on your own experiences and mentor and coach others, if that was felt to be appropriate. It might well, too, be a good idea to outline your goals and ambitions very clearly, in essence showing a potential employer that you are unlikely to be wanting to move on after a year or two years unlike, perhaps, a younger employee, even if you don't spell it out that explicitly.

It may even be tactful to tackle the 'R' word – retirement – head on. So, how long do you intend to stick around for and, barring the unforeseen, what do you see happening when you reach, say, 65? Being able to show that you are happy to work flexibly, particularly as you may now have fewer dependent or childcare responsibilities than many younger workers, can be another potent selling point.

Similarly, it might be a good idea to address the issue of money upfront, as this is one of the stumbling blocks employers most often assume will get in the way of them employing an older worker. Of course you don't want to do yourself down and you want to be paid the going wage for the work you will be doing but, if starting this new career is clearly going to mean a pay cut, it can make sense to spell out that this is something you accept and is not an issue for you because other factors are more important at this point in your life.

Finally, as a person of mature years you are likely to be able to emphasise your level-headed reliability as a potential future employee. It is all really just about actively showing the employer the advantages of taking on an older worker really do outweigh the advantages of taking on a younger worker or graduate.

The latter may well be a blank piece of paper that can be moulded to fit the organisation but what you need to be getting across is that you will bring a richness of experience, and wider skills, with you rather than having to be taught. You will also bring greater flexibility in how and when you work, the motivation and commitment to make the most of this opportunity later in your life and a 'still young' attitude to change and new ideas.

Key points

- Recognise that getting the qualification is only half the journey
- Try to get as much work experience of your new field as you can while you are retraining
- Use whatever contacts or networks that are available to help you break into your new career
- Focus on selling your new skills, but don't discount your old ones
- Be prepared to be asked about why you are giving up on your old career
- Show what you can still bring to the workplace and the advantages in terms of flexibility, motivation, commitment and experience an employer might gain from you as an older worker

PART TWO

BEING YOUR OWN BOSS

Part 2: Chapter One

GOING IT ALONE

We've just gone through perhaps the toughest year economically since the 1930s, with businesses large and small folding in their thousands, and you want to leave the security of employed life to start out in self-employment – are you mad? Maybe. But, as we've also seen, with unemployment inexorably spiralling upwards month after month, the concept of 'the security of employed life' has been somewhat shredded in the past 18 months. At one level, then, it's arguable that, if you can get it right and make it work, becoming self-employed, whether through running a business or other form of enterprise, can be a more secure long-term career choice these days. No one is going to fire you, you can't get made redundant, you call the shots. What have you got to lose? Apart, that is, from all your money, maybe your house, even perhaps your health if it goes wrong. So, no pressure then.

In this chapter we will be covering what you should be thinking about before you venture out into the world of business and self-employment, in many respects before you even think about going for that first meeting with the bank manager. As ever, you will probably be able to find examples of people who've done completely the opposite and managed to make a success of it, but the intention here is to offer a few basic building blocks that will, hopefully, help you anticipate and avoid some of the more common pitfalls that people make when, eager, excited and completely naïve, they rush out into business. In Chapter Two we will then look in more detail at the practicalities of setting up and launching a business, particularly becoming a limited company, and then keeping the momentum going to make it thrive and survive.

Whichever way you cut it, starting up in business or self-employment is a big deal. If you want something that isn't going to disrupt your family life, give you sleepless nights, mar your weekends or upset those regular skiing holidays, then perhaps it's a good idea to think again. Having said that, a successful business can, in time, mean those expensive holidays come your way, that you can delegate those long hours to someone else and even pass on a comfortable living to the next generation, should they show even the remotest interest in 'your baby'. The entrepreneurial spirit is something that does seem to be innate within the British psyche. We may laugh at the next hopelessly deluded case on *Dragons' Den* but we're equally likely to give a little cheer to those who, against the odds, through sheer guts, hard work or inspiration, make their fortune. And, after all, the vast majority of the UK's working population are employed by small businesses, often run by just the sort of enterprising people who have at some point turned their backs on a 'safe' corporate career and decided to go it alone.

Five reality checks

The best starting point here is simply to take a look at yourself – at your skills, attributes, ambitions and, at its most basic, whether you are the sort of person who is likely to be cut out for the challenges and vicissitudes of self-employed life. The business advice and support service BusinessLink **www.businesslink.gov.uk**, perhaps one of the most useful resources out there for anyone thinking about or in the process of taking the plunge, provides a good list of five day-to-day 'reality checks'. Tick these off before you start rushing down to the bank:

1: Is it the right move for *you*?

In essence, what BusinessLink is saying is, ignore whatever your exciting business idea is for the moment, take a step back and look realistically and coldly at what it is you might lose and whether that's a risk you are prepared to take. So, before even getting to the nitty gritty of the business plan, market research or profit projections, you need to look at your knowledge and skills, your finances, the personal attributes you can bring to your business, how committed and driven you feel about it and the level of support you can count on from friends and family.

For instance, if you're going into this because you want a better work/life balance, how realistic is that going to be – cutting your hours might be something achievable as a freelancer or contractor, for example, but as a small business owner you are likely to be working much longer hours, at least at first, than you ever did in employed life. Are you prepared to make the personal and emotional sacrifices that may be required to make your great idea a reality?

2: How much can you afford to risk?

Financially, what have you got and what can you afford to risk? We're not even talking here about detailed financial planning – that will come later – but you need to take a good, long look at your financial situation. Do you have savings or a generous redundancy cheque that you could invest? Will a partner still be bringing in an income and so taking the pressure off in the early days? Would you be prepared to use your home as security for a loan, with all the risks that that could entail? Can you sell any investments or 'downshift' to get more flexibility that way – or will you endlessly miss those posh evenings out?

Similarly, it's worth having a realistic think about your attitude towards money and debt – are you cautious, chaotic, a risk-taker or an obsessive planner? You can, of course, pay other people to manage your financial affairs or it might be that you're the creative one and your partner will be dealing with that side of it, but if going a few pounds overdrawn at the end of each month starts you hyperventilating, it's worth considering whether the financial precariousness of being self-employed is going to be for you.

3: Can you cope without your company perks?

Consider what the loss of company perks you have perhaps got used to is likely to mean. We're not really talking about the subsidised gym here, but rather the really important stuff such as company pension, private healthcare provision for your nearest and dearest, sick and holiday pay or the loss of a swanky company car. OK, you might have to put up with a lot of grief at the office in return for all this, but is losing it going to feel liberating or loathsome?

4: Are your family on your side?

It goes without saying that you need to have your family or partner absolutely behind you when you take this step. Even if they are not going to be directly involved in the business or venture, they will be affected; whether it's because one half of the household income has suddenly gone and they are now propping up the mortgage, or because they now never see you. They will perhaps also be staying up late helping you plough through the books, watching you stress about the latest obstacle or knock-back and supporting you in other ways. At the same time, it may be that,

MAKING THE CHANGE

Cath McIlwham, 49, gave up a high-powered career as a buyer with Tesco to set up her own online business Just Horse Gifts **www.justhorsegifts.com** based in Welwyn Garden City, selling horse-themed gifts from around the world.

I've always loved shopping and really enjoyed the career I had with Tesco. But by the end of 2007 I had spent two decades in corporate life and just had a desire to do something for myself. It had been growing on me for a long time – I had first had the idea for the business five years before – so when the offer of taking voluntary redundancy came along, I jumped at it.

I have a horse and a lot of friends who I only know through horse-riding but when it came to buying them gifts, while you can always find dog and cat-themed things I found it was much harder to find anything horsey. I'd seen at a gift trade fair that there were quality, well-designed gifts out there you could buy and so I did a lot of research on the size of the market and assessing how it might work. If anything I probably did too much because it took me longer to get set up, around six months, than I had originally intended, meaning that it wasn't until April 2008 that I launched the business. I think I probably had the most comprehensive business plan anyone has ever seen!

I got loads of advice from BusinessLink and spent a lot of time choosing a name for the business. One of the key things was finding a domain name that had not already been taken. So if you have an idea, it can be worth buying and registering its domain even if you are not yet ready to launch. It only costs a few pounds to do but can save you a lot of hassle later on.

It was also important to get the feel and design of the site right. I decided to pay someone to build the site for me but when you go online there are so many businesses out there offering this type of service that it can be very hard to tell them apart. I eventually went for a local designer who I knew was at the end of a phone and who, if necessary, I could actually go along and meet. It is always a good idea to ask for examples of their work and speak to people who they have done business for.

When it comes to trading as an online business, it's important that payment is smooth and secure. You need to have a payment service provider and a merchant account. The merchant account is something that all retailers need in order to take credit cards and can be organised through one of the big banks. In addition, the payment service provider enables you to take payment over the internet in a secure format. This can also be organised through the banks or through a specialist provider. It's worth bearing in mind therefore that there will be two sets of charges – two set-up fees, two annual fees and two sets of transaction charges. For postage, as most of what I sell is quite small, I simply use my local post office. But for bulkier items I use a parcel firm, though at the moment I just do it on an ad hoc basis rather than having an account. I also hire a storage unit for the stock.

Getting noticed online

A big challenge, and probably the biggest surprise, was how difficult it is to get yourself noticed online. When you type in a search term on Google what you are doing is what is called a 'natural search'. So if you were to type in 'horse gifts' you might expect my business to come up. But it doesn't always work that way because there is just so much information out there, and you might have someone come up before you who sells the occasional product. Your search for 'horse gifts', for example, will throw up something like 13.6 million results worldwide! It's a bit like setting up shop and discovering your premises is down a side alley and no one knows you are there.

So what I did was sign up to Google AdWords, which helps businesses advertise to people searching on the web. I pay a few pence to Google every time someone clicks through on my advert – which will be one of those search terms that come up in a tinted box – and probably average a sale every 25 clicks, which I believe is actually pretty good. I'd say that I get about three-quarters of my online sales through this, so it has been really worthwhile doing. Apart from that I have run banner advertisements on some of the various horse magazine websites, done some product-based PR and in my first summer I physically went around some of the big horse shows selling stock. Because the business is still new, running it is completely full-on, which is a bit ironic as one of the reasons I left Tesco was to get a better work/life balance. For the first time in 20 years I didn't take a holiday during the summer! Also don't necessarily expect it to go as you intended after you launch. In the first six months the traffic was quite slow across the site and, if it hadn't been for going around the shows and seeing how much people liked the products, I might have worried I had done completely the wrong thing.

You need to get out there and network and meet real people – there is a danger with any online business that you just sit in your back bedroom worrying. It's a good idea if you can to try and get some feedback from customers about what they think of the business and your products. You also need to be disciplined with yourself about what hours you are going to work – as being online you can end up working all hours of the day and night.

At the moment I'm barely even making a salary, let alone anything like I was at Tesco. But I wouldn't go back to corporate life and the business is growing all the time, so I am really optimistic about the future. After 20 years of working for other people the best bit about it is that I am now working for myself. It is hard, you have to have a huge amount of belief in yourself and your idea and you really have to want to do it. But it is worth it.

if (or let's be optimistic and say when) it starts to go well, you are imagining they will become involved in the business too and perhaps even give up their own day job – but has that ever explicitly been spelled out?

5: Are you likely to feel isolated?

As the boss, whether you have a business partner, employees or are working as a one-man band, the responsibility for success or failure will lie squarely on your shoulders. Is dealing with that level of responsibility or potential isolation something you will be happy with? Do you have people, perhaps someone you're working with or is at the company you've just left, or who you simply admire or trust, who you can bounce ideas off, who can act as mentor and cool head to your excited entrepreneur? Longer term you may want to think about joining a local business group, federation or chamber of commerce that will provide much-needed ongoing advice and mentoring.

What skills will you need?

All businesses, of course, are different. Yet it's also true to say that all businesses, at their core, have much in common. As someone who is self-employed and in business you will need to have certain skills to survive, or at the very least be in a position to delegate such skills to someone else if need be. The first key skill is probably product development – in other words delivering on whatever product it is you are making or skill or service you are offering. Given that the whole point of this exercise is to end up doing something you feel truly passionate about, this should be a no-brainer. But it is worth considering whether the product will be something you are physically going to make or deliver or whether you will be paying someone else to produce it and, if so, who or what will do this for you, at what sort of cost and where. You will also want to consider what sorts of processes, materials and protections (all of which more of later) you might need, what supplier relationships you are likely to have to build and so on.

Then you will also need to have some basic financial management skills. Yes, you can offload some of the details of this to your bank adviser or accountant but if you are going to be in business you really do need to have at least a modicum of financial savvy. You will be coming into contact with, or having to manage, things such as cash flow planning and credit control and will need to keep in good standing with your bank manager, accountant and the taxman. Within this, it's good to have the ability to be clear-sighted about your business and where it's going and what markets it might need to evolve into as time goes on.

Marketing, promotion and selling are likely to be other key attributes required of you. You may not be physically cold-calling people but any business needs to get out there and chase its markets and customers, particularly in a tough economic climate. So an ability to identify your market and know it inside out, as well as an ability to identify any gaps, is important. Similarly, you will, clearly, need to be good at dealing with customers – just think Basil Fawlty and do the opposite. Even if you are unlikely to be dealing with the general public directly or spending most of the time hiding behind a computer, being able to interact and communicate properly and authoritatively with your customers is vitally important.

People skills may also become an important part of the equation if and when you start to employ people. If you've spent your whole corporate life working within a team, suddenly finding yourself having to dole out orders, keep people motivated or hold difficult conversations about someone's performance can be challenging. You won't necessarily need to be a star at all of these all at once, and these are skills you can learn as you go along, but for most businesses they will come into play at some point.

To MBA or not to MBA?

Some of our best-known and most successful businessmen and women have made their millions without a business qualification. Sir Richard Branson and Sir Alan Sugar both famously started out with just the 'university of life' after their names. So a business qualification is neither a prerequisite nor a guarantee of success. Nevertheless, a good business qualification may be worth considering if you want that extra bit of confidence, a better understanding of the jargon and a clearer perspective on where you have come from and where you need to go with your business.

As Anne Woodhead, director of the executive MBA programme at Durham Business School, argues, learning on the hoof after a lifetime in a corporate environment can be an uphill struggle.

> 'It is quite common that people who have had a corporate career and reached their mid to late 30s or early 40s often start to get frustrated and feel they want to do something more with their skills and be more in control of their life and career. But if you have been in a single organisation or a corporate environment all your working life, even if you have been managing people, the sort of skills you are likely to need to become a successful entrepreneur, business owner or self-employed business person can be very different,' she says.

Of course this does not necessarily mean you need to go the whole hog and get an expensive, 'gold standard' MBA. Tap the words 'business qualification' into Google and you will come up with an array of courses, from short tasters through to diplomas, undergraduate degrees and specialist master's courses. The important thing is to think what you're going to need it for – do you just want to gain some basic financial, management, business and accounting skills or do you want something with a bit more meat behind it?

Woodhead makes the valid point, too, that a good business qualification such as an MBA can open doors and give you greater credibility, not simply because of the letters that will be after your name but because of how you will come across, who you will now know, how you will speak and what you will understand when you are spoken to.

'An MBA can give you a "helicopter view", a better understanding of what to expect, a familiarity with the language of business and a better awareness of where the pitfalls may lie,' she explains.

'What we find an MBA does is that it helps people to talk with more confidence to people in other areas, it gives you the key skills you will need to ask the right questions and get the right answers. So you will have a much better understanding, for example, of what your accountant is saying to you, and what in turn to ask. You will understand more clearly, too, how your suppliers are operating, whether the business is running in a financially sound way and how to see your future path and direction more clearly. While you can get individual skills from many business courses, what an MBA can give you is across-the-piece consistency. It shows you are both serious about your business and someone to be taken seriously,' Woodhead adds.

What sort of business?

You may know in your head what sort of business is going to work for you but is it, in reality, viable? We will look in the next chapter at some of the different ways you can structure self-employment, including being a sole trader, a partnership, a limited company and a social enterprise. Then in following chapters we will look at the ins and outs of franchising and freelancing but, whatever final physical and financial shape your business takes, it's a good idea to spend some considerable time researching your market, your customer base, your 'unique selling point' and how you will actually make your money.

Market research is much more than just thumbing through your local Yellow Pages to see if there is anyone else doing what you intend to do. You may, for example, think you have spotted a gap in the market – but has someone got there first, even if the product they are pushing is not exactly the same as yours? Is there, then, enough differentiation, or enough of a potential customer base, for two similar products and businesses to survive in relatively close proximity?

In days gone by customer base used to mean either where you could physically get to, or the distance from which your customers could realistically come to you. Nowadays, of course, with the internet, businesses can be instantly global but that still may not necessarily mean there is a market out there for you. Conversely, is your product or area going to be so specialist and niche that it either simply does not have a sustainable market or, and this can happen, it will be self-sustaining because it will tap into highly expert individuals, clients or communities who will keep coming back for more? Could your idea, too, be affected (for good or ill) by unforeseen events, such as demographic or social trends – or even the weather? If you can avoid it, it's a good idea not to base your USP on simply being cheaper at whatever it is you are aiming to do than everyone else. This is because a) you'll probably have to slog really hard to ever make any money out of it and b) once you have set your prices low it is much harder to raise them than if they were never set at rock-bottom in the first place.

So, some key questions to consider should include: Does my product or service create its own market? Is it going to be local, national or international? Who will be its potential customers? You'll also want to think about whether there will be the possibility of repeat business, whether it will need to evolve quickly (for instance if it is tapping into a passing fad), how it will differ to that of its competitors and, if it is superior, how to convey that to your customers. Clearly, too, you need to be sure that if you are selling a product, it is safe for public use and that it is legal and compliant with any relevant rules and regulations.

A good place to start when it comes to gathering market research is simply with those closest to you, your friends and family and any trusted colleagues. If the general consensus is sniggers rather than a look of 'Why did I never think of that?' amazement you might want to go back to the drawing board, though you may also find that in time you can prove them all wrong. You may also want to consider shelling out some cash on proper market research through a research agency or run focus groups. And, in fact, thumbing through the Yellow Pages or relevant trade magazines and journals can have its merits in that you should be able to get a good steer on the number of rivals or competitors in your area of business and your geographic area.

If, for example, there is a glut of driving instructors in the streets around you all vying for the same business, simply adding to their numbers is perhaps not the most imaginative way forward. Alternatively, there may be mileage in speaking to your accountant, if you already have one, or a small business banking adviser, even if it's just on an informal basis, to tap into their knowledge and expertise and, at the very least, to find out what they will require from you when things get more serious.

Keeping your idea protected

If you are developing a new, physical product to sell there may be a process of designing and prototyping to go through, which can become quite expensive. You may also need to look into patenting your idea or protecting your intellectual property (the intellectual or creative activity behind your venture), so that no one can steal it or steal a march on you. The government's Intellectual Property Office **www.ipo.gov.uk** has loads of information on its website explaining what patents are, whether you need one and how to go about securing one.

Having a patent does not just protect you from competitors but will also give you the licence to sell your invention and any intellectual property rights, license it to someone else but retain all the IP rights and discuss the invention with others in order to set up a business based around it. And the cost? At the very least you are going to have spend £200 on this because that is what it costs the office (at time of writing) to process a UK patent application, though fees for international patents are much higher.

Beyond protecting your physical product or invention or your intellectual property, you may need to consider whether your product, logo or company name – the choosing and registering of which we will look at in more detail in the next chapter – needs to be trademarked. Again, the IPO can help with this and you can, again, expect to pay a fee of around £200. Other 'rights' you may need to look at protecting include your copyright, if what you are producing are original literary, dramatic, musical or artistic works and your 'design rights' if you just need to protect a product's appearance.

Be realistic

An important part of this market research and planning is the need to be honest with yourself. You may have set your heart on something but if the market research consistently shows that it doesn't stack up and is not commercially viable, perhaps because it is going to be too expensive or time-consuming to produce, you'll have to make some tough decisions.

Don't forget to consider the wider economic circumstances. If it's clear the industry or sector you are trying to break into has been suffering hugely from the recession, is it wise to join that profession's ranks at this time, however well qualified you have become or however hard you have worked to build up experience in that field? Is your business therefore likely to be affected by a tighter availability, or no availability at all, of loan finance in the current climate? Or, conversely, is it, if not recession-proof (few businesses are, except perhaps bailiffs and locksmiths), then recession resilient? Might it be something for which demand increases during a downturn? In that case you may need to get your skates on to make the most of the current economic conditions.

MAKING THE CHANGE:

After a varied career in the offshore industry, a serious accident, redundancy and the discovery of long-term disability forced Jane Barnes, 61, to completely change direction, and she now runs a successful multi-media company, Yakkety-Yak **www.yakkety-yak-multimedia.com**, based in Stevenage.

Before my accident in 1995 I had been super fit, doing martial arts and long-distance running, dancing on stage and gymnastics. But it was in hospital that they discovered I had osteoporosis, arthritis and a disabled hip. I was on my back for more than a year and, though I managed eventually to go back to work as a salesperson and trainer to the offshore gas and oil industry, I ended up being made redundant in 1997.

It was a very low time. From being a bubbly and outgoing person who used to go out with friends and to clubs, I was now classified disabled, out-of-work, depressed and when I did apply for jobs constantly being told I was over-qualified. At that time there was not the same awareness of disability that there is now, so people tended to shy away when they saw I was disabled. I also believe there was an element of ageism there too, even though I never put my age on my CV.

A completely new start

Things started to turn around in 1998 when my adviser at Jobcentre Plus told me about a return-to-work course specifically for women, which I did and it immediately helped to boost my self-confidence and started to give me some new skills. I then went on to do a one-year postgraduate certificate at the University of Hertfordshire in management skills. My parents had run their own business so that had always been in the background when I had been growing up so, at one level, it seemed a natural progression.

Because I was unemployed and got Disability Living Allowance it enabled me to buy the course materials and cover my travel expenses. I also managed to get funding from the university and some financial support from Hertfordshire Training and

Enterprise Council. It was really just a question of asking what was available and not being afraid to put myself forward. The university, too, was very helpful and had a dedicated person to deal with issues for students with disabilities.

The other support that proved really helpful, and still is, has been the Access to Work Scheme which, when it came to setting up in business, helped me with my office equipment. It provided me with a desk that rises up so I can work at it standing up if I need to, which sometimes I do because of the arthritis. It also provided me with a special ball chair that I can use to whizz between the desks. I was provided with an Access to Work support worker, who I still regularly turn to for advice and help.

Once I'd finished the course I was still trying to get jobs but with no luck and began to get demoralised again. If you have always been employed it is very easy to forget the impact that being out of work has, and how suddenly things can go downhill when you do not have an income, how quickly your savings deplete and how much it costs running around to interviews. But then one time I was sitting down and rewriting my CV and it just hit me that I actually had quite good communication and writing skills. I had also always been interested in films, acting and media and, again with the help of Job Centre Plus, which helped me to go on another course, on entrepreneurship, began to start the company.

After two years of researching it, and all the while unsuccessfully looking for jobs as an alternative, I finally launched Yakkety-Yak in 2003, turning it into a limited company a year later. From small beginnings, the business now employs four people full-time and another three on an ad hoc basis, and the turnover is £100,000 plus, something I am really proud of.

For me, the best advice for anyone thinking that they want to change their career would be talk it through not only with family and friends but also people who understand the area you want to go into. Family and friends, while they may have your best interests at heart, may not understand exactly what it is you want to do. There is a huge amount of support out there now, particularly from organisations such as BusinessLink, a lot of people who can give you advice and loads of courses that are available.

But it is still up to you to make it happen. If you're hankering after change, you should do it sooner rather than later. There will always be obstacles and challenges, but if you're set on a path, follow it. You may need a new qualification, you may need to start back down at the bottom, or you may need to take a financial risk to get there, but if you have the belief in your own ability, the belief that it is the right course for you and you have to do it, then you should pursue it. If you do have a dream, go for it.

The business plan

Assuming the feedback you have been getting is that, yes, there is a potential market out there for you to win, the next important step is to draw up a business plan. There is going to be some overlap here with the following chapter, in that by this point you will probably already have decided on your business name and what type of business you are proposing. But even if you haven't it is a good idea to start working on your business plan as early as possible, as it will form an absolutely central part of any later discussions you have with accountants, bank managers and so on.

A business plan needs to be as comprehensive as possible, but that does not mean it has to be a long document, particularly if the business idea is quite straightforward. In fact the exercise of keeping it short and concise can focus your mind on what you are trying to achieve, and it will probably come as a relief for the time-pressed business banking adviser or manager! The key to any good business plan is clarity and realism. To this end, ensure it is professionally presented and clearly legible, with clear headings and page numbers, that it is grammatically correct and accurately spelt (get someone who knows about these things to proofread it) and that if it is being emailed it is in a friendly format.

At its most basic a business plan is simply a document that describes a business, its objectives, its strategy, market and how it will be funded and fund itself. This is a more important point than it first seems because, while a business plan can be and often is used as a tool to secure funding, once the money is in the bank account it shouldn't just be filed away and forgotten about. Ideally a good business plan is a 'live' document, something you dig out periodically and revisit to see if you are on track or whether you need to change tack. It is also, at a practical level, a key document for any other partners or potential investors in your business, whether private or institutional, any grant or funding bodies or, of course, anyone who subsequently wants to buy your business from you.

Six steps to a perfect business plan

BusinessLink provides a helpful list of what a strong business plan should include:

1) An executive summary

The executive summary is probably the most important part of your document. It is the first bit that will get read and so will have to make an impact, and if you are unlucky and your potential partner, investor or bank manager is in a hurry, it may be the only bit that gets read!

So, what you should endeavour to do within the summary is to break down your plan into key points, highlighting and condensing what you are going to say in the rest of the document. Ideally, anyone reading the document should be able to walk away with an educated view and understanding of what your business is about – though of course the whole idea is that they don't walk away at that point.

A common mistake people often make is to see the extended summary as a glorified table of contents, or overhype the business before it's even clear what its credibility is likely to be. People are sometimes so close to the subject that they can fall into impenetrable jargon that will put any reader off going further. So, work out perhaps how you would explain your plan, in 30 seconds, to your best friend – or your mother – if they knew nothing about it.

2) A short description of the business

Next, you need to outline what the business will actually do, so it's a question of saying as clearly as you can what your products or services will be and who you see as your market. Good things to incorporate here might include any trading to date, the business sector, any business history (for example if you've bought the business off someone else) and your key idea, ambition or vision for it. You should look to outline its USP, why customers would buy from it, how you plan to develop it and any issues around patents or property protection.

Within this you'll also, of course, need to give a good overview of your position vis-a-vis your competitors. So, it's really summarising what you've learned during your market research: what challenges you are likely to have to overcome, what gap in the market you are filling, your target customer and customer base, your likely competitors, and how you see your market changing and evolving over time particularly if there are any technological innovations that will be a threat or opportunity.

3) Your marketing, sales and promotional strategy

The next element – marketing and promotional activity – can sometimes be a bit of a weak link within the business plan. However, Mark Stuart, head of research at the Chartered Institute of Marketing argues that it is so important that in fact, alongside including it in the main business plan, you should consider writing a separate marketing plan.

'This isn't as onerous a task as it sounds. Consider how you're going to price your products and how you will target your market. If your product is likely to appeal, say, to women in their 20s and 30s, think about the best ways to reach your target audience. Avoid a scattergun marketing approach that will use up resources without effective payback. Get the product right, and communicate your offering appropriately,' he recommends.

'In this day and age your brand, both bricks and mortar and online, and the image you present to the public and your customers has become hugely important,' he points out.

'If you're operating in a crowded marketplace, a strong brand can be the best way to distinguish yourself from the competition. And if building a brand seems irrelevant when you're starting out, bear in mind that all great brands started out as small companies. Less than 100 years ago, Tesco was a single market stall in the East End of London,' he adds.

As well as pricing, you should look to include information on how you are going to promote your business, whether it'll be through online, viral marketing, social networking sites, direct marketing, conventional advertising, word of mouth or public relations – and so on. How, in effect, will you reach, communicate with and retain your customers? How will you actually sell to them – face-to-face, online, over the phone, through a shop, or a combination of all of the above?

4) Who is going to be running the business?

Next on the business plan list should be you and your team. This should include an outline of your background, and that of anyone in your management team, your credentials, skills and strengths. Describe how you intend to plug any gaps or weaknesses, such as perhaps appointing an accountant to do the bookkeeping or someone to manage your software or design your website. If there are going to be employees in the business, it would be a good idea at this point to outline how many, doing what and how the workforce will be structured.

5) Your operations

At the same time, you'll need to outline where the business will be based, particularly if you are going to need to set up in dedicated premises that will require funding. What sort of facilities will you need now and in the future? Similarly, what sort of IT and technology will you require, how will you manage, receive and deliver stock and how will you maintain quality control around this?

6) Financial forecasts

Finally, the business plan needs to include robust and realistic financial forecasts and projections. These should include how much capital you need (assuming you are seeking external funding), what security you can offer lenders and how you will repay or service any borrowings or debt. You should also mention what you expect your revenue and income to be at specific points of time, normally after six months and then a year. You may want to include projections for the next three or even five years, though it is important if you do so to ensure your projections are as realistic and achievable as possible.

Within this section, you will probably need to include an illustration of your cash balance and monthly cash flow patterns for at least the first 12 to 18 months. This is simply to show that you have enough working capital to survive and pay any salaries. Then you should include a profit and loss forecast and a sales forecast, showing the level of profit you expect to make, the probable cost of providing services, and other overheads. You should also include the margin you expect to make from your sales.

Err on the side of caution and don't be over-optimistic, particularly in the current climate. It may even be a good idea, and show admirable realism, to outline a few 'worst case' forecasts and projections to show that the business plan can still stack up even if your existing projections do not come to pass.

Steer clear of potential pitfalls

It is estimated that around a fifth of new businesses fold within their first year, and that a half fold within their first three years – and that's without having a recession to factor in. So, to make sure that your business is not one of them, it's worth briefly highlighting a few of the more common mistakes people can make when planning and starting up.

Don't neglect your research

The first and most obvious mistake, as we made clear earlier, is not doing enough market research. It is impossible to over-emphasise the importance of putting in the legwork to build a realistic picture of what you are likely to be able to capture in terms of market share and who you are likely to be up against. Many businesses, when they fold, blame recalcitrant banks or a lack of funding. But while, yes, banks have been guilty recently of sitting on their hands and sometimes allowing perfectly well-run businesses to suffer, more often than not it was simply that the owners were over-optimistic about their market research.

Just as commonly, business owners can make the error of failing to react swiftly enough when their market shifts, perhaps because a recession changes people's spending patterns and choices. All good businesses, especially small ones, need to be nimble enough to react to changing economic conditions and, if necessary, you may need completely to rethink your business model to follow the contracts. If a sideline is the part of your business that is holding up best it needs to stop becoming non-core as rapidly as possible.

Keep your feet on the ground

Over-optimism can be a key failing for many would-be entrepreneurs. It's probably human nature to dwell on the positives, the reasons you can make something work, but it is important, as we have already stressed, to be realistic about the potential of your business or your would-be market.

Especially in the early days, it is all too easy to rely on over-optimistic forecasts or projections of where you are going to be in three or six months, or a year's time. Similarly, it is easy to take a rose-tinted view about how much money you will need to get up and running, for working capital and to live off.

Remember your budget

This all brings us neatly to the sin of weak financial planning. Businesses that fail will often have run through what cash they had much too quickly, perhaps spending injudiciously at the beginning and then slamming the brakes on too late or, worse, just at the point they should have been spending to maximise the nascent potential their business is beginning to show.

So, while forecasting what is going to happen in the future will never be an exact science, it's imperative to be as accurate, realistic and even downright pessimistic as you can be on cash flow and income forecasting. Remember, no business ever went bust because it was suddenly doing better than expected. The one corollary to this is that if you do too well too early you can run into difficulty if things get ahead of the capabilities of your suppliers and staff and you are no longer able to meet demand.

Spread the risk

Other common pitfalls include failing to plan for the unexpected, such as sudden interest rate rises or political, international, technological or even weather-related disruptions. Similarly, while it's a good idea not to be overly reliant on one market or client, being full of wonderful ideas that lead you off on too many tangents or into new markets runs the risk of overstretching the business and making it run before it can walk. Being overly focused on the volume of sales you are making as opposed to their value to the business, or relying on debt-fuelled expansion at the expense of solid profits can imperil a business of any size if things suddenly turn sour. Just ask the banks.

Credit control can make or break you

Finally, failing to keep a proper hand on your credit control or your stock levels, on what your suppliers are doing or charging you and even on what your competitors are up to can all be a recipe for disaster, particularly if the wider economic picture suddenly darkens. Suddenly money you thought was coming in doesn't, you realise too late suppliers are fleecing you, or a competitor muscles in on a market or suddenly launches a new product that leaves you gasping in its wake.

MAKING THE CHANGE:

John Dunsmure is managing director of the British Chambers of Commerce **www.britishchambers.org.uk**

Starting a business, even in a benign economic climate and certainly nowadays, is not easy and will require a lot of work, so you have to serious about it. If you want to be successful and to generate a proper income it is not something you can do just as a hobby; you have to recognise this is going to be your life from now on.

You will need to sit down and think very carefully about your reasons for starting up a business, whether it is something you are cut out to do, whether you have the right skills, outlook, ambition and temperament to do it.

The more planning and thinking you do before actually launching, the better – it is amazing the number of people who launch a business without even having done a business plan. You should have planned out carefully what you are going to do, who your customers are, who your likely competition is going to be, where your income is going to come from and what you will live off while it gets on its feet. It does not have to be planned to the nth degree but there does have to be some realistic thinking behind it.

Seek out support and advice

It is also important to recognise that, while it will be your business and yours alone, you are not alone. There is a lot of help you can call on, both from national and governmental organisations and on the ground more locally, which is where chambers of commerce can come in.

You'll normally expect to pay around £150 to £200 a year to be a member of your local chamber of commerce, which can sound a lot when you are trying to get a business off the ground, but what you will get is immediate access to an invaluable network of like-minded people who have been through this all before. Just as importantly some of these people, as well as being useful sounding boards, may turn out to be potential customers and clients.

There is also a lot of formal support and advice available. For example, we offer small business start-up packs, which include deals offering things such as free business banking, plus insurance and legal support as well as advice on areas such as health and safety and HR, both very important if you are going to be employing people. Chambers of commerce also run business growth clubs, regular business clinics and workshops and networking and social events. If your business has the potential to trade overseas there is also an international chamber of commerce network that can help you to develop opportunities in other countries.

Being you own boss is something many people dream about, but it is important to realise that running your own business is likely to mean long hours, hard work and a lot of dedication. You might in principle be in charge of your own working hours but in practice, especially at the beginning, it is unlikely to be something you can switch on and off. Especially if your business is online or international it may mean you are effectively 'on call' 24/7. Unlike when you are employed everything will be up to you. It will be you who makes things happen and sorts out problems, so it is not an easy way to change your career.

So, while you may well be getting out of the rat race, in a way, when you start your own business you are just getting into another rat race. The big difference is, this time, it will be a rat race where you are in control.

Keeping it in the family

For many people starting up a business, particularly a small or micro one, the resource sitting around the table looking at you – your family – is an obvious one to be tapped. It may be that you just use your family members on an ad hoc basis to do some leafleting, perhaps some cold-calling on your behalf, checking the books, proofing the business plan and so on. In this scenario, where the work is done largely as a favour, it is going to be very much up to you and the sort of relationship you have as to whether you pay them and need to put it through your books.

But if you are looking to use your family members, whether it is your partner, children or another relation in a more formal way, there are a few things you need to take note of. Technically, the term 'family-run business' means one in which more than half the shares are controlled by members of the same family, or where it has been passed down between generations.

Family dynamics

As the Scottish Family Business Association **www.sfba.co.uk** points out, while there can be clear benefits in turning your business into a family business, it can also bring its own challenges, and there will probably be quite a few questions you need to resolve at any early stage.

One of the key advantages is that you will be employing people you know and trust and who have the same outlook and values as you do, as well as being loyal to you. Because they will have an emotional as well as a financial stake in the business, they will probably feel more committed to it and therefore prepared to put in the hours – and possibly for a lower wage than people you would have simply hired to do a job. There is, potentially, also a ready-made line of succession.

But these relationships can also cause their own problems, not the least of which is the issue of succession. Family dynamics are rarely simple and adding the pressure of being in business together, with all the financial gamble (or inheritance) that that can entail, can be like dropping a match to a powder keg. Unlike a 'normal' employee, a family member cannot simply walk away and, of course, any business-related fracturing of the relationship can have profound repercussions on the family set-up.

If you are not careful there can be all sorts of assumptions made about people's roles within the business and their expectations for the future – essentially the succession again. There can also be issues around people's titles or why they are not being paid the same as, say, Uncle Bob who hasn't even turned up to a board meeting for months. You probably won't be able to rely indefinitely on the goodwill of family members to work all hours for a pittance, and you will need to take it on the chin when the daughter you thought you were grooming for a senior position or eventual ownership decides she'd much rather train as a vet.

According to the SFBA, the key questions for parents within a family business are whether shares should be divided equally, whether and how much individuals should be paid, what security they may have outside the business and issues around any planned retirement date. You will also want to consider who should be running the business in your absence or incapacity, how the business will be sold or passed on, what will happen to it if you die unexpectedly and, ultimately, if the benefit it might bring to the family is going to be worth the possible cost?

Similarly, for any children, key questions are likely to be simply whether they want to be involved with the business at all and, if so, what skills they will need, what they will get paid, whether they will get shares and what hours they should work. For family members who are not in the immediate family but are still involved, think about whether they will feel excluded, what their promotion prospects will be, their stake in the business now and in the future and how much voice or clout they will have.

Communication is key

It makes sense therefore to have lots of clear conversations about how it is going to work right from the earliest point – in other words don't do that common family thing of assuming you've said something or that everyone has understood what you *really* meant even if you didn't exactly spell it out.

For example, even if you and your partner are both keen on the marketing or promotional side of the business, it makes no sense for you both to be doing it, as that will probably just lead to confusion or doubling up. Similarly, if one of you has taken responsibility for the administration or bookkeeping, it's probably not politic to be double checking or redoing it just because it is 'your' business.

Financially, it makes sense to decide early on how you are going to allocate any shares in the business and whether there will be any non-family stakeholders – who can, incidentally, act as a good cool head and counterweight if things start to get a bit heated within the family. You will also, without question, have to work hard to separate business and family life. This can be anything from ensuring you don't let family dynamics or arguments cloud your business judgment to having a rule that business is never discussed around the dinner table, and especially not on Sundays.

It is also a good idea to be transparent about remuneration, particularly what you are paying to non-family members, and that it is clear why someone is being paid significantly more or less than someone else. It might well make sense to have a written remuneration policy that is regularly reviewed and to draw up a family business constitution, also sometimes referred to as a family creed. Your accountant should be able to advise you on this, or point you in the direction of an expert who can.

Decide on an exit strategy

Hang on, you've not even launched yet, surely it's way too soon to be thinking of how and when you are going to wind up your exciting new venture and life? Strangely enough, no. One of the best reasons for sitting down and having a think about how you intend eventually to exit the business is that it can help to focus your mind on what it is you want to achieve with it up to that point. If you know where you want to get to you are much more likely to be able to make clear decisions about how you should get there.

For example, do you want the business ultimately to keep you in comfortable retirement, float as a publicly listed company, be bought for vast sums of cash at some point or simply provide enough of an income to let you live relatively frugally while pursuing all your other hobbies or ambitions? Whatever your answer is may well govern your whole strategy for the business, how fast you look to grow and expand, the sort of people you employ or agree partnerships with and so forth.

Similarly, do you have a timeframe in which you are likely to want to step back from or sell the business? A common pitfall for small business owners is that they get so wrapped up in the day-to-day running of the business that they never prepare in time for the moment they will eventually sell up, and therefore perhaps fail to get the most from it financially in return. Or they suddenly decide 'Oh yes, I'll retire next summer' and then take their foot off the pedal and run the business down just at the point they should actually be building and strengthening it so that they can get the best price from any potential buyer.

There may also be legal issues to consider – it is, for example, much easier to sell or pass on a limited company than it is to pass on business where you are a sole trader, even if it has just been you and your son running it for years. Similarly, the 'cleaner' your accounts and the better your record keeping, generally the easier and less expensive it will be to pass a business on. As we have just seen, the question of family succession can be a thorny issue and it's best if you can address it early on. If you pass your business on to a son or daughter do you risk upsetting their siblings? Could it also mean you lose out on that retirement income you had assumed you would get from the sale of the business? Alternatively, if you are going to sell to someone external, what sort of person should you be looking out for, when should you bring them in and in what sort of role? These are all hard questions and ones you may not have a ready answer to at this point but they do need to be considered and, ideally, sooner rather than later.

Who can help?

The more people that you can turn to for help when you are setting up, the better. The key message here is that, a bit like *Close Encounters of the Third Kind*, you are not alone, so don't simply shoulder the entire burden yourself, and don't be afraid to access the resources that are out there. Accountants, small business banking teams, solicitors, BusinessLink advisers, your local chamber of commerce, organisations such as the Federation of Small Businesses **www.fsb.org.uk** or the Forum of Private Business **www.fpb.org**, even bodies such as the Confederation of British Industry **www.cbi.org.uk** can all help or, at the very least, offer useful pointers.

There are also vast resources out there on the internet and a myriad of self-help books on the ins and outs of setting up in business. More specifically, there are also a range of resources and organisations that have been set up to encourage under-represented groups, including women, ethnic minorities and people with disabilities, to start up in business and help them on their way.

For women, organisations such as the networking body Women in Business Network **www.wibn.co.uk** have a great track record in helping and mentoring women who want to set up in business, as do the bodies Prowess **www.prowess.org.uk/**, Opportunity Now **www.opportunitynow. org.uk/** and the Women's Enterprise Ambassador Network **www.womens enterprisetaskforce.co.uk/ambassadors.html**.

Similarly, it may well be worth checking out what organisations there are near to you locally. In the West Midlands, for instance, there is the Women's Business Development Agency **www.wbda.co.uk**, in Scotland there is the Association of Scottish Businesswomen **www.scottishbusinesswomen.com** while in Northern Ireland there is Women in Business **www.womenin**

businessni.com, though there are many, many others around the country.

For entrepreneurs from ethnic minorities, there are bodies such as the government's Ethnic Minority Business Task Force www.embtf.org.uk and the Make Your Mark campaign **www.enterpriseuk.org**, among others, while bodies such as DiversityNow **www.diversitynow.net** support and mentor people from diverse backgrounds. For older potential business owners, a good resource is the Prime initiative **www.primeinitiative.co.uk** which supports the over-50s in starting up.

For entrepreneurs with disabilities, the Employers Forum on Disability **www.efd.org.uk** can be a good starting point while the Leonard Cheshire association runs, along with Barclays, an initiative called Ready to Start **www.readytostart.org.uk** aimed at encouraging people with disabilities to go it alone. Similarly the Business Ability network **www.business ability.co.uk** does good work in this area. More widely, the government's Access to Work scheme **www.direct.gov.uk/en/DisabledPeople/Employment support/WorkSchemesAndProgrammes/DG_4000347**, which has contact centres around the country or can be contacted through Jobcentre Plus, provides invaluable support and funding for many people with disabilities, both to help them back into employment or set up in business. AbilityNet **www.abilitynet.org.uk** works to improve access to computers and the internet for people with disabilities.

Key points

- Think whether you are cut out for self-employed life
- Be sure about what you are risking or could lose if it goes wrong
- Plan it carefully, particularly your market research
- Be realistic, even pessimistic, about how you are likely to do, especially at the beginning
- Use all the help and advice that is out there

SETTING UP

What's in a name? When you're starting out in business, pretty much everything, along with your location, your unique selling point, your relationship with your customers and your delivery on results. This chapter explores how you actually go about setting up in business once the initial thinking, legwork and planning is done. So it will be looking at things such as the different business structures you can consider, how to choose a name, setting up your website, finding the right premises, getting the bank (or others) to stump up, tax and accounting issues, how to pay yourself and the ins and outs of actually launching and then building and maintaining momentum.

Getting a name, and a domain

Choosing your name, then, first. Choosing a name for your business is, quite obviously, likely to be one of the first big decisions about your business that you will make. You might keep it simple and just choose your own name, or a combination of you and your partner or someone else's name, such as Jack Cohen combining with the initials of tea supplier TE Stockwell to come up with Tesco. Or you might be looking for something that simply explains what you do or gets you to the front of the phonebook – witness the ubiquitious Aardvark this and that or AAAAA Cabs that seem to pepper most directories these days. You might want to choose something that your target customer base will understand and relate to, with the surf and beach clothing chain Second Skin a good case in point. Or it might just be something catchy or which has personal resonance.

If you're setting up as a sole trader, and probably in a limited geographical area, it probably isn't going to matter hugely if it's a name that's already taken somewhere else in the country, unless of course it's going to end up putting you at a competitive disadvantage or if you court trouble by calling your venture, say, M&S. But if you're planning to go the limited company route, you will need to check that it is available. The best place to go for this is to Companies House **www.companieshouse.gov.uk**.

This outlines a number of restrictions that might stop you choosing a preferred name, for example if it is the same as one already on its index or if you are foolish enough to try and call yourself 'Limited limited' or something obscene. It also prevents people calling companies names that are effectively the same as another, even if they are not the exact same wording. Companies House gives the example that, if there is an existing company called Hands Limited, then you would not be allowed to call your company Hands Public Limited Company, H and S Limited, H and S Public Limited Company or H&S Limited. Similarly you are not going to be able to include a word such as 'chartered' or 'charity' (among others) in your name unless that is what you actually are. It's all pretty much common sense.

Alongside this, these days, it makes sense to make sure your chosen name is available on the internet so you can create a suitable website and email address. There are an array of companies out there that will allow you to search for and buy domain names, with some of the best established being BT **www.business.bt.com/domains-and-web-hosting/domains**, Nominet **www.nominet.org.uk** which is the registry for .uk names and Netbenefit **www.netbenefit.com**, though there are many others. With the importance of the internet to marketing and branding it probably makes sense to do both the online and Companies House name checks at much the same time, although of course even if your preferred name is already taken online you may well be able to come up with a suitable variant that is not too far off.

Once you've bought and registered your domain name, the company will normally 'host' it for you and you should be able to buy any number of email addresses to go with it. With the internet now such an important resource for many small businesses, we will come back to some of the practicalities around designing your site, maximising traffic and getting noticed online a little bit later on in this chapter.

What kind of business is yours?

The next big decision you will need to make is exactly what sort of business you wish to be. There are a number of options to choose from, including sole trader, partnership, social enterprise and limited company, or even floating on the stock market as a public limited company. Less common variants include right-to-manage companies (or companies normally set up to represent the interest of owners in a shared block of flats) and limited liability partnerships. However, forming as a sole trader or partnership and, most of all, as a limited company, tend to be the business vehicles most commonly used by entrepreneurs and small business owners.

Sole trader

A sole trader is by far the simplest way to run a business or be self-employed. You do not have to pay any registration fee to set up and you get to keep all the profits. The main downside is that, unlike being 'employed' by a limited company (even if the company is only you) or working within a partnership where the liability is shared, you will be personally liable for any debts that your business runs up. This could feasibly mean your house or other assets are at risk if the business fails and also means it can be a risky option if it is going to be the sort of business that burns a lot of cash or runs up a lot of debt at the beginning.

Having said that, you have no shareholders, so you alone get to run the business and make all the decisions, including how to raise money. When it comes to tax, you have to inform HM Revenue & Customs within three months of starting in any form of self-employment that you have changed your status in this way – and if you don't you risk a £100 fine. As a sole trader, all your profits will be taxed as income and it will be up to you to keep records of your business income and expenses and file an annual self-assesment tax return to HMRC, although of course you can get an accountant to do it for you if you'd rather. You will also need to pay National Insurance contributions, both what are called Class 2 and, if your profits are above £5,715, Class 4 NICs. If your turnover goes above £68,000 you will be required to register for VAT. As many freelancers and contractors tend to be sole traders, there is a more detailed look at all this within the chapter on freelancing later on.

Partnership

A partnership is the next stage on from sole trader but still a step down from turning into a full-blown limited company. In a partnership, which will need a minimum of two people, the risk, costs and responsibilities are shared evenly between the partners. Each partner within it is self-employed and will take a share of the profits. The decision making will also normally be shared between partners, and partners, like sole traders, will be responsible for any debts the business runs up. The main difference here is that it will be joint

MAKING THE CHANGE

CASE STUDY: Auctioning on eBay

Former council electoral officer Niki Rae, 38, has turned a hobby of buying and selling clothing on eBay into a full-time job, and now runs two successful businesses, Fourgiraffeshugging and Heatwaveshack, on the auction site from her home in Aylesbury, Buckinghamshire.

I'd always been a keen shopper on eBay – it was something I did in my spare time, just for fun initially but, increasingly, as a way of earning a little extra money in the evenings and at weekends. I also always enjoyed going to car boot sales and picking up nearly-new clothes, so it just seemed a natural thing to do.

I was an electoral officer at Aylesbury Vale District Council and a qualified secretary but it wasn't what I wanted to do – it wasn't particularly well paid and I wasn't happy there. The good thing was that, when I decided to hand in my notice in August 2007, eBay was already there as an alternative; it was something I had been building up gradually and I knew it was what I wanted to do. The Fourgiraffeshugging name really came about by accident. It used to be my password on eBay – we have a limestone ornament of four giraffes hugging – and it just stuck. It's a bit silly but it is a name people remember, which is what counts.

Building a reputation

If you want to trade successfully on eBay you really need to become what is known as a 'PowerSeller' (**http://pages.ebay.co.uk/services/buyandsell/powersellers.html**) because when you hit that the fees you have to pay can plummet by as much as 40 per cent. You build up your 'Detailed Seller Rating' by gradually increasing how much you are buying and selling, and the amount of positive feedback you are getting from customers, and eventually, once you are earning above a certain amount each month (at the moment it's £750 or 100 items for three consecutive months), you get listed as a PowerSeller. I'm currently a Silver PowerSeller but the highest you can go is Titanium. When you become a PowerSeller you get access to lots of other support, such as phone and email help and a PowerSeller Board.

One of the great things about building up a business through eBay is that so much of it is done for you. You do have to be careful to abide by its rules, as it is quite easy to get thrown off, but they make it much easier than if you were trying to set up as an independent trader online. What's more, there's an automatic marketplace – people know eBay, so it's easier for people to find you rather than having to hunt you out online.

I set up the templates for my stores myself, though I did get some help from another eBay trader I met who was selling men's clothing and who was very helpful. It's sensible to look at what other shops selling the same stuff as you are doing. It's also a good idea to set up a Google Base Store Connector, which is a free download that puts information about your store into Google's index and helps direct shoppers to your site.

Stock levels and pricing

For the first four months I did wonder what I had let myself in for. I worried about my stock levels in particular. I'm only now sorting out a dedicated storage unit for the stock as it's got too much having it stored all over the house. You do need to be organised if you are going to run a business properly, and to get on top of things like the packaging and parcelling. I probably spend about an hour and a half each morning packaging up stock and then sending it out via Royal Mail, which can be tedious but it's just what you have to do. Another good thing about doing it through eBay is that you can print off packaging slips provided by them. Most people who buy through eBay will pay through PayPal, which means that once you have set up the account with them that side of the business is pretty straightforward. I also spend quite a lot of time comparing prices with other shops to make sure I am not over-pricing or under-pricing myself.

I've now reached the point where the business is at a bit of a plateau. Between the two businesses I'm turning over around £4,000 to £6,000 a month and I am starting to think whether I need to employ someone else, although that brings all sorts of other complications, so it is a big step. It's still not a huge business but I've doubled my income from when I was at the council.

The next stage is to launch my own brand, something I am right in the middle of trying to sort out now. I'm also trying to spread myself out a bit more by getting on some other e-commerce websites, comparison sites and places such as Amazon. It's not that I ever expect eBay to get into difficulty, it's so popular, but I always think it's a good idea not to rely on one source of income.

Maintaining a work/life balance

One downside is that I have found it hard to separate my home and work life, not that I really mind as I like to keep busy. I worked four days a week at the council but now, especially because it's online, the shop is never really shut. I've not had a proper holiday in two years and I even took the laptop with me when we went camping. But I've never been happier. It's a lot of hard work but I love it.

The only other downside is that, from having been an avid eBay shopper, I hardly ever go on the site just for myself anymore! I used to sit there for hours after work but now if I go on it's because of the businesses.

or shared responsibility rather than sole responsibility. Nevertheless if the business fails completely they will all be liable. To this end, both the partnership and sole trader format offer less protection than being a limited company, but they are also more flexible to run and easier to set up.

On the issue of liability, it is worth being aware that there are some differences around the country. In England, Wales and Northern Ireland partners are jointly liable for debts owed by the partnership, and so will be responsible for paying off the whole debt between them. But they are not severally liable for that debt (meaning each partner might potentially have to pay off the entire debt). In Scotland, however, partners are both jointly and severally liable.

When starting up a partnership, it is normally a good idea for a written partnership agreement to be drawn up by an accountant or solicitor. It is also possible to have what's called a 'sleeping partner' who contributes money to the business but is not directly involved in running it – as well as possibly being happy to be the butt of many a lame joke. If a partner decides they have had enough and wants to leave or resign, or if they die or go bankrupt, then the partnership has to dissolve. If a partner leaves the partnership, the remaining partners may be liable for the entire debt of that partnership. Also, a creditor chasing a debt can choose to pursue any of the partners for it.

As each partner is self-employed, it is up to them to make annual self-assesment returns to HMRC but the partnership as a whole must maintain records of its business income and expenses. Their NI status, too, will be the same as if they were sole traders.

Limited liability partnership

A limited liability partnership, commonly known as an LLP, is similar to a partnership but the main difference is that individual partners, as the name suggests, have lower or limited liability for any debts that may arise from the running of that business. In many respects it is more similar to a limited company in how it operates, in that the LLP is liable for any debts run up, rather than the individual members. What this does mean, therefore, is that LLPs really need to be businesses running at a profit rather than ones that are heavily geared or indebted.

Like a partnership, the LLP must have at least two partners, with the rights and responsibilities of its members normally laid out in what is known as a 'Deed of Partnership'. To form an LLP you, again, need to contact Companies House and fill in an incorporation form, or get an accountant to do it for you. Companies House will normally levy a fee of between £20 and £50, with the latter being for its 'premium' service.

In terms of running it, the LLP will normally designate a member or members to be responsible for maintaining communications with Companies House, preparing the accounts or acting for the partnership if it needs to be dissolved for whatever reason. All profits from LLPs are split between the members, with tax liability falling on the individual partners rather than the LLP itself.

Because most LLP partners will be self-employed – one of the reasons why so often accountancy firms consisting of a number of partners are LLPs – declaring for tax will normally be done through self-assessment, with partners only paying corporation tax on their income if they are also registered as a business. As with sole traders, and as of writing, an LLP will also need to register for VAT if its income exceeds £68,000 in a calendar year.

Social enterprise

Counting Jamie Oliver's Fifteen and the Eden Project among their numbers, social enterprises are businesses, normally ones with specific social or community aims, where any profits are reinvested back into the business or the community rather than given to shareholders or the business owners. They are also becoming an increasingly common part of the UK business landscape, and now contribute an estimated £8.4bn to the UK economy each year.

Last year, in fact, the government set out a 'Future Investment Plan' for such enterprises to make it easier for them to tender for public sector contracts. The National Endowment for Science, Technology and the Arts, along with the government, also last year launched a programme to help social enterprises access finance more easily.

To make life more complicated, social enterprises can take a number of different legal and business forms, though all still under the social enterprise umbrella. Without wanting to get too bogged down, you can have unincorporated associations where a number of individuals simply agree or 'contract' to come together for a common purpose, which may be of a social or community-based nature. You can also get social enterprise trusts, essentially unincorporated bodies that do not distribute their profits and are managed by trustees. Then there are social enterprises that take the form of a limited company (of which more later) with the main difference between it and a normal limited company being that it will include a clause setting out its aim and purpose, often again social or community-based.

If that wasn't enough, you can get social enterprises that have been set up as community benefit societies, where profits are solely returned to the community. Then they can also be set up as community interest companies, essentially limited companies that exist solely to provide benefits to a community or a specific section of a community. Probably the key thing to know about these is that they have an asset lock, which means they cannot normally transfer any profits or assets for less than their full market value. Lastly, many social enterprises are set up as charities and, as of late last year, in England and Wales could even become what are called charitable incorporated organisations, a hybrid between an incorporated company and a charity.

Good starting points for finding out more about social enterprises are the Social Enterprise Foundation **www.socialenterprisefoundation.org** and the Social Enterprise Coalition **www.socialenterprise.org.uk**, although BusinessLink also has a comprehensive section on its website about them and how to form them.

Limited company

For anyone looking beyond being a relatively small one-man band or partnership, a limited company is probably the most logical step. The first thing to recognise about becoming a limited company is that it is not hard to do or that expensive – Companies House charges the same £20 to £50 registration fee as for setting up an LLP. Then the various memorandum and articles of association forms (see below) that you will need to incorporate, the technical term for becoming a company, will probably set you back about £30, while you may also have to pay a nominal fee to get your forms witnessed.

But you also have to recognise that a limited company is a legal entity governed by strict rules. So, although it is more than possible to do it all yourself, what many people do, especially if they are busy working out the business plan and completing their market research, is get a specialist company formation agent to help them set them up. These agents will often charge around £30–40, and can be found online or in the phone book. Alternatively, a solicitor should be able to help you get things under way – though it will be worth agreeing your fee beforehand – or, if you're appointing one anyway, it may make just as much sense to get your accountant to sort out all the paperwork for you. For all these sorts of people this should be pretty basic bread-and-butter work.

What incorporation means is, very simply, that your business has been registered, or incorporated, on the Companies House Registrar of Companies. In Northern Ireland, incidentally, up until October last year, you would have needed to have sent your documents to the Companies Registry for Northern Ireland, but the implementation of the Companies Act 2006 in that month has meant a single company law regime now applies for the whole of the UK. Companies are therefore UK companies rather than being Great British or Northern Ireland ones. This has also meant the Companies Registry for Northern Ireland has now merged with Companies House.

What Companies House will need from you

You'll be asked for a Memorandum of Association outlining your company's name, location and what it will do. Companies House will also require Articles of Association, which basically describe how the company will be run and the powers of the company's directors, and what is called a Form 10 or Statement of the First Directors, Secretary and Registered Office, which gives the details of your registered office – which can be different from the office from which you trade. They will also need the names and address of the company's director and company secretary.

By law, companies must have officers in place at all times, and their

MAKING THE CHANGE

Entrepreneur Alex Hoye is chief executive of digital marketing agency Latitude and acts as an adviser to private equity fund Vitruvian Partners as well as being a business angel and investor in a variety of technology and internet-based projects.

What we have seen over the past two years is that corporations are no longer necessarily a safe place to be anymore. If you look at what happened in the 1930s in some countries, and what may well happen this time around, it was not the big companies that survived but the ones run by entrepreneurs. And business angels are there to help these small, entrepreneurial businesses, businesses often run by people setting out on a new career, to get off the ground and stay there.

What is a business angel?

A business angel is normally an individual who has become successful and knows a lot about entrepreneurs and setting up businesses. They will be people who love the opportunity to participate in an early-stage venture but, having done the hard graft themselves before, don't want to do it with the boot-strap lifestyle.

If you go to a bank you will probably be able to get a limited sum of money, perhaps £20,000 to £50,000, assuming your business plan stands up. The difference with business angels is that, while any one of them may only offer a similar amount, what often happens is that they will be working in a group – I for instance am a member of the Cambridge Angels network **http://cambridgeangels.angelgroups.net/** – and so together you might be able to access anything from £20,000 to perhaps £500,000.

In return, the angels, to a greater or lesser degree, will become participatory in the decision-making process of your business, they will take an equity stake and they will also normally act in an advisory and mentoring role. There's a lot about it that is different to *Dragons' Den* but what the dragons are, essentially, are business angels. When it comes to how much equity you should be prepared to give away, the angel will not want to take a majority stake and you should want to keep some room for manoeuvre and something to offer to later investors, so about 20 per cent I'd say is about right.

What we will be looking to do is to make an assessment of you as an individual, whether the business stacks up, what potential there will be for it to grow, whether the opportunities and strategy that you see are solid and really there or whether it is a complete leap of faith, and what the exit strategy – whether it's a future sale of the business or just that it's going to make a whole lot of money – is likely to be.

Don't come to a business angel if the business is still just an idea on a piece of paper. It needs to be a credible business before most angels will be willing to invest, it needs to have a proven market and some clients, or at very least the firm prospect of some customers. Most of the key questions that an angel investor needs to know will be fairly obvious and, to be honest, you should be telling them before they ask. So it's things like what is the market (and please don't say 1 per cent of the trillion pound global economy), what are the realistic opportunities for growth, who will the management team be, how exactly do you intend to use the funds, what is your competitive advantage, what is your exit strategy and so on?

Take your time and show your commitment

Beyond that we want to be sure you are credible as an individual, that we are confident not only that you have a good idea but that you are someone who is going to be capable of growing the business. Unlike on *Dragons' Den*, you're unlikely to get an immediate decision. Normally what happens is there will be an initial meeting, then a process of due diligence and some discussions about what is the likely road map for the business.

While passion for your business and business idea will clearly help, what we really look for is if you have passionate customers. Having even just two or three really satisfied customers who see the need for your business and will come back time and again is better than just having pure passion yourself for your concept. We also need to be sure you are committed to it. While at the start of a venture it is sometimes possible to do it alongside the day job, by the time you get to the level of business angel funding you need to be absolutely focused on it.

names and addresses must be printed on the registration documents. If any resign or new ones are appointed, or even if their personal details change, the Companies House registrar must be informed. If you're going the private limited company route – and for most start-ups this will be the case – your company will need to have at least one director (who must be over 16) and, ideally, a company secretary, although that is not a legal requirement. If there is only one director this must be stated in the articles of association.

If you're launching as a public limited company (PLC) there will need to be at least two directors and a company secretary, who must be formally qualified. At the other end of the scale, it is possible to create what are known as 'single member' companies consisting of just one person, though that person cannot also be the company secretary. The key difference between a PLC and a limited company, incidentally, is that the PLC can raise money by selling its shares on the stock market – as well of course having the fun of watching them crash through the floor when the banks snarl everything up. A PLC must also have share capital of at least £50,000.

Within all this, there are two forms of limited company – a limited company by shares and a limited company by guarantee. A company that is owned by its shareholders is one limited by shares and is the most common structure – and it also means shareholders who have paid in full for their shares are not liable for the company's debt. One that is limited by guarantee is slightly different, in that those forming it agree on liability limits when they incorporate. It is a structure more commonly used by social enterprises when setting themselves up as limited companies.

Tax issues

When it comes to tax and salaries, the basic fact you need to know is that limited companies pay corporation tax on their income and profits. They will also pay their employees, which means their directors as well as anyone directly employed, through a Pay as You Earn or PAYE system. But shareholders in the company can also pay themselves dividends based on the taxable profit of their company. What many directors end up doing is paying themselves a low salary, because such payments are taxed more highly, then dividing up the rest of the profit, or any profit that is not required to be re-invested back into the business at a later date, as dividends.

Dividends can be paid at any time, as long as you have the money in your business bank account to do so, with the only problematic area being that you should ensure the total of all your dividends taken has been covered by the profits earned by your company after all its expenses have been taken out. Taking dividends from untaxed earnings or having an overdrawn director's current account is technically a breach of the Companies Act and so is something you should pay back or reverse as soon as you can or the HMRC will be able to penalise you for doing so.

Just on a housekeeping note, while Companies House will pass on your details to the HMRC, it is also up to you to contact your local office and failure to do this can result in a penalty being levied. Like all the other business forms mentioned, if your turnover goes above £68,000 in a 12-month period (or you expect it to do so within the next 30 days) you will need to register for VAT, although you can register voluntarily if your turnover is below this level.

Once you are up and running as a limited company you must display your registered address on any letter-headed paper, invoices, letters of credit, websites and emails, at the registered address itself and at any other place where the business is carried out. If you are just working from home you won't need to do this as long as customers or employees are not actually going to be coming to the house.

The accountant

There are many ways of finding a good accountant for your business. Word-of-mouth and personal recommendation can go a long way, though it is still worth making sure the accountant will be right for your business. If your friend is in a completely different type of business, or your business is likely to have specialist accounting needs (for example if it is a franchise), a generalist, high-street accountant may not be as appropriate as someone, even if they are not local, who has expertise in that area.

So it's worth asking any prospective accountants whether they have any similar businesses on their roster or have worked with businesses in your sector or area before. You should also ask them about their qualifications, the size of the practice and number of partners, who will be in charge of looking after you on a day-to-day basis, whether they will remind you to submit accounts or other documents or whether it will be left up to you, whether they offer any specialist services or more general business advice and, not least of all, what their fee will be! Often you might be able to haggle a fixed fee for the first year. Fees are, of course, going to vary, depending on what you want, the complexity of your requirements and how many accounting transactions you are likely to do a month, but a good rule of thumb for a small business is between £80 and £150 a month. Whether or not your accountant is local can, of course, make a difference too, but may not matter hugely if you don't expect to need physically to drop in.

Either way, there are a number of bodies that should be able to help, including the Institute of Chartered Accountants in England and Wales **www.icaewfirms.co.uk**, the Association of Chartered Certified Accountants **www.accaglobal.com** and the Chartered Institute of Management Accountants **www.cimaglobal.com**. In Scotland, there is the Institute of Chartered Accountants of Scotland **www.icas.org.uk/directory** and Ireland is covered by the Institute of Chartered Accountants in Ireland **www.icai.ie**.

One thing an accountant will definitely be able to advise you on are the various tax advantages of taking particular steps or actions and what tax reliefs you might be able to claim on renting or leasing assets, for example a company car, or on any borrowing that you need to take out to rent or lease an asset. Which brings us rather nicely to that bone-quaking moment – going cap in hand to the bank or other financial institutions.

Money, money, money

We've all seen the headlines over the past year of how the banks have been screwing small businesses when it comes to funding. In many newspapers, not least the *Guardian*, small businesses have complained frequently about banks denying them access to finance, even to the new government-backed Enterprise Finance Guarantee, or offering them finance on such expensive terms that it is as good as impossible.

Bodies such as the Federation of Small Businesses have been vociferous in their criticisms of banks that have continued to sit on their hands while entrepreneurs and business owners struggle. So the first, pretty obvious, thing to say here is a) don't expect to be able to rely on the banks right now and b) think seriously about whether you even need to go to the bank at all. It may be, if you are starting up a business with relatively low overheads, that you can tap some savings, stick something temporarily on the credit card or borrow money from friends, family or colleagues. If you can access funds from a personal source such as this it's likely to be substantially cheaper than doing it commercially through a bank or other lender, depending on the relationship you have with the family member, relative or friend. There may, too, be more flexibility around payment terms and the repayment period. But tapping a family member or friend is not without its risks either.

The main one is, of course, that they will lose their investment and you will lose a friend. So it makes sense to ensure they are going into it with their eyes open and not simply being charitable because of who you are – try therefore as much as you can to put it on a 'commercial footing'. It may, for example, be a good idea to draw up a formal agreement or set down the terms of the loan in writing, including whether any interest is being charged. Beyond the family orbit, you may, as we will also come to shortly, be able to access grants or cash from business angels or venture capitalists. Nevertheless, for most start-ups, the bank is the first port of call for that first cash call.

What your bank may be able to offer

Banks will normally be able to provide two sorts of 'funding' to your businesses: loans and overdrafts. The overdraft, much as in your personal life, is simply a facility attached to your business bank account to allow you to go into the red to an agreed limit within an agreed timeframe. Its main advantage is that, as with a personal overdraft, it provides flexibility and is easy to set up. Its main disadvantage is that it can be expensive to service, with high interest rates, and so is probably not a good long-term funding solution. If you exceed your limit you are likely to get hammered with charges and the bank also has the right to withdraw it at any time. It is possible to secure overdrafts against your business assets – although this does of course mean the bank will be able to take control of these assets if you subsequently default.

Most small businesses will run an overdraft on a fairly regular, day-to-day basis but will also be funded by a bank loan, often to cover their start-up costs, the purchase of any assets, such as computers, cars or other equipment and for their initial working capital. This will normally be a set amount borrowed for a set period, and to be repaid within a set time, normally between three and 10 years. You may still be able to negotiate things such as early repayment holidays or initial discretionary lending rates, but in the current climate don't count on it. You should also expect to pay an arrangement fee at the start of the loan. It may well be, too, that the loan is secured on the assets of your business or even your personal possessions, such as your house, though, clearly, that significantly raises the stakes if things subsequently go bad.

If you think you might need to provide security on a loan it makes sense to have worked out in advance as many contingency plans as possible and what you would be prepared to offer as security if asked. It's also worth recognising this should not all be a one-way street and that you may have some room to negotiate on the terms of your loan, such as the due date, interest rate, whether you can make overpayments or take payment holidays and so on.

Alternative loans out there

As BusinessLink points out, it is worth knowing there are other sources of loan finance apart from the high-street banks and building societies. The Islamic Bank of Britain, **www.islamic-bank.com** for example, offers specialist loans to Muslim business owners, while organisations such as Prime **www.primeinitiative.co.uk** can offer loans for the over-50s. There is the Co-operative and Community Finance scheme **www.icof.co.uk**, aimed at co-operatives and social enterprises, and the Community Development Finance Association **www.cdfa.org.uk** which offers funding to organisations trying to create wealth in disadvantaged communities. BusinessLink also recommends the website of the British Bankers' Association **www.bba.org.uk** as a good place to go to check out the various business accounts available.

Post-credit crunch, the government's flagship lending scheme for small businesses is the Enterprise Finance Guarantee, which replaced the Small Firms Loan Guarantee scheme. Under the scheme – which has still not been without its critics, who have argued it is either not widely available enough or only offered with too many strings attached – the government has stepped in to guarantee 75 per cent of the loan amount to the lender, for which the borrower (ie you) pays a 2 per cent premium on the outstanding balance of the loan. It is available on loans from £1,000 to £1m with terms of up to 10 years and to any UK business with a turnover of up to £25m. More details on it, including a list of current lenders, can be found here: **www.berr.gov.uk/whatwedo/enterprise/enterprisesmes/info-business-owners/access-to-finance/sflg/page37607.html**.

The bank interview

So, how should you 'do' the bank interview and what should you expect? The main thing to bear in mind is that it's nothing personal. Yes, the bank may ask all sorts of searching questions and want to find out about you and your track record and aspirations but, ultimately, it should only be interested in whether it's likely to see its money (with interest of course) back again. So selling the business through the business plan is likely to be key point of discussion. If you've done your legwork on the business plan and have it all clear in your head, it's going to be much, much easier.

You may, however, also be asked for some other documentation, such as personal tax returns, a personal financial statement listing all your assets and liabilities or debts, an explanation of any criminal records you may have, a credit report (although the bank will run its own one) and proof of identity. It goes without saying that you should make an appointment, rather than barge in speculatively and expect to be seen, dress smartly to make a good impression, and ensure all the relevant paperwork is legible and easily accessible. It is often a good idea, too, to put your contact details on all your paperwork.

How much you should offer to put in yourself, or expect to have to put up, is a moot point and, once again, will depend on how much you are asking for and how much of a risk the bank considers you to be. The banks will normally look for you to commit something of your own, whether actual cash or simply security on lending. It is worth bearing in mind here are that, while it may be tempting to reduce your borrowing by ploughing in everything you have, that may not be the most sensible course of action if you don't then have a fall-back position for if things go bad. Also, under-borrowing and then having to come back to the bank in six months to a year can often be as bad as trying to borrow too much, as the banks may look askance on your apparent lack of planning and foresight. So it is very important that you try and get it right from the off which, again, comes back to realistic planning and projections.

Could a grant be the answer?

As we've mentioned, the banks and building societies are not the only source of potential funding out there for you. Grants are one increasingly popular alternative and often, if you can get them, the equivalent of 'free money'. A grant will normally be given for a specific project or purpose, usually covering a part of the total costs involved. You can get grants from the government, but also the European Union, regional development agencies, bodies such as BusinessLink, local authorities and various charitable organisations. In fact, one of the main challenges with grants is finding the right one for you and working your way through the maze of information . Another common misconception is that grants are evenly distributed around the country all of the time. In fact funding schemes come and go as priorities change, for instance focusing on a specific area needing regeneration, or as schemes simply run out of money.

Most government grants will require you to match the funds you are being awarded, meaning you will need to be able to demonstrate your business can provide its share of the total costs. It may also be a good

MAKING THE CHANGE

Paul Hickson is a partner at London and South East England chartered accountants Menzies LLP.

People generally are much more financially astute than they used to be and a lot of people setting up in business will use their own bookkeeping or accounting software. Twenty or 30 years ago you might get someone coming in and asking, 'How much profit have I made?', but nowadays small business owners are expected to have much more control and understanding of how they are doing financially on a day-to-day basis.

What this can mean, though, is that people often assume they do not need an accountant. While no one wants to pay for something they don't require, the law dictates that, if you are a limited company, you have to file accounts and a corporation tax return. Even if you are not a limited company you will still have to file a tax return. Companies House has recently increased its penalties for not filing accounts quite severely, and HMRC is getting much stricter about ensuring what people and businesses pay in tax is right. So you do need to make sure you are crossing the Ts and dotting the Is.

A helping hand to get you started

At the same time many people come out of employment and don't really know that much about finance or managing money. It will always have been done for them, but you have to get on top of it when you are running a business. You are also probably going to be working flat out to get the business off the ground and established, so it is very easy to let it slip and get out of hand.

People often think of an accountant as just providing the basic bookkeeping, tax and accountancy services, but most accountants these days can provide a lot more than that. We offer a range of consultancy services and advice to small businesses, so it is a question of judging what you need and what you can afford as a small, start-up business. Your accountant should be able to sort out all the paperwork around setting up as a limited company, such as the articles of incorporation, registering the business and so on, and if you get to the point of employing people, you may require a lot of advice about things such as payroll and insurance. Similarly, becoming VAT registered can be quite a big and challenging step for many small businesses.

It's surprising, too, how many people start up a business as a knee-jerk reaction to being made redundant without knowing where it is going to go and, as a consequence, find it is quickly drifting. So what you need to have is a business plan that focuses on what the business is going to look like after one year, two years and three years – and this is something a good accountant should be able to help with or at the very least give advice on.

You don't want necessarily to be worrying that every email or letter you send is going to cost you money, so what a lot of small businesses do is arrange a budget for consultancy work for, say, a 12-month period and then they know they can pick up the phone without it costing more than it should. And having someone knowledgeable at the end of the phone or email can be absolutely crucial in those first six to 12 months.

Making the right choice

When it comes to choosing your accountant, a personal recommendation from someone you know and trust is always a good idea, though bear in mind the requirement of their business and what they need from their accountant might be very different to what you require. It's important, too, to consider where the accountant is based. That may sound obvious, but if you are going to be needing to go in to see them regularly you don't want them to be a pain to get to. But if you're mostly going to be communicating by phone or email, which is often the case now anyway, that consideration may be less important.

You also have to gel with the partner, as the relationship between the business owner and their accountant can be a very close one. So you need to understand each other and trust each other's judgment. It is important to ask about what experience the firm has had with your type of business. Ask if they have other clients similar to you and if you can get a referral. You need to be sure the accountant understands the dynamics of your business, and in particular any financial or tax issues – for example if you are going to be trading overseas – that you might be likely to encounter.

One of the most common traps that people fall into when starting up a business is under-valuing themselves. They plan it from the top down, valuing everything else first and putting themselves at the bottom. But you need to work into your plan a proper reward for your efforts, even if for the first few months or even years you do not draw much of a salary.

If after the first nine or 10 months you are earning far less than you were before that's not going to be a huge issue as it's common with a small business starting up, but if the situation is still the same after two or three years it may be a good idea to sit down and have a proper look at the business model. Here, too, an accountant can be a good sounding board, because they will have seen a lot of different businesses and will not be as closely wrapped up with it as you are. A good accountant needs to be someone who is prepared to say no to a client from time to time – they may not listen and go ahead anyway, but as well as ensuring the books are all in order, an accountant should be prepared to challenge their client from time to time and help keep them on track.

idea to look at whether your business has a particular selling point that might open it up to a grant, for example if it is a rural or women-only business, a social enterprise or you are planning, perhaps, an environmental or sustainable project or a project related to research and development.

When it comes to resources, BusinessLink has a wealth of information on its website within its 'grants and support' directory. There are also various commercial grant-finding services available, though they may not be free or at the very least may require you to register. Some of these, and this is by no means a comprehensive list, include **www.j4b.co.uk** and **www.grantfinder.co.uk**, while the website **www.access-funds.co.uk** has information on charitable and not-for-profit grants and **www.grants online.org.uk** includes information on EU, UK and National Lottery grants. The Department for Business, Enterprise and Regulatory Reform also regularly announces the creation (and closure) of various grants.

For younger entrepreneurs in particular, there are often organisations such as Shell LiveWIRE **www.shell-livewire.org**, which offers help and some financial support, as well as the Make Your Mark campaign **www.enterpriseuk.org** and the Prince's Trust Million Makers initiative **www.princes-trust.org.uk/support_us/million_makers.aspx**, which challenges teams of employees to set up in business to raise money for the trust – mini-enterprises that can sometimes lead to people deciding to go it alone more permanently. If you have been doing a course at university, particularly a business-related course, it makes sense to check out what resources might be available there – many universities and business schools now have 'business incubator' centres, offering students with business ideas access to things such as office space, phone lines, broadband access, conference and meeting rooms, photocopying and phone answering services and so on. Some may even offer some 'seed funding' for new start-ups or run competitions with a financial reward at the end.

Business angels and venture capitalists

Another key source of funding are business angels and venture capitalists. These are easily confused, as both will normally want some form of equity stake in return for their investment. The key difference is that business angels – wealthy individuals who invest in high-growth businesses – will normally invest their own money (think *Dragons' Den*) or pool money if they are acting as part of an angel network. If it's a single individual you might be looking at anything from the £10,000 mark upwards, with networks able to invest much more, often as much as half a million.

As with everything, you need to come to them with a well-thought-through, well costed business plan and, ideally, some evidence of a track record, which can mean it's not the sort of funding you are going to need to get started but more the sort of injection that might help you get to the next level. With business angels you may also be able to tap into their invaluable 'been there, done that' expertise. Organisations such as the British Business Angels Association **www.bbaa.org.uk** should be able to help you find relevant angels or networks near you.

Venture capitalists, meanwhile, are more likely to use pooled money held in a professionally-managed fund and may want to take a more hands-on role as a director or board member. The size of investment is often higher, with a minimum of £2m not uncommon. The main advantages of securing VC funding are the larger sums as well as, again, the potential to bring expertise on board and so make it easier to secure further funding.

The main disadvantage is that securing a deal can be a long and complex process and you'll have to pay legal and accounting fees, whether successful or not. Useful bodies include the British Venture Capital Association **www.bvca.co.uk** and the European Private Equity and Venture Capital Association **www.evca.com**. A 'third way' here is what are called Enterprise Capital Funds, essentially a government-backed equity finance scheme aimed at small and medium enterprises (SMEs) **www.berr.gov.uk/**

bbf/enterprise-smes/info-business-owners/access-to-finance/enterprise-capital-funds/page37473.html though it makes sense to check what is running and when. There may also be the option of Regional Venture Capital Funds, which provide up to £500,000 for SMEs that have good growth prospects, with funding split between the government, the European Investment Fund **www.eif.org** and private sector investors. More information on this is available at **www.berr.gov.uk/bbf/enterprise-smes/info-business-owners/access-to-finance/regional-venture-capital-funds/page37596.html**.

Finding your 'shop window'

If we'd been writing this a decade ago, this section would have been predominantly about bricks and mortar and finding the right high street, side street or business park location for your business. To an extent, of course, it still is. But these days your 'shop window' also needs to be as much about the virtual, internet presence that you are showing to the public as it is about how many people will be physically walking past, stopping to browse or coming in your door. And for some businesses, particularly home-based ones, the website has become all or nothing – it will be your brand, your word-of-mouth, your shop window and your till combined.

According to the Interactive Media in Retail Group, which monitors online sales, web-based shopping in the UK has risen by a staggering 5,000 per cent since 2000, with shoppers now spending an average of £43.8bn a year online – so getting the site right, bringing traffic to it (perhaps through search engine optimisation) and having a 'shop' that will keep customers happy and engaged is as important now in the online world as it is in the physical one.

As Mark Stuart, head of research at the Chartered Institute of Marketing points out, the virtual image you project to the public, and the reach that a good website can give your business, can be the difference these days between success and failure.

> 'The internet means you can expand your horizons and easily sell abroad if you decide that's the right thing to do. If the recession means that you struggle to get the market to come to you, then you must go to the market. A property agent going solo, for example, might consider buying or selling in Bulgaria or Romania, where the markets are still flourishing,' he says.

Unless you are very confident that you can get it right yourself, it can make sense to get a professional in to design your site – particularly if there need to be functions such as a checkout or some other form of customer interactivity. We've all been there and know how frustrating it is finally to track down a site only for it to be impossible to navigate or not give us what we want. There is so much competition out there, too, that start-up businesses cannot afford to lose traffic to rivals simply because their website is not up to scratch, as Stuart also makes clear.

'Once you have set up a strong site, you need to attract customers to it. Invest in pay-per-click advertising, which are the sponsored results that appear at the top and side of search engines such as Google. Also get a web designer who can implement effective search engine optimisation, ways of designing and writing the site so that your company appears higher up the listings when customers search for the kind of thing you offer,' he advises.

'Consider, too, using social networking sites such as Facebook or YouTube to promote your company. Viral campaigns can be inexpensive and highly effective – people will forward video clips that they like and which are funny, and you effectively get free word-of-mouth publicity when they do so,' he adds.

There are a huge number of designers out there who can put sites together for you – as there are many self-help and do-it-yourself tools if you want to go that route – but the key, along with their price and affordability, will be whether they understand what it is you want the site to achieve. Be very clear – designing a good website is not about the technology, however excited your designer gets about that side of it.

Getting the technology right is, of course, vital but business is business is business – a site can have the most advanced wizardry in the world but if it is not right for your business or is not doing what your business requires or is not reliable or easy to navigate, it has failed. The other potential pitfall of using a third-party designer is that you risk relinquishing an element of control over your site – if you cannot update it yourself or manage or amend the site on a daily basis you are going to have to be absolutely sure you have someone you trust to do it for you, and properly.

You will also need to be sure, if you are accepting payments online, that you have secure credit and debit card payment systems, a procedure for refunds, proper systems for managing customer data and details, a reliable distribution and supply chain, a proper 'cooling off' period after purchase for customers to change their mind, accessible contact details and so on.

Your premises

All these elements are equally important within any physical premises or outlet that you operate from. Things to consider when choosing a physical premises should include where exactly it needs to be, so if it is likely to need a lot of passing trade a high-street site might work best. If that's of less importance, a cheaper secondary or side street site might work. Realistically it's probably going to be a toss up between what you can afford and what'll be best for the survival of your business.

Similarly, an out-of-town site might work if what you are selling will mostly need to be transported by car. Or if you are unlikely to have that many customers physically coming to you, you might want to consider a site in a business park or serviced office block, rent space in a convenient unit, or even operate from home. You will also need to consider whether you want to buy or rent your premises. There are, as ever, advantages and disadvantages to each. With renting, what normally happens is that you will lease a premises for a fixed number of years and pay an agreed rent, which will be periodically reviewed.

The advantage of this is that your upfront costs will be much lower, the downside is that you may have to pay through the nose if you want to terminate or change your agreement before the term is up (for instance if you quickly need to expand or downshift), rents can often rise unexpectedly and if you fall out with the landlord (perhaps because of the last point) it can get nasty. You will also still be responsible for the health and safety of any employees or customers using the premises, even if you are only the lessee.

In some sectors, such as the pub trade, there can be industry-specific issues to consider too. If you, for example, become a tied pub owner – generally considered one of the cheapest ways into an industry that attracts many career changers – you will lease the premises off your brewer but you will then be contractually 'tied' to buy their beer, at their price, and accept their regular rent reviews, a business model that, in an industry already struggling to cope over the past couple of years with recession, cheap supermarket beer and the smoking ban, has created considerable disgruntlement among tenant publicans.

With buying, the main advantage, of course, is that you will own your premises and be able to stay there as long as you like, rent it to someone else, alter it yourself (as long as there are no legal or planning restrictions on it), sell it on (hopefully at a profit) and so on. There can also be tax benefits in buying, in that you may be able to claim capital allowances towards the cost of renovating or converting the premises.

The downside is that you'll have to find the money to buy it in the first place, or be prepared to stump up for a commercial mortgage as well as probably shell out for things such as stamp duty and solicitor's fees. You will be responsible for repairs and maintenance and, as we have seen over the past year, there is no guarantee that it will be an asset whose price will rise inexorably.

If you are planning to work from home, the main premises-specific things you will need to consider will be whether customers or employees will be coming to you on a regular basis, in which case there may be health and safety stipulations you need to take into account, whether your insurance and mortgage will need to change, whether your home will become liable for business rates, whether you may, for example, need to convert a garage or another room into a storage area or whether you will need any specific equipment.

Becoming an employer

If your business premises is going to be staffed just by you, or possibly you and your partner, it should (hopefully) be pretty straightforward to manage. But if you are going to be employing other people (as opposed simply to contracting them to do a job) it opens up a whole new set of complications. In a guide such as this, it's only possible to scratch the surface of what you'll need to be thinking about for this but, essentially, you'll need to ensure you supply them with a written statement of employment, that you understand their employment status, that you recruit fairly and without discrimination, that you carry out any relevant criminal or pre-employment checks and that you have a legally watertight employment contract.

You'll also need to understand what their and your rights are, how to register as an employer (which you will need to do in order to pay their tax and National Insurance Contributions and to operate a proper payroll system), that you are paying above the national minimum wage, that you are paying appropriate sick, maternity or paternity pay, that you are keeping proper staff records and personal information (but also that you are only keeping data you are supposed to keep), that you are offering any appropriate benefits or pensions, that your premises (and working practices) comply with health and safety rules and that you have proper employers' liability insurance. For much of this, it is a good idea to get specialist legal, financial and even personnel/HR advice though, again, organisations such as BusinessLink or websites such as **www.smallbusiness. co.uk** can offer a lot of good basic advice.

The launch... and what comes next

For many would-be entrepreneurs the vast majority of their time and effort will go into the launch of the business, the moment when they first open their door to the public or their website goes live. That, of course, is a hugely important bridge to cross and it is vital that you have the infrastructure in place to cope with immediate demand, to meet (and exceed) customer expectations and, simply, to function as a proper, professional business. You'll probably need to have a marketing and promotional budget in place and, as we have seen, a proper marketing strategy for how you are going to get your name, product or service out there.

If you're operating from a shop or some other physical premises you may want to make a big event of it, perhaps with balloons, people in costumes, advertisements in your local paper and so on. Or perhaps you can offer first-day discounts, product sampling or other promotional giveaways. Online it's harder to make a splash when you launch and is more likely to be something you may have to grind away at until you gradually build up your virtual reputation and traffic to your site, but it should come. Either way, hopefully in time you'll be working all hours not because you are desperately trying to make ends meet but because you are rushing to meet intense customer demand, chasing suppliers, following up invoices and seeing the money starting to come in.

But the launch is, and should be, just the start. It's very easy to get overly focused on D-Day and forget this is something where the intention is that it should be your life from now on. Therefore, as a final point, it makes sense to have a plan for expansion and how you are going to build on or, at the very least, maintain your launch momentum.

Some of this should, of course, have been built into your business plan, but both the wonderful as well as intensely challenging thing about being in business is that it never stays still, or should never do so if you are successfully driving it forward every day. So from day one you need to be thinking about new markets and opportunities, even if they are ones you will not get to for a year or more, better ways of managing your processes or costs, ways of improving your margins or investing in new goods and services and how you are going to compete with or even beat the big players out there.

Most of all, though, every day remember why you're doing this. It's not because you want to be spending an evening humping stock around your garage or labouring over the books at midnight – though you may end up doing both (hopefully not consecutively). It's because this is one of the best ways there is to take control of your life.

Being in business can be one of the most exhilarating, as well as one of the most white-knuckle, rides there is. But if you can make it the success *you* want it to be, which may mean anything from having a Rolls-Royce in the drive to bringing in just enough income to enable you to live your new life, then as a way of changing your career it takes some beating.

Key points

- There are many different business formats you can choose from
- Don't assume you have to rely on the banks for funding, but if you do be very clear what you want funding for and why
- Your internet 'shop window' is now as important as your physical premises
- The launch needs to be just the beginning

FRANCHISING

Walk down most British high streets and, while you may not have been aware of it, you will probably have been surrounded by franchises. McDonald's, Costa Coffee, Domino's Pizza, Prontaprint, perhaps the 02 mobile shop or the énergie fitness club – all of these are chains that are either predominantly or partly franchised. Similarly, if you are letting out or selling a property through Bairstow Eves or Belvoir! lettings, it may well be a franchise. Or the Drain Doctor you call in a panic to sort out that blocked drain on Christmas Day, or the Kumon after-school maths class you send your children to – and so it goes on. In fact, according to last year's annual survey of the industry by the British Franchise Association (BFA) and NatWest, franchising is now an £11.4bn business, with some 838 different types of franchised business operating around the country.

Franchising is also an industry that is actively geared towards career changers and people looking to start a second or third career. The average age for a franchisee in the UK is mid-40s and, while you do get some younger entrepreneurial types running franchises, the vast majority come to franchising after a period in corporate employment in some shape or form, often starting a franchise in a sector or industry in which they had absolutely no prior experience. The past few months have also, perhaps unsurprisingly, seen an upsurge of interest in franchising, often from people who now have a redundancy cheque burning in their pocket.

So, what exactly is a franchise?

Franchising in its most common form – technically known as business format franchising – comes about when an individual or organisation (known as the franchisor) either buys or creates a licence to sell businesses under a set trademark or name to other individuals, who becomes franchisees. Agreements normally last for a minimum of five to 10 years, after which they need to be renewed. In practice, this might mean the franchisee buys the right to set up under that company's name (with their logo, look, equipment and so on) on a high street or it could mean they acquire the right to operate that business in a particular geographic area or territory. This will particularly be the case for mobile, or so-called 'man-and-van', franchises where you might buy, say, north Hampshire or west Leeds and then that will be your 'patch', although you may also get national jobs supplied through your franchisor.

A variation of this is the growing number of online-based franchises where, while you might be operating from a room at home, you could be running a website based around your specific local area. Another option is to buy what is called a 'resale'. This is where you simply buy an existing franchise that someone else is selling. Generally speaking, as a franchised network becomes more established and so has fewer new territories or units to offer, resales become more common. The downside with a resale is that, because it is already an established business, it will normally be more expensive. The upside, of course, is that it will already be an established business and so will probably already be profitable, have a client base and a local reputation (hopefully a good one).

What you get, or should get, for your upfront fee is, first and foremost, the fact that you are buying into an established, tried-and-tested business model that is, perhaps, also a well-known name with the general public. This may well, as we will see, help when it comes to agreeing finance with the bank, and many franchisors offer a 'turnkey' package where a lot of the contractual and financial leg work and issues such as finding the right premises and fitting out are all done for you. What you should also get is comprehensive training in both the technical side of the business and, normally, some of the more general sales and business skills you will need.

On top of this, most well-established franchises will be able to offer access to national advertising campaigns, or even national contracts or a ready-made supply of clients in your area to get you up and running. There may also be economy of scale, bulk-buying agreements with suppliers that you can tap into, unlike smaller independent operators.

Just as attractively, a growing number of franchisors offer, for a fee, access to a central credit control and invoicing service so you don't have to spend your time chasing tardy payers and know you will get payment for what you have invoiced coming through each month, even if the client has not yet physically paid up. You will own the business and it will be yours to grow, expand or ultimately sell on, with some people eventually buying more than one territory or unit or even, if the business model will support it, buying their own regional master licences to sell franchises on to others.

In return, the franchisor will receive an initial fee, normally payable once you sign on the dotted line, together with on-going management service fees, sometimes called royalties. This will usually be based on a percentage of the annual turnover or might be calculated as a mark-up on the supplies you buy. As part of the ongoing relationship, the franchisor should provide support to you and others in the franchise network, whether it be through training updates, new product development, advertising, promotional activities or other management services.

Buyer beware

Because you are going to have a big brand name behind you, as well as an established business model, many people when they go into franchising see it as something of a licence to print money. It is true that the failure rate for franchised businesses is lower than for stand-alone independents and it has been an established part of the UK business landscape for more than 30 years now. Yet there are two words that you as a career changer need to bear in mind, both before you purchase a franchise and all the way through the recruitment process – buyer beware.

This is because, for all the well-known franchised names up and down the country, franchising is an unregulated industry. The best it gets is the oversight of the BFA but – and many potential franchisees get confused by this – the BFA is not an industry regulator but simply an accreditor of franchisors. In other words, it operates a code of conduct and monitors how franchisors are running their operations and that their business model stacks up. But it does not represent or offer protection to individual franchisees, though this is something it has been looking at and could feasibly do in the future. Having said that, and this is something we will examine more closely a little later on, what BFA accreditation does mean is that, if you're buying into that business, it will have been given the once over by experienced BFA assessors, something that should probably help you to sleep a little easier at night.

This is not to say, of course, that all non-BFA franchised businesses are spivs, far from it. There are many highly reputable, successful franchised businesses that operate and thrive outside the BFA umbrella, though it may well be worth asking them why they have decided to go down this route. Similarly, there have been occasions where the BFA has had to unaccredit businesses when problems have become apparent.

The point is that, before taking the plunge into franchising, you need to be aware it is an industry that can attract dodgy operators trying to take advantage of people's desperation to get out of the rat race and become their own boss. Whether it's someone who makes their money by crookedly 'churning' – where an operator simply recruits a load of franchisees, pockets their fees and leaves them to sink or swim – or someone who means well but has not thought through the margins, has been over-optimistic on projections or has not put in place the right support infrastructure, you need to be careful, diligent and questioning when you are buying a franchise. After all, given that a franchise can often cost anything between around £10,000 and more than £100,000, it may be the biggest purchase you ever make – sometimes even bigger than buying your house – and an investment at a point of your life where it is going to be much harder to recover financially if it all goes wrong. Ultimately, if it looks and sounds too good to be true, it probably is.

Finding the right franchise for you

The BFA has a lot of information about franchising on its website **www.thebfa.org**, plus a bookshop where you can buy guides on subjects such as how to evaluate and choose the right franchise for you. It regularly runs seminars around the country, again listed on its website, that offer an introduction to franchising and what it's all about. There are also a number of websites and magazines that offer advice, though a lot of it tends to be rather uncritical. Perhaps one of the best sites for both general advice and to find out about individual franchised businesses is **www.whichfranchise. com**. Apart from going online, one of the most common places where people interested in franchising end up at is one of the BFA-organised regional franchise exhibitions that are held up and down the country each year.

These tend to be, like any exhibition, busy, hot and stuffy affairs where you will be presented with row upon row of franchised businesses touting their wares. So the key if you are going to go to one is to do at least some initial leg work, or even just thinking, beforehand about what sort of business you are interested in. If you can, for example, immediately discount man-and-van or gardening/outdoors franchises, that's inevitably going to help in narrowing down your search. It's worth mentioning here a common misconception that many potential franchisees slip up on – just because it is a BFA-organised exhibition does not necessarily mean that all the businesses exhibiting will be BFA members, so it can be worth checking this out afterwards on the BFA website.

Another thing to watch out for is the hard sell. The people on the stands will often be sales people and it will be their job to reel people in. But if

MAKING THE CHANGE

Running a camping club franchise

Greg Baines, 45, and his wife Karen, 44, gave up successful teaching careers to buy and start up a Camping and Caravanning Club franchise in Polstead, Suffolk. The club, which has been running for 108 years and has 450,000 members, operates 109 parks, 16 of which are run as franchises.

We'd both been keen campers and caravanners for many years and about four years ago we were on holiday in Dorset, sitting out one evening and just got talking about what a great idea it would be to run a holiday park rather than just visiting one from year to year. Although we had established careers as teachers, me in a secondary school and Karen in a primary school in Preston, we were both feeling slightly restless. It wasn't that we were desperate to get out, but we were at the point where it was either stick it to retirement or get out and do something different.

But we knew it was a huge decision to make so we didn't rush it. We toyed with a lot of different possibilities – running a holiday cottage complex, a touring park, holiday lets and so on. There was also a lot to think through. Were we sure we wanted to go from a profession where you get long, set holidays each year to one where holidays are non-existent except in the closed period between January and February? There were our four children to consider too, then aged between seven and 15, who were happy and settled in Preston – how would they feel about being uprooted and relocating halfway across the country? There were so many variables to consider and it seemed such a big leap that it would be impossible to do. But we also knew there is never a good time to make this sort of decision and you can always find good reasons for not doing it.

Inspiration

Then Karen saw an advertisement in a franchising magazine for the Camping and Caravanning Club franchises and so we started digging around and looking into it. We filled in the application form and, very tentatively, put it in the post. We didn't necessarily think much would come of it and were really just testing the water. We also knew nothing about franchising and how it worked. But it was clear that you would be running and owning a park yourself, but doing it under the flag and brand of the club, using their signage and so on, and that you'd potentially have a ready-made market out there of club members.

We also realised that there was no way we could afford to buy a park by ourselves, but doing it through the club could be a more viable option. We had a fairly good idea that most banks would be unlikely to lend us the sort of money we would need as individuals, but if we had the club name and record behind us, which the banks knew, it could make a big difference.

We were initially asked to come to an introductory day to get to know the club, and for them to get to know us. They simply ran through how the franchise worked, the history of the club, what would happen if we were accepted and what would be expected of us. That gave us a better idea and allowed us to go away and do some more research. We then had a more formal interview, where they asked us things such as our ambitions and aspirations for the club, how we would guarantee the income was there and so on. There were also various psychometric tests to see if we were the right sort of people for them and compatible with what they wanted. It was quite extensive and rigorous. They wanted to gauge how we would handle the move, the loss of secure careers in teaching and how we would cope with some of the worse-case scenarios that a site might experience or when we were dealing with the public. The only criticism of the process I would have is that, at the time, the club was not overly proactive when it came to us speaking to other franchisees. It was left up to us to get in touch with people, which of course we did. That has now changed and people are encouraged to speak to others in the network, which makes a lot of sense, because when we spoke to franchisees it was real eye-opener; they were so positive about it and it was really helpful.

Choosing a location

The next challenge was finding a site. Though we had been accepted as franchisees in principle we still had to do things such as sell the house and move into rented accommodation while we then found the right site and put down a deposit. We found the Polstead site simply by getting out there and going round sites and doing letter drops around various counties. We initially thought of Devon and Dorset but when the Polstead site came up, which was an existing park, though it had been run independently, it just seemed right, though it still needed a lot of work to bring it up to club standards. At this point we also had to put together a quite comprehensive business plan because, although we had sold the house and were putting that into the park, we were still going to need to invest around £100,000 to get the site up to scratch, with the bank lending us around 80 per cent for the purchase and the improvements.

We started trading in August 2008, but did not start as a club site until the following February, and because we had started in the second half of the year, which is normally when things start to slow down, for the first few months the income was incredibly tight. There were a lot of decisions to be made about how best to spend the money, where to get the best deals from tradespeople and so on.

But since we opened as a club site it has just been fantastic. It has been phenomenally busy, we have exceeded our occupancy level expectations by around 100 per cent and advance bookings across the network have been up 27 per cent. The club has put a lot of effort into marketing us as a new arrival – there are never enough clubs in the network to cope with demand from members – in particular through the club magazine. So we do not have to worry about promoting the park or reaching out to our audience which, if we were an independent park, could be a big challenge I'd have thought.

There are days when you have been working non-stop and you feel really shattered, and there are always a huge amount of decisions to make and challenges to be met for the week ahead, so your mind is always busy. Sometimes I find myself nodding off by 9.30 pm because it is so exhausting. But I would never go back – I have no regrets, my lifestyle is now so much better. I don't get that Sunday evening growing sense of dread at the week ahead. In fact last year in our closed season I went back to visit the school where I used to teach and I was in the staff room, the bell went and I couldn't help but smile to myself as everyone trudged wearily off to their classrooms.

Changing your career can be a long process and sometimes if you try and look at it from beginning to end, at all the things you have to achieve and the stages you may have to go through, it can seem impossible and you end up completely daunted. So you need to take it in steps and see it as a journey. You also need to be sure you are asking the most searching questions possible. You need to make sure you do your groundwork and, if you are going into franchising, that you speak to existing franchisees in your network. Also, make sure the training you are going to be given is well-established, as that can make a huge difference.

When we told people this is what we were doing they either said they were completely jealous or that we were absolutely mad. But the satisfaction that you get when you walk in on the first day and you're finally in your new career or new business is amazing.

you do sign up for anything, make sure it's just to being contacted or to have a chat at a later date. This will normally be all any reputable franchisor will be wanting to do anyway, but just be wary of anyone who is trying to get you to sign anything more binding or (an absolute no-no) trying to get you to put down a deposit in the heat and stress of an exhibition. The exhibition should just be the first part of a much longer recruitment process.

What BFA membership means

It's probably worth touching briefly at this point on what BFA membership actually means if you see a franchise advertising this at an exhibition or in its promotional literature. The BFA has four levels of membership: full, associate, provisional and affiliate. Businesses that sign up and pay their dues commit themselves to agreeing to the BFA's code of ethical conduct and its disciplinary, complaints and appeals procedures. They will have provided the association with any non-confidential information relating to their franchise business, the standing and qualifications of their directors and so on. They will also have agreed to provide the association with any confidential information it has deemed reasonable to ask for.

A business that is a full member will have demonstrated that it has a proven trading and franchising record, that it is viable and that there is an established method of transferring knowledge to new operators. It will need to have shown that it is operating in accordance with the European Code of Ethics for Franchising, which outlines criteria for advertising, recruiting, selecting and dealing with franchises, and that all information relevant to the business's franchise proposition has been disclosed. Associate members have to demonstrate all the above but do not need to prove they have a proven trading and franchising record. They also have to commit themselves to abide by the Advertising Standards Authority's code of practice and also to the BFA's own complaints and disciplinary, appeals and re-accreditation rules.

Provisional listing is available to firms that have a track record of at least a year but which are new to or in the process of developing a franchised model. They should have their documentation, including the franchise agreement (which, again, meets the European code), already prepared and should be taking appropriate professional advice – often from a specialist franchising consultant – in the development of the franchise. They will also need to commit to complying with the conditions of BFA membership and to work to achieving the standards for associate membership.

Finally, affiliate membership is available to any organisation or individual offering professional advice to the franchising community and who can 'show evidence of professional standing' and that their staff are qualified in their profession and are experienced in the application of that profession to franchising. The reality is that most BFA affiliates are specialist franchise lawyers, banking teams, consultants and accountants.

Choosing the right franchise

More generally, and much as when deciding on a choice of new career, when it comes to choosing the right franchise, you will probably need to do a good bit of a 'self-audit' beforehand. First, you will need to think very basically about what sort of business you want to be involved in. To make a success of franchising you will have to expect to work ferociously hard, particularly at the beginning, and be completely passionate about it, so it has to be something that is likely to fire you up each morning.

If for example, you're not a great salesperson or are nervous about face-to-face communication, then a retail or public/consumer-based franchise may not be the best one for you. Similarly, if you are a gregarious, outgoing type, a home-based business might end up driving you up the wall. While you may well be venturing into a whole new sector, do you have any skills that might be transferable from your old career that will make the change that much easier?

Then you need to think about the financial implications. Yes, you may have a redundancy cheque or savings that you are happy to spend, but it's not a good idea to gamble everything on this one throw of the dice. How much therefore, realistically, will you be able to afford to invest, how much debt are you comfortable taking on and, just as importantly, how much debt are you feasibly going to be able to service, given any other family, personal or financial commitments? Will you need to invest in a premises or a van? Similarly, how much will you be needing or expect realistically to make from the business, whatever the promotional guff says – will it, for example, need to be a primary income or secondary pin money? There is no point falling in love with a business, or the idea of a business, that is not set up as something that will enable you to be the main breadwinner if that is what your role needs to be.

It goes without saying you should carefully research the franchise and its business model – what will you actually be doing on a day-to-day basis and how will you make your money? But you should also look at where you will be operating, particularly if you are intending to move to another part of the country (or even abroad). What is the population demographic like, what is the potential market for your business, what sort of competitors are there likely to be, and so on. It's absolutely vital within this research that you speak to current franchisees – these should ideally be ones you have chosen not just ones that have been offered to you by the franchisor. This may not happen until you are going through the recruitment/ application process, or you may be encouraged to speak to people much earlier on, but you absolutely must do it. If the franchisor is reluctant or cagey or, at worst, obstructive about this, you should be very cautious.

You should also investigate the franchisor themselves. What is their business background, what is the track record of the business, both before it became a franchise and subsequently, how fast has it grown (and does such growth appear sustainable), has it had any failures along the way and, if so, why? What exactly are they offering in the way of support and training? A lot of these questions should come out during the recruitment and application process, where it will be as much about you assessing the franchisor as them assessing you. It is to this that we shall now turn.

The recruitment process

So, you've exchanged details on a stand, pinged off an exploratory email or sent for an information pack. What happens next? The recruitment process will, inevitably, vary from franchise to franchise but you will

MAKING THE CHANGE

Chris Gillam is the franchise consultant for Mail Boxes Etc, which oversees more than 100 franchises in the UK and 6,000 worldwide, offering parcels packaging and delivery, postal services, mailboxes and printing and copying.

A lot of franchisors have been reporting increased interest in the past few months from people who have been made redundant and see franchising as a possible alternative. But investing in a franchise is potentially one of the biggest financial decisions you can make, so it is not something you should rush into.

All ethically operated franchises should have a set recruitment process. If the franchisor only seems keen to get their fee off you, walk away. You should go through a process of extensive due diligence before you buy into a franchise, so if you come under pressure to make a quick decision or, even worse, put down a deposit, perhaps at a franchise show or an exhibition, again, walk away.

One of the great advantages of franchising as a career move is that you can do something you have no previous experience in, as all franchisors will train you in your new role and career. But that also means you have to be sure it is the right sort of franchise for you – a lot of franchises require at least some sales savvy or marketing awareness and confident communication skills. So you need to be sure that is something you will enjoy and be capable of. Or it may be that, if you are going to do it as a husband-and-wife team, one of you will do the sales side and one the paperwork and administration. That's fine, but you do need to talk through how it is going to work for you. Similarly, if it's a man-and-a-van franchise, you need to think about how you will enjoy being out on the road all day.

Using what happens at Mail Boxes Etc as an example, there will normally be a number of stages you will go through as part of the recruitment process. After the first meeting or enquiry we would send you some information simply explaining the franchise proposition and how it works. After that it'll be a question of speaking to us, normally over the phone initially, about the franchise in a broad sense, the sorts of qualities we look for and your aspirations.

Taking things further

If you are still interested, we'll set up a face-to-face meeting to discuss things in more detail. About half the people who express interest in us will have said no by or before this point, so it is a useful vetting process for both sides. At this point, too, we encourage people to go and speak to other franchisees to find out what the business is like from their perspective. Meeting other franchisees is an absolutely vital part of the recruitment process and if a franchisor, for whatever reason, is reluctant to let you do that, it should set alarm bells ringing.

Assuming you are still keen, what happens next is that we will hold a structured interview, at which point there will be full disclosure of the company, its accounts, business model and so forth. That would then lead to a review of the franchise agreement and some initial business planning and, eventually, a decision on whether or not to go ahead. We do encourage prospective franchisees to take advice from a British Franchise Association lawyer and to get some independent financial and business advice too, ideally from someone who understands the concept of franchising.

Once the decision is made to go ahead we will ask for a deposit and that then heralds the process of the acquisition of the franchise. While the amount of deposit you might be asked to pay to a franchisor can vary, somewhere between 10–30 per cent of the initial franchise fee is normally a pretty reasonable level to expect. Our fee is currently £16,500 but you should budget for total set-up costs of around £60,000.

After that you will start the training process – for us it's about four weeks and is a combination of classroom-based and on-the-job training. Normally you'd expect it to take about three to six months from signing to getting up and running, with finding a suitable premises to lease the thing that most commonly slows the process down. As an established franchise that has been doing this in the UK since 1997, we offer a 'turnkey' service so we will be able to help in finding the right site for you – normally what is called a prime secondary site, so a location perhaps to the side or just off a high street. We will also help with fitting out the premises, legal fees, supplies and inventory.

Making it work for you

When it comes to turning in a profit, our maxim is that the business really needs to be moving into positive territory in some shape or form by the second year of trading. If you are following the business plan, you should be becoming cash positive between 12 and 18 months from opening.

You can normally expect quite a bit of physical field support, as well as online and intranet support, from us once you are up and running. Inevitably we find the support is quite intensive at the beginning – perhaps seeing people once a month – and then gradually tails off as they get established. After the first year it's normally just a case of popping in from time to time. You will also be able to access support from your fellow franchisees through regional meetings, informal communication and our national conference. One of the things franchisees say to us is how good it is to be able to speak to others in the network and share information, something you could not do so easily if you were an independent business.

There is no one type of person who makes a successful franchisee, and franchisees come from all walks of life and backgrounds and have different ambitions and aspirations. But in general, curiously, we tend to find that being highly entrepreneurial is less of asset than you might think. The point of a franchise is to follow an established, tried-and-tested business model so, if you are full of your own ideas for the business and highly entrepreneurial you can find the harness of a franchise frustrating. You might be running your own business but you are still part of a larger, national operation and so there may be occasions where you have to toe the line or, at the very least, try not to reinvent the wheel.

Similarly, we sometimes find people who have been in very senior management positions can struggle to make the transition because they are less used to dealing with the day-to-day. As a franchisee, you can be emptying the litter bins in the morning, dealing with a supplier over lunch and, hopefully, sealing a deal with a customer in the afternoon. What we find is that if you have a good business head, are sales savvy, commercially oriented, prepared to work hard and, most importantly, passionate about making a success of it, then franchising can be a great way to change your life.

probably be asked to come in for an informal chat and, perhaps, a 'getting to know each other' day where you will be given an overview of the business model and how it all works. This is likely to be followed by a more formal, and more rigorous, interview though, again, neither side will have made any formal commitment to the other.

This interview is a hugely important part of the process, and it is likely you will be asked about your background, ambitions and aspirations, previous employment and educational history – key questions might include why you think you would make a success of the franchise and what your three-year goals will be. You may at this point be asked to supply some credit and personal references. Essentially the franchisor is looking to see that you are good a fit for their brand, that you have the right sort of temperament to be a franchisee, the ability to learn and yet follow an established model and the right sort of business acumen and ambition. While you will not necessarily be expected to have any of the technical skills needed – as those will be taught later – they may well want to gauge that you have the right sales, marketing, management, customer service or financial skills for them.

The questions you'll need to ask

But the interview should be very much a two-way process, and **whichfranchise.com** suggests you should come armed with 20 questions with which to grill your prospective franchisor. To help you out, it suggests the following which, as they are all absolutely key questions, we have taken the liberty to reproduce in full:

- Will you supply me with a breakdown of all costs necessary to open the business?
- Are there any other costs I can expect to be asked for?
- Do I have to pay a deposit or upfront payment, and if I do not proceed will I lose my deposit or any part of it?
- How much working capital do you think I need, and what help can you give me in estimating my projections?
- How long will it take to start trading from the time I sign the contract?
- What will training consist of, how long will it last and are all training costs included in my franchise fee?
- What is my expected break-even and how long should it take me to reach this figure?
- Do you charge ongoing franchise fees and if so what are they and how are they calculated?

- Do I have to contribute to any other costs such as advertising and promotional expenditure that you incur, and if so how much?
- What help, if any, will I receive if I want to do some advertising and promotion on my own?
- After I have opened, what ongoing support will I be provided with?
- What help and guidance do you offer in site selection?
- Can I be provided with a full list of all franchisees in the network and can I contact them?
- Do you provide instructional and operational manuals and can I see them prior to signing?
- Have any franchisees failed, and if so why?
- How thoroughly do you vet prospective franchisees to maintain a high standard in the network?
- Will the territory offered be for my sole and exclusive use?
- Are you currently operating in areas with similar demographics as my proposed territory?
- How do you handle grievances with existing franchisees?
- Does your company see any threats in the current marketplace?

The next steps

Assuming all these questions have been answered to your satisfaction you will probably be sent off to be given time to speak to franchisees, go over the franchise agreement and speak to the bank. It is worth getting a specialist franchising solicitor to look over the agreement (who will often do this for a fixed fee) and, probably, to speak to one of the specialist franchise teams at some of the big banks, notably HSBC, Lloyds and Royal Bank of Scotland, which owns NatWest of course. The BFA, again, has lists of specialist franchise solicitors, bankers and accountants on its website.

As there is no specific regulation of franchising, as we have seen, the franchise agreement is a very important part of the agreement process and so should not be something you sign without careful consideration. While agreements will vary, as a rule of thumb the franchise agreement should at its most basic set out clearly the rules that will be observed by each side. It should probably include a commitment from the franchisor to train you, supply goods and services, be responsible for advertising, marketing and promotion, help you find and if need be acquire and fit out your premises and generally help you to set up the business. It will probably include clauses allowing the franchisor to monitor your performance, protect any intellectual property or particular innovation and impose a range of obligations on you once you have been granted the franchise.

Very importantly, it should outline the grounds on which each side can terminate the agreement, the consequences of any such termination and the payment and timing of any upfront and ongoing fees. A good agreement should also include a clause on what will happen in the event of your death or your becoming permanently incapacitated. It is a good idea, even if it is not included in the formal agreement, to get agreement on what will happen if and when you wish to sell the business, particularly if this is midway through your franchise contract.

Once you are happy with the agreement and have sorted out (at least in principle) your funds and initial business plan, what will normally happen is that a further interview will be held, at which point the franchisor will outline any information about the business that has up to then been confidential for commercial reasons, there will be a further review of the agreement and a decision will be made on whether to go ahead. At which point you sign in blood – just kidding.

Funding and the business plan

Securing funding and getting the business plan right are, clearly, two of the most important elements of any successful franchise, as they are of any successful business venture. The point at which you are asked to draw up a business plan is likely to vary, and may be any time from the middle of the recruitment process to nearer the end, but you will be expected to draw one up, both for the franchisor to assess and, just as importantly, to convince the bank to stump up to fund your venture. As we have seen in earlier chapters, there is a lot of mystique about business plans but at their most basic all they are doing is outlining what the business will do and how it will make money, what you hope to do with whatever money is invested in your business, how much you will need (and why), a profit forecast and projections, and a cash flow model.

The exercise of drawing up a business plan can in itself be very useful in helping to clarify your thoughts, ideas and objectives about the business – and you may be able to get some useful pointers and advice from the franchisor. You should look to be as realistic as possible, particularly around what you will need to live off for the first six months to a year and your long-term forecasts. The temptation is always to assume you'll be able to live off half what you have been – fight it.

As well as outlining the main aims and objectives of the business and its products and services, you will probably be asked to outline who else will be involved in it with you and what their background is – so if it's your partner, they need to be prepared to reveal that information. You will probably need to give clear and detailed information on your proposed market, your likely competitors, your promotional and launch strategy for the business, what you are going to do for premises, your profit and loss forecast for the first year, when you expect to break even (and why), when you expect to get money from sales and when you have to pay suppliers, any likely overheads and any capital equipment needs.

One of the good things about a franchise is that the bank, particularly if you are dealing with one of the specialist franchising teams, will probably be aware of your franchise already, know its track record and have dealt with many such similar applications. So they will not only have a good idea of how it all stacks up and be able to compare you with other applicants, but may well see you as a much sounder financial bet than if you were just sitting in front of them as an individual with a bright idea.

How much you can borrow will, again, depend on your personal circumstances and the reputation of the franchise, with banks more inclined, naturally, to look more favourably on well-established brands with a proven return. A common proportion is the bank lending up to 70 per cent of the total set-up costs, including any working capital. You will need to retain a cash stake in the business and probably provide some form of security to cover the lending. Even if you have a lump sum or redundancy to blow, it is worth being careful how much of your own money you put in, particularly if the bank is laying money on the table, so you are not putting all your eggs in one basket.

It's also worth checking out the government's new Enterprise Finance Guarantee scheme, which we looked at in the setting up in business chapters. This has replaced the Small Firms Loan Guarantee scheme, which tended to be very popular with prospective franchisees. Under the EFG scheme, to recap, the government will guarantee 75 per cent of any loans made, with the bank covering the remaining 25 per cent. The guarantees will mean the government will pick up three-quarters of the tab for any bad loans, with loans available of up to £1m (rather than a maximum of £250,000 under the previous scheme) for businesses with a turnover of less than £25m.

What the life is like, and knowing when it's time to go

Once you're up and running, operating a franchise should be pretty similar to running any other small business – in other words you'll be expected to do everything, be everywhere and be a jack of all trades. Franchising is, of course, different, in that you will retain the backing and support of the franchisor, although normally the hand-holding tapers off as you become more established. The other thing to note with a lot of franchises is that, while many may well be hands-on, muck-in operations, others will expect you over time to step back and essentially become more of a manager of a workforce or team – this will particularly be the case where you are juggling a number of franchises or running a multi-unit operation.

Another curious thing about franchising is that, while franchisors look for people with drive and enterprise, they often shy away from people with a strong entrepreneurial streak. This is because they are looking for people who, once it is up and running, will be happy to follow the model and not get all creative reinventing an (already successful) wheel. So the key to happy franchising is to recognise that, if you follow what has already been bedded down, it should probably, hopefully, fingers crossed, touch wood etc. – work.

It's not a happy subject but it's worth a brief word at this point on what happens if it all goes wrong. Even the BFA admits that franchise disputes arise quite frequently, normally simply because franchise agreements are complex contracts with a lot of money and vested interests at stake. Often franchisees can feel they have not received what has been promised to them, the promises of the business do not stack up or the franchisor has failed to keep their side of the bargain. Similarly, franchisors complain of franchisees who expect the earth, have unrealistic profit expectations or simply did not understand what they were getting themselves into. Common pitfalls can be franchisees deciding to branch out on their own or franchisors terminating the contract. Tensions can often arise when times are tough and businesses are more likely to be struggling.

Another bone of contention, particularly in tougher times, can be around management fees. If your business is suffering, perhaps because of recession, you will still have to pay your management fee, however poor the cash flow. Your franchisors may, of course, be prepared to be flexible but, bearing in mind it will probably be their own main income and the only way they can afford to maintain their network, there is no guarantee of this and, in the worst case scenario, it is possible to get caught between the rock of a downturn and the hard place of an immovable franchisor demanding their cash. The other side of the coin, though, is that, unlike an independent business faced with similarly tough conditions, as a franchisee you will have access to a national network and brand. Perhaps (as we have seen) with that will come national contracts and advertising,

MAKING THE CHANGE

THE EXPERT'S VIEW

Graeme Jones is head of franchising at NatWest Bank, now owned by Royal Bank of Scotland, and one of the sector's longest established specialist franchising lenders.

There's no 'best' time to come and see a team like ours, although the earlier you do it the better. We have a presence at most of the specialist franchise exhibitions across the country and give seminars and talks throughout the year as well. We tend to find that a lot of people who approach us at exhibitions are at a fairly early stage in their decision-making process, which is absolutely fine as we are able to provide expert advice about what questions to ask and how to go about researching the franchise market. The important thing we always emphasise is that you must do your research and your due diligence as thoroughly as you can. Generally, the earlier you engage with your bank, the more informed decision you are likely to make.

Discussing your plans

When discussing finance, what we will want to see from you is that you have put together a proper, realistic, well-costed business plan and, crucially, that it is your business plan, not just one that has been supplied as a template by the franchisor. We want to be sure you understand the dynamics of the business and exactly what it is you will be doing. We will talk to you about your product and your market, and we will want to see how it will work in your town, not how it might have worked somewhere else. We will want to be sure you understand what competitors you are likely to be up against and how you are going to differentiate yourself from those competitors. We will also want to be confident that you are clear about the challenges you will undoubtedly face as you set your business up. Essentially, we need to be sure that you completely understand the contract and the business you are entering into.

How much money you should put into your business is, of course, a very personal decision and will vary according to individual circumstance. However, we will want to look at not only your ability to borrow but what contingencies you have in place if things don't pan out the way you planned. Even if you have savings or redundancy to invest, it's not a good idea to commit all your capital resources otherwise you won't have a financial cushion. If your projections are not being met, you do need contingency plans and it's essential that you are realistic about how much you will need to live off in those first weeks and months. Sometimes the only reason why you may not be able to get a loan is down to the fact that you do not have any security to offer the bank.

To this end, the introduction of the Enterprise Finance Guarantee scheme has made a difference, particularly in helping franchisees structure their deals more effectively. To date, NatWest and RBS have led the field in taking applications for the scheme. Of all EFG lending across the industry, NatWest and RBS are responsible for half of all loans drawn down. What's more, if we are presented with the right information, applications can be processed very quickly. For example, four out of every five EFG loans are processed and drawn down within three weeks.

Be realistic about your goals

In the current climate one trend we have seen is that people are being more realistic about their financial projections. Someone approaching us several years ago for example, when the economy was more buoyant, might have made projections for that growth to continue and then found it harder to match them. We now find that customers are more aware of the volatility of the economic cycle, and this helps them with their risk assessment, in terms of financial planning.

One of the mistakes that is commonly made by those embarking on a career in franchising is to underestimate just how hard it is going to be to meet their turnover projections. Yes, you will have the backing of a larger network and the support of a franchisor behind you, but if you have previously been employed and are used to having sales, marketing, HR and accounting done by others it will be necessary very quickly to move out of your comfort zone. All the decisions are going to end with you and you may have to learn to react decisively when unforeseen problems arise. You will need energy, enthusiasm and total commitment to make it work.

People often underestimate the effort it will take to get their sales up to a reasonable level – it is really important to research your market properly and identify how your business is going to grow, not only at its launch or in the first six months but over the first few years. Yes, you need to focus on the launch of the business and getting it established, but building and maintaining momentum, growing your customer base and then, critically, not losing it can often be just as challenging. So you need to be aware that you will need to be refreshing the business over time, revisiting your business plans, and ensure you keep the franchise fresh in customers' minds.

advice and support from an experienced franchisor (as it is clearly not in their interests that you go down) and, sometimes just as importantly, access to a network of other franchisees who you can share best practice (and gossip) with.

Either way, disputes can get acrimonious and costly for both sides, and often the only people who benefit from them are the lawyers each side end up calling in. The BFA, though technically an organisation for franchisors, does also run a mediation and arbitration service to try and resolve disputes, which of course may or may not work but is probably worth a try. If the franchisee is a member of a BFA-accredited franchise he or she can also write to the BFA to complain. It may be, for example, that it is not the first complaint of its kind about a particular franchise and could in turn prompt a closer investigation into that business. Franchise disputes, unfortunately, can tend to get very messy and therefore highlight even more the importance of doing as much legwork and research as you can beforehand.

Think about your way out early on

It may sound counter-intuitive, but just as in business generally it can be a good idea when starting out in franchising to be thinking about your exit strategy early on. Yes, you may have just signed a contract that will run for five or 10 years, but there are still questions about the future that it's beneficial for you to be considering now. Do you intend the business to become your retirement nest-egg, or intend to expand into multiple units or territories? Do you hope to pass it on to another family member in time? Of course, things can change, but these are issues worth thinking about because they will help you look at the business in a more realistic way and may even colour how you run and expand it.

Speak to franchisees and you'll normally get the same bit of advice back – it's bloody hard work but is ultimately worth it. Particularly in the first few years you will probably end up working much harder than you ever did in your old corporate career and not be making that much money to boot, although the rewards further down the line can sometimes be substantial. But if you do your research carefully, go into the venture with open eyes, stick with it, and have the drive and commitment to succeed, it can be a way of becoming your own boss that has a high chance of success, as well as being potentially very satisfying and rewarding.

Key points

- You will own your business but operate as part of a larger network/brand
- Just because you will have a big name behind you is not in itself a guarantee of success; you will still have to work hard to make it work
- Franchising has a better success rate than being an independent but 'buyer beware'
- It is geared toward career changers
- Look for, or at least ask about, BFA membership/accreditation

Part 2: Chapter Four

FREELANCING

At this point I need to get personal and declare an interest. I am a freelance journalist and have been for the past nine years, therefore freelancing is something I have personal knowledge of as well as a professional interest in. Within journalism and the media generally, freelancing has long been an alternative to a corporate, 'employed' career and many journalists, particularly those who have built up a few years' experience in staff jobs, will at some point make the transition to freelance status, sometimes going back and forth between the two. Many well-known TV and print journalism names, such as *Question Time's* David Dimbleby, the *Today* programme's John Humphrys and columnist and author Max Hastings, are or have been freelance at one time, even though they may be 'retained' on a long-term basis by some of the outlets they work for. Many backroom media workers, such as camera crews, sub-editors, producers and so on will be employed on a freelance or contract basis.

But becoming a freelance can be an option in many other industries and sectors, too. IT and telecommunications, for example, use a lot of freelance contractors, as do engineering and construction, public relations and marketing, entertainment, management consultancy, financial services and the pharmaceuticals sectors, among others. In fact, though you may not have been able to tell, you will probably have come across freelancers in many walks of life, from many hairdressers and beauty therapists through to the supply teacher who was covering your child's class while their regular teacher was away. So freelancing can be a very viable option for anyone thinking of changing their career or, more accurately, taking control of their career and how, where, when and for whom they work.

That last point is a pertinent one. It's not a cast-iron rule but, in the context of changing your career, it's important to recognise that going freelance is normally not something you do as a way of changing tack or direction. Your freelance career may well evolve into new areas and fields as you become more established, and indeed it is desirable that it does so if you are to cushion yourself against the unexpected. Yet most freelancers, at least at the beginning, will launch their freelance career by doing much the same sort of job or role as when they were employed. The 'change' is about who you are working for, ie yourself.

As Gay Turner, who started out as a freelance PR and now runs an agency based in South Warwickshire, explains, within her industry at least the norm is very much to get experience under your belt first before striking out into the world of freelance.

'Most people who become freelance PRs will have worked in an agency in some shape or form beforehand. You really can't just go out and be a freelance PR because first you must have an understanding of the processes, of how the media works and what clients and journalists both want,' she says.

Having said that, if you do have that experience, one of the attractions of freelancing is that it need not cost vast sums of money or take years of retraining to make the transition.

'With the advent of new technology and increased working from home or remotely, more and more women in particular have found going freelance to be something they can fit around their children.'

Getting off the ground

So, how do you get started? There are no hard and fast rules here, as every industry is likely to employ freelancers in different ways. But probably the one constant is that successful freelancing will normally be as much about the contacts and networks you already have as about the people you will approach for work in the future. How many freelancers get established is simply by going back to work for the employer or employers they were most recently employed by, but simply on a freelance basis.

After all, they know you, you know them and they've seen first-hand that you know what you are doing. So it's potentially a very easy win/win. One of the first things to do, therefore, if you are considering going freelance is to sit down and think about, or write down a list of, who you might be likely to be able to get work off. There is no guarantee they will come up with the goods, but if you go back over the people you know, or know they know, or the organisations or agencies you have come across in your employed life, it is likely to give you a much clearer idea of the potential opportunities out there. You may well find yourself pleasantly surprised at how many people or possible sources of income you identify.

There may be mileage, too, in having an exploratory chat with a current or previous manager along the lines of, if you were to go freelance, would he or she be interested in taking you on on a freelance basis, and how might that work? Of course, if this is a conversation with your current manager it probably needs to be phrased a little delicately! If there is already the possibility of work in place, or even actual agreements or contracts, it is clearly going to make the transition to freelancing much less fraught and worrisome. Once you have some regular 'bread and butter' work in place it is also much easier to start casting around for new opportunities or looking at completely new areas that you might be able to venture into.

The freelance life

Freelancing can be as big or as small as you want it to be: anything from a cottage industry – you at a computer at home or simply hiring out your knowledge or skills to whoever wants and is prepared to pay for it – right up to you as an employee of your own VAT-registered limited company, perhaps in partnership with someone else and 'employing' a bank of other freelancers or contractors.

There are of course almost as many reasons for going freelance as there are freelancers themselves. But it does make sense, as it has all the way through this guide, to sit down and think carefully about whether freelance life is going to be right for you before you go for it.

Freelancing can be physically lonely, especially if it is just you working from home. It can also be lonely in the sense that it will just be you against the world without any corporate safety net or support. Sure, that can be liberating in that you will be your own boss and it will be up to you and you alone to make a success of things. But, equally, it will be up to you constantly to make things happen, to promote and market yourself, to network and make your chances, to chase up payments (of which more later), to make sure your tax and financial affairs are in order (of which also more later), to keep all your disparate, and often demanding, clients and customers happy, right down to getting down on your knees to change the toner cartridge on the printer, emptying the bins or sitting on the helpline working out why your internet connection keeps going down. So you need to think long and hard about whether you are that sort of person.

Ideally, what I've found from my own experience is that it helps to be a self-starter, particularly if you are working from home, and to be good at managing your time. By keeping on top of the financial and tax stuff you can ensure it doesn't get in the way of the important business of making money from your main freelance activities. But I also know freelancers, curiously enough specialist financial journalists among them, who claim to be spectacularly bad at these sides of freelance life, and yet manage to make a success of their jobs.

Living the dream... or is it? Pay and holidays

There will be other significant adjustments to make too. Perhaps the biggest, and most obvious, is simply the fact that you will no longer have a regular pay cheque coming in every month. This is something that, clearly, is a financial issue but can also take quite a lot of getting your head around.

I will come on to some of the practicalities of credit control – or in lay terms chasing the sods, sorry important customers, for the money they owe you – in a moment, but living from cheque to cheque or only having work booked in for the next week or two and then pages and pages of empty diary can take some getting used to. Again from my own experience, I found it simply was a case of a) breathing deeply and trying not to wake up in a cold funk in the night and b) living each week and month as it came. As long as the work was coming in regularly, even if it was just dribbling in, and I was keeping on pushing, marketing and promoting myself, I knew the longer term would (probably) take care of itself.

As a freelance you never completely stop worrying about where the next cheque is going to come from, but the longer you do it the less of a nagging voice it tends to become – if you know that you have successfully negotiated one year or two years in this weird way of working then you will know, at its most basic, that the business model you are following is working.

Similarly, there will probably need to be an adjustment to make in your thinking around working hours and holidays. As a freelance, technically, the world is your oyster – you can go and do anything, work for anyone, any time and anywhere. The reality, however, is likely to be quite different, especially in the early days. First, on working hours, yes, nominally you will be in charge of when, where and for how long you work, but in practical terms if you have a client that needs something done by yesterday or, say, over a weekend it will either be a question of saying 'no' (in which case you may risk losing future business) or agreeing to their unreasonable demands through gritted teeth and delivering come what may. If I had a pound for every time someone had said to me how great it must be to be in charge of my hours as I must be able to drop everything and swan off

MAKING THE CHANGE

CASE STUDY:
Setting up as freelance contractors

Redundancy forced Selby-based software developer Craig Gilchrist, 26, to re-evaluate his career and, with colleague Andy Litherland, 32, set up as freelance contractors.

It had always been at the back of my mind that this was something I might want to do at some point. But normally when you go into contracting or freelance work you need to have quite a few years of experience and a bit of capital behind you. As I'd only been working for my employer of the time for about two years, I reckoned it would be a while before it happened.

The redundancy when it came was a definite surprise because our most recent figures had been quite rosy. Basically our office in York, which had a team of about eight people, was merged with the head office in Manchester. But it turned out for the best because the redundancy money that Andy and I got, about three months salary each, was an invaluable financial cushion that allowed us to get trading.

Going into it together

I didn't want to set up as a one-man band because I knew a lot of the bigger clients, which were the sort of organisations we would be targeting, like to deal with what they at least feel are established companies. I knew his skills were complementary to mine, too. He is very level-headed while I tend to go at things hammer and tongs. We also simply get on very well, which is important when you are working so closely together.

We were made redundant in December 2007 and Got Focus Solutions www.gotfocussolutions.com was up and running within three weeks. We chose to go the limited company route because we felt there was less risk in being structured that way but also if you are tendering for big contracts in the sorts of sectors we knew we would be working in, you really need to be a limited company. It can be a good idea to get some advice from a bank or a small business adviser on this — many banks offer a free advice service as part of setting up your business account.

We chose our accountant through a personal recommendation but it makes sense to go for one who specialises in your area, as this will reduce costs and, hopefully, provide a more decent service. It's the same with a solicitor, if you need one. We, for example, made the mistake of initially adopting an expensive solicitor who didn't understand software contracts and so we didn't get very good value for money. Joining a guild or other professional group can also be a good idea as it can provide advice, networking and sometimes even discounts on things such as insurance, legal advice and training.

One of our first contracts was from our former Manchester head office, which shows the importance of using your existing networks to get established. A big hurdle for many freelancers when they start is simply getting known and trusted by clients, so if you can work for someone where that relationship already exists, all the better.

When it comes to late payments we do not have any fail-safe route other than just to keep chasing people. We try to build up and maintain good relations with the people who will be paying the invoice so if you need to call them up you do it as a colleague or friend. It's also worth knowing that the Inland Revenue offers courses on things such as bookkeeping as well as seminars on being VAT registered. If you have a client who is a prolific offender, however, it may be worth seeking legal advice or simply making a judgment call as to whether you want to keep working for them.

A lot of larger companies don't appreciate what a problem late payment can be for contractors when you need to rely on your cash flow. If we do an invoice for, say, £9,000 that is a lot of money for us and it will make a world of difference when it comes through, but for a big company it's not a big deal.

The key to being a successful freelance, I think, is keeping your focus on acquiring new clients. It is hard, especially if you are busy with what you already have, but you can never rely on anything continuing forever. It is easy to get complacent and, in fact, we need to be doing more ourselves because we really rely on two major clients and so if one of them stopped our capacity could go down considerably.

Ideally you need to have a lot of different sources of income or, if not, a good contingency fund that you can call on if or when things slow down. You also need to be constantly on the top of your game because when you are freelance you are competing with everyone, including big companies. So, while it is a change of career in the sense that you are taking charge and control of your career, it's often a good idea to stick with and specialise in what you do best.

Having said that, being self-employed does give you the scope to look at doing things that are completely different to what you have been doing previously. We, for example, have recently branched out into running a franchised pretzel shop in Newcastle which is a certainly a major departure from software and IT, but a new and exciting challenge nevertheless.

to the beach/pool/park etc. at the first sign of the sun coming out, well, I'd probably be able to do just that!

Which brings us rather nicely on to holidays. The first thing I did when I went freelance was take a week's holiday which, at one level, was completely mad and at another made absolute sense, at least to me. It was mad because I now no longer had a regular income or even the prospect of one and so really ought to have been getting out there straight away and chasing jobs. But it made sense, first, because I was knackered from the staff job I had been doing and wanted to start off in this new life feeling refreshed and recharged and, second, because technically (as I had tagged some holiday on to my notice period) I knew it was going to be the last paid holiday I ever got.

The serious point to be made here is that freelancers do not get paid holidays – it is, after all, one of the reasons employers like to employ them (along with not having to pay for their pensions, National Insurance, desk space and so on). So, yes, you might be able to take the whole of the summer holidays off or over-eat for the duration of the Christmas/New Year break, but you have to recognise you won't get paid for the privilege. Similarly, you'll be quite at liberty to work through weekends, evenings and bank holidays and will have no one to complain to but yourself. The same will go for sick pay – you may be able to take out income protection insurance or illness insurance but either way you'll need to recognise that lying in bed moaning is not going to pay the bills.

This is also precisely the reason why, in a kind of quid pro quo way, freelancers may often be paid a better hourly rate than their employed counterparts, something that can sometimes lead to grumbles around the coffee machine – though in the current recesssion there have been many examples of rates being squeezed or, at best, frozen. No one expects you to work 365 days a year or to be free of illness year after year after year, so it's a good idea that freelancers build up a cash 'buffer' to tide them over such eventualities, or even just help them through any fallow periods.

The freelance buffer

Particularly in the early days when cash is tight, building up a financial buffer might appear like a demand too many on your already stretched finances, but it is important to have one if you can. The Professional Contractors' Group (PCG), which represents freelancers across many industries and sectors, advises freelancers to have built up a fund sufficient to cover expenses for six months. If that feels impossible you should at the very minimum try to have a month's income put aside somewhere. This can of course also be used as a 'float' if cash flow runs tight (though it is important to be disciplined and remember to pay it back) but its primary purpose should be as a fund to help you sleep more soundly at night.

A financial buffer is also very important when you start out in freelancing. In an ideal world everyone would pay by or before 30 days from invoicing but, as any small business owner or self-employed contractor will tell you, that is often rarely the case. The Federation of Small Businesses, for one, has estimated that a quarter of business failures can be attributed to late payment, and that an average of £38,000 is owed to individual small businesses at any one time.

All industries will be different in how swiftly they pay and, once you're up and running, you'll probably quickly work out the foibles of your sector and, just as importantly, whether particular clients are good or bad payers. A good example in my own industry of print journalism is that once an invoice is with a paper's accounts' department it can take from around a fortnight (well done, the *Guardian*) to anything from six weeks to three months to grind out the other end.

The difficulty for many freelance journalists is that, more often than not, it only gets to go to accounts once the commissioned article has been published, which assuming it's not particularly time-sensitive may be weeks (or in some cases months) after it has been submitted to an editor, so it is easy to end up in a financial limbo. The freelancer can rage and complain all they like, but ultimately if you want to keep on working you have to accept that is how the system works – and there are probably equally frustrating systems in every other industry and sector.

MAKING THE CHANGE

After working in a range of management roles in Scotland, north east England, Africa and the Middle East, Alasdair Drysdale, 62, became a freelance, interim manager in the mid-1990s, and since then has worked on more than 40 assignments on five continents. Based near Jedburgh on the Scottish borders, he also works through, among others, interim agency Interim Partners.

There is some overlap between the role of interim managers and management consultants, in that they will both go in and advise a business. But while consultants generally work as specialists from the outside inward, interims usually work as generalists from the inside out. Interims are usually members of the management team, bringing to bear their extensive experience of different industries and situations. They need to be able to adapt rapidly to the style of the client's board or management team and decide whether to adopt that style or counterbalance it. Most importantly, interims should leave behind all the improvements they have brought to client businesses once they have completed their assignments – so a large part of the job is imparting knowledge and giving people the skills to take that knowledge on.

Adaptability is everything

The jobs vary immensely. You may be involved in a reorganisation or working as a temporary finance director or picking up the reins because someone has been relocated, fired, or has died, for example. Sometimes you will be required to change something or turn something around; other times it will just be a case of acting as a stop-gap and keeping things sailing along smoothly until a permanent resource is found. Or it could be about installing a particular system or passing on some specific expertise. I've even, as an interim, appointed other interims to a company and helped to recruit a permanent director to replace me!

The shortest job I have had is a single day and the longest lasted for 13 months. But the average is about seven months and even the shortest ones can take quite a lot of advance preparation. I've also gone from sleeping on an airport floor en route from a job in Yorkshire to one in California the next day, to having periods where I haven't worked for five or six months. So it is important as an interim to put money aside and have a financial reserve in place either to cover fallow periods or simply to cover the preparation time before you start a job. A management training project, for example, can involve weeks of preparation.

The pay rate for an interim will inevitably vary a lot, largely depending on your seniority and experience and what it is you are being asked to do. At the top end, people can command up to £2,000 a day and then, at the bottom, where it merges with the mass temporary market, there are people on around £300 a day. But the average daily rate is probably between £600 and £1,000. There is also a strong networking element to being an interim – I'd say that in the past 15 years about three-quarters of my income has come from the same small group of people. It may not necessarily be directly, in that it could be from someone who knows someone you know, but the contacts you build up and maintain are vital.

Skills you will need

When it comes to what makes a good interim, it helps if you are a fast learner. Every business is unique and you are always going into a new and sometimes problematic environment. But there are normally some items that will be the same regardless, such as the need to keep inventory tight, collect debt quickly, eliminate waste and so on. So your first priority is the basic ground-rules of business, after which you will normally have a very short time to grasp the specifics of your new client.

Sometimes, too, there can be hostility, particularly if people think you are coming in to change or, even worse, get rid of their jobs. So what I try and do early on is to get people to express their fears to me and then try and put them at their ease (except in the few cases where a shake-up in attitude is needed!).

If you think this life is for you it makes sense to sit down and ask what is it that you are good at, what is that you will be able to convince someone else to give you a go at doing. Also, are you going to do it as a stop-gap or do you intend to do it for an extended period? You might need to look at the range of skills you have and whether you need to widen them to become more of a generalist or, conversely, narrow them down to become an absolute expert in a field which you can market to clients.

One thing that has happened during the recession is that the interim market is now swarming with new people, some of them simply between jobs and others who have decided that this is now how they are going to want to make their living. That has meant that clients can be more particular and they may look for someone with very specific skills, perhaps experience of particular software or a particular industry. So how you position and market yourself, and the skills and experience you can offer, have all become even more important. Any interim's CV will say they are highly motivated and results-orientated, and the usual clichés. But you have to zone in on exactly what it is that you have achieved, and what it is that you can offer.

So, when you are starting out it makes sense to have built up a financial buffer of a few weeks – ideally three months' worth but six months will be even better – to tide you over until the first cheques start to arrive. I should know, as I made the mistake of not having one when I went freelance. What I quickly found was that, while on paper I was already making quite good money, I only 'earned' about £600 in the first two months because very little came through until at least the third month. Not an experience I would ever recommend anyone to try and repeat.

A 'cash flow' of freelancers

If there was such a thing as a collective noun for freelancers, it'd probably be a 'cash flow', such is the importance chasing and receiving payment from recalcitrant customers and clients can often assume in our lives. It is a good idea to include some set terms of payment on your invoice, whether 15 days or 30 days or whatever is the norm for your industry, and the option or threat of fines or charging interest for late payment. The key is to keep your invoices clear and consistent so there is less opportunity for employers to drag their feet by querying them.

The dilemma freelancers often face (like any small business or contractor) is that, if they complain or, worse, issue an invoice for payment of interest or a fine, will they ever be asked to work for that employer again? It's a classic case of having to bite the hand that feeds, because it hasn't been feeding you and you are hungry! And there's no easy answer to this.

There are various tactics you can use to try and speed up payment. You might, for example, ask for a deposit in advance of delivery or offer a discount for early payment. There is also the option of pursing a debt through the Small Claims Court, though you will probably need to accept that any relationship you have had with the company involved will be irreparably broken as a result.

What I find works best is simply keeping on top of things – if you don't chase it they're not going to rush – and politely but firmly and professionally chase that payment to the ground. You may want to send an email across a few days before the month is up gently reminding them that it will be due imminently, then gradually ratchet up the reminders, if necessary giving a set time for payment, and then pester them until they pay up just to make you go away.

Building up a rapport with the accounts department can also help oil the wheels sometimes. Without wanting to give away too many professional secrets (or drop myself in it for the future), I often try to depersonalise it by casting the blame elsewhere. So, if I'm chasing a payment with an accounts department, I might suggest, no doubt, that it was the fault of the commissioning editor for failing to sign off the outstanding invoice and, when I'm speaking to the editor, blame the accounts department for, no doubt, dragging its feet! The Better Payment Practice campaign **www.payon time.co.uk** also has a wealth of useful advice on this issue.

The other big issue that raises its head time and again with freelancers is tax. It's a thorny and complicated issue that we are really only able to skim over in a publication such as this, but the PCG, for one, has published a comprehensive guide to some of the tax and finance issues freelancers are likely to encounter, which can be downloaded from its website, **www.pcg.org.uk**. Other organisations such as BusinessLink also offer useful advice online.

The right business for you?

To get to tax, accounting and VAT issues, it is necessary to follow a bit of a circuitous route, covering first what sort of business you will be as a freelance, as all have different tax and accounting needs. As we have seen, freelancers can work in a range of settings and be small or large operations. So in deciding what business structure is right for you, you will need to look at a range of factors.

First there will be your own personal circumstances: is this something you are going to be doing full-time, during school hours, or in tandem with a regular part-time job? What's more, you should look at what sort of freelance structure tends to be the norm within your industry. Within journalism, for example, a lot of freelancers will be sole traders, often working from a room at home or physically working in the client's office.

But in other industries it may well be more the norm, or even expected if you are going to make headway, that you set yourself up as a limited company or work, say, through established agencies. So it's worth looking closely at what others do in your sector. As we've seen in the setting up in business chapters, there are a range of different business structures that you can work within when becoming self-employed, including sole trader, limited company or partnership, so don't just assume you will always have to be one or the other. You can also, of course, set up as one structure – perhaps sole trader – and then convert into something more complex as your business grows and expands.

Whatever structure you choose, the key thing to remember is that being self-employed, in whatever shape or form, brings with it a whole raft of legal and financial rules and responsibilities. For example, if you become a limited company, you will need to have a registered office (often your accountant's) and to have the company registration details on all correspondence (including emails) and publicly displayed if customers are coming to your premises. Similarly, if you are going to present a professional image, you'll need to think about getting letterheads made, business cards, a website or online presence and a company name.

You may need to set up a separate business account or if you are sole trading, at the very least look at how you are going to keep business and personal finances separate. Will you also need a separate phone line, a dedicated office (whether at home or in another premises), any specific equipment such as a computer or photocopier or somewhere to store stock if you are going to be supplying goods to people? And will you need a loan for any of this?

Similarly, what insurance will you need – you may, for example, require professional indemnity insurance or employers' liability insurance (which you will need when you start to employ anyone). You may need to look at your house insurance if you are setting up from home, your car and life insurance and perhaps, as we have seen, income protection, critical illness and private medical insurance. You should also think about how you are going to fund your retirement, as you will clearly no longer be paying into any employers' scheme. What many freelancers do is simply set up a personal pension, such as a stakeholder pension. The main point is, however you do it, you do need to be making provision for your old age, as now no one else will be.

What will you charge?

Other issues to consider include how you are going to pay yourself, a pretty simple calculation if you are a sole trader but a more complex one if you have become a limited company that will require you to take either a salary or dividends, or a combination of both. Then there is the issue of what you should be charging your potential clients. This is not as straightforward as it might at first seem.

In some industries, and freelance journalism is one, you will nine times out of 10 be working for a rate set by the client, and so it's simply up to you to decide whether you are prepared to work for the miserly penny pinchers or not. But in others it will be up to you to quote, perhaps for a day or project rate.

So it's worth doing some research to find out what is the going rate for your industry and location. You may of course be tempted to steal a march and undercut your rivals, but do bear in mind they probably charge that amount for a reason and it may be hard to raise your rates once they have been set, so you need to set a rate that is reasonable for the work involved, that does not under-sell your skills and reputation and which stacks up financially.

You may also be required to draw up a contract with your client, although more often it will probably be you signing their contracts. If it is up to you, it may be something you require specialist legal help with to ensure you have a watertight standard contract in place, particularly one that is not going to let clients wriggle out of payment.

The dreaded issue of tax

So, at last, gird yourself – on to tax. Whichever way you cut it as a freelance you are not going to be able to avoid paying tax so you may as well face it and get on with it. To reiterate from earlier chapters, the first thing you have to remember is that, even if you have already been filling in a self-assessment tax return you need to tell HM Revenue & Customs within three months of going self-employed that that is what you have done.

MAKING THE CHANGE

THE EXPERT'S VIEW

John Brazier is managing director of the Professional Contractors'
Group, which supports and represents contractors and freelancers
in a range of sectors, including oil and gas, engineering,
information technology, management consultancy, marketing,
telecommunications, construction and pharmaceuticals.

Freelancing is as much an attitude and a way of thinking as a means of working. If you
go into it half-heartedly you may well find it hard. People do use freelancing as a
stop-gap or even as a way into a permanent position, but to do it properly, you need
to embrace it and relish the fact that you are never going to be an employee again.

Before you take the plunge you need to plan it out carefully. You need to think about
what sort of 'business' you are going to be. If it is relatively small-scale, simply setting
up as a sole trader might well work. But in other areas, such as IT or engineering
for example, being a limited company is much more common.

You need to look at it from a tax and regulatory point of view, too. If you are just
going to be earning a few thousand a year as, say, a freelance swimming coach, you
are going to be in a very different financial and tax situation to a freelance IT consultant
earning £100,000. So you need to think about these issues and it may be good to
get some professional advice. It can be well worth using an accountant. They may
not cost as much as you think and may save a lot of hassle – and you will almost certainly
need to if you are going the limited company route. A good rule of thumb is to ask them
whether they have many other freelance contractors on their books and how much
they know both about your sector and this type of working.

Be organised – and assertive

Don't assume all freelancers work from home. Many do but in some sectors it is
more common for freelancers and contractors to work on-site and, again, there may
well be tax issues, for instance if you are being paid through the organisation's PAYE
payroll, that you will need to take into account. You need to think about what you are
going to do for a pension and how you are going to put money aside for tax.

Similarly, while a lot of freelance contractors go into it for a better work/life balance, it is important to recognise that, while you will have much more control over how and when you work, you are also likely to be at the beck and call of, sometimes demanding, customers and clients. Many freelancers find it difficult, particularly in the beginning, to take time off or go on holiday. You won't of course get holiday pay when you do and you risk losing out on a job to someone else. You may also have to be prepared to get out there and market yourself, often aggressively.

If you are going to set up from home you need to think about how it is going to work. Where will you work, what equipment will you need, what are the tax, mortgage and insurance implications of doing this? What distractions are there likely to be, what hours are you going to work? You may need to consider whether you need professional indemnity or other insurance. Joining an organisation such as ours, or one specific to your sector, may help you to get some good deals, as well as access to forums, events, support and even perhaps potential clients.

Be proactive

Think who your likely clients and customers will be – a lot of freelancers start off by working for people they have known and worked with in the past. But think, too, how you are going to chase up debts and late payers. You have to be very, very disciplined about financial control. If your invoice says payment within seven days and by the end of the seventh day it has not arrived you need to be sending out that email. It can be difficult, particularly if you are working for someone who is also a friend or who is a lucrative client, but you do have to keep on top of it.

Because you will be your own boss you do need to be self-motivated and a self-starter. It also helps if you are pretty adaptable and flexible and prepared all the time to look at your skills and your markets. Particularly in recessionary times it becomes much more important to be proactive and to be thinking about and searching out your next job all the time. Freelancing will not suit everyone, but it is something more and more people are looking at.

You may decide that, in the long run, it makes sense to appoint an accountant to handle your tax and accounting affairs or you may prefer to do it yourself through self-assessment, in which case you will need to fill it in by September 30 of the following tax year if you want HMRC to calculate your tax liability for you, or by January 31 (as well as paying it) if you are going the whole hog yourself.

If you go the accountant route, it's a good idea, if you can, to go to one that has been personally recommended to you, but even if they have been, it makes sense to quiz them on how much they know about freelancing and whether they have any other freelancers on their books. There may be good deals you can get if you decide to become a member of your industry guild or association, or a body such as the PCG – and in fact such bodies also often have a good record on deals for things such as insurance – but it is also worth weighing up whether you'll be wanting to go and see them in person, in which case it obviously needs to be someone local.

While many accountancy firms do now offer a range of 'add on' business advice services, they all add up. So for most freelancers, whether in a simple limited company, partnership or sole trader structure, what you're likely to want is end-of-year accounts and the peace of mind that, assuming the figures you have given are correct, all the Is have been dotted and Ts crossed.

Often people when they go freelance baulk at the potential cost – it will vary, but a good rule of thumb is probably between £80 and £150 a month plus VAT – but, given that for any freelancer time is most definitely money, you have to weigh this cost against the amount of time and hassle it is going to cost you if you decide to go down the self-assessment route. Ultimately it will probably come down to how confident you are in your own bookkeeping and accounting skills. The same time/work equation, incidentally, will probably come into play in terms of whether you decide to fork out to get someone professional to design your website, do your bookkeeping, mail-shots and so on, or you do it yourself.

Plan for your tax bill

How much tax you will pay, and whether it's corporation tax or income tax, will inevitably depend on the size of your business and its structure. But, and again it's only a rule of thumb, the PCG calculates that you should probably be looking to set aside between 25 per cent and 30 per cent of your gross income each month to cover your tax liabilities.

It is only too easy to forget about tax but, while you may effectively get a year's grace when you first start trading, in that you are always paying tax for the previous tax year, if you don't get into the habit of setting money aside from the off, ideally into a separate account, it can come up and bite you remarkably rapidly. Certainly, for me, setting aside money for tax was one of the hardest things to be disciplined about in the early years and I have found what works for me is effectively to 'write off' a number of jobs each month, which I then pretend don't exist and are firmly allocated as tax money. But everyone will have their own strategy for dealing with this.

It's also common sense to be bearing in mind any late payment issues for your sector. If you know money tends to take a couple of months to dribble through, and you know you are going to need to be paying a tax bill at the end of January, there's no point in allocating a wad of cash to the taxman in what you are invoicing in December as all you will end up doing is having an even more miserable and penniless January while you scrabble to get together the shortfall.

Ultimately, the best advice that I can give from experience here is don't hide from your tax affairs; if you plan for it, put money aside and are organised about getting your affairs in order, it shouldn't be a problem. And if you do find you're getting into problems with it, go and speak to an accountant and if necessary, don't be afraid to get advice from HM Revenue & Customs. HMRC's website **www.hmrc.gov.uk** also includes a lot of good general information about tax and self-assessment.

It's worth being aware of the potential pitfall of the classily titled IR35. This is a tax issue that can appear arcane but can get freelancers caught in it frothing at the mouth. It's hugely complex but essentially IR35 was introduced by HMRC in 2000 as a way to crack down on some tax avoidance schemes, with the effect of it being to penalise freelancers who did not meet its definition of 'self-employment', often those working via an intermediary such as a company or partnership and often solely for one client.

If the HMRC determines that the freelance would in effect be an 'employee' if they were contracted directly with the client, rather than using the intermediary, they can come under IR35 and end up paying higher National Insurance Contributions (NICs) and higher levels of tax. If you find yourself snarled up in this it is probably worth getting specialist accountancy advice and help to extricate yourself.

I appreciate you may be chewing the carpet by now but there are a couple of other key tax issues to bear in mind as a freelance: NICs and VAT. Self-employed people and those working as partnerships will generally pay two different types of NI, Class 2 and Class 4. Class 2 NI contributions in 2009/10 were set at a weekly rate of £2.40 and need to be paid either monthly to HMRC by direct debit or through a quarterly bill, unless your expected earnings have been below £5,075 in which case you can apply to be exempted. The other exceptions for Class 2 are those under 16, those over state pension age, married women or widows entitled to Class 1 NICs. Class 4 NICs are paid in addition to Class 2 NICs by self-employed people who make a profit above, in 2009/10, £5,715 and will be included within their self-assessment tax return. If you have become a limited company, you will generally be paying Class 1 NICs, both on your earnings as a director and the company itself as your 'employer'.

VAT

When it comes to VAT, the main thing to bear in mind as a freelance is that, even if you are a sole trader, if your turnover goes over £68,000 during a 12 month period you will need to become registered for VAT. In other words you will need to add 17.5 per cent (as the temporary reduction to 15 per cent imposed in December 2008 ended at the start of this year) to your bills. If you are a limited company and your turnover is below this you do not have to be VAT registered but you can voluntarily choose to be so.

It's also worth being aware that becoming VAT registered need not necessarily mean filling in onerous VAT returns and making payments every three months. While this is indeed the standard way of doing VAT, HMRC does offer a number of schemes aimed specifically at making being VAT registered easier for smaller businesses. In particular it may well be worth checking out its annual accounting scheme, which is open to all businesses with a turnover of less than £1.35m. This allows you to make nine interim payments a year (or three quarterly ones) and then complete one VAT return at the end of your year. At this point you either make a balancing payment or receive a balancing refund.

There is also what is called the 'cash accounting' scheme that allows firms not to pay VAT until a customer has paid, rather than having to do so irrespective. If your customer never pays, you never have to pay the VAT. Finally, there is the flat rate VAT scheme, for any business with a taxable turnover of less than £150,000. This works by allowing you to calculate your VAT payments as a percentage of your total (VAT inclusive) turnover. The downside is that you cannot reclaim VAT on any purchases you make but it also means you don't have to record the VAT you pay on those purchases either. You can get a discount on the flat rate you pay in your first year on the scheme. HMRC and organisations such as

BusinessLink both include detailed sections on their websites about all these issues.

Step away from the keyboard!

Finally, a brief word on working from home. As we have seen, this is something many freelancers do (and indeed is often one of the attractions of the freelance life), but is not without its pitfalls. Alongside issues around insurance and the mortgage (particularly if you are going to have people visiting the house or be storing stock on the premises), you need to think where in the house you are going to work and how you are going to shut work off from home and family life.

Balancing a laptop on the edge of the kitchen table may seem like a cheap option but it is unlikely to make for a quiet working environment. Similarly, setting up an 'office' in the corner of the bedroom is not going to work if you are constantly needing to work late and your partner can't sleep with the light on, or it means that your desk is the first thing you see when you wake up at the weekend. Being able to close the door on the office at night or at the weekend is also important if you are to get that valuable work-life balance that was probably one of the main reasons why you were tempted to go down the freelance route in the first place.

And then there are kids and pets to factor in. A barking dog or squalling toddler may be part and parcel of family life but it's unlikely to be something a potential client wants to hear down the phone or at a meeting. Home-working has become much more accepted over the years yet you still need to present a professional face to the world.

As PR Gay Turner cautions:

'When you are freelance or running a small company you are competing with everyone, including the big agencies, so you have to give clients the same level of service, or even better, than they would get from a big organisation.

'It's important to get yourself into work mode and maintain high personal as well as business standards when you operate from home. Personally, I have always believed in putting on smart clothes and make-up to put me in the right frame of mind to begin the day. You may in theory be able to shuffle down to your office in your pyjamas but you should never ever let that show to your clients – you never know when one might pop in unexpectedly. You need to be super professional and super efficient at all times,' she adds.

'For me the golden rule is that, even if you are juggling your work with the kids, you have to make sure the children cannot get near the computer, and don't let them answer your phone – make sure you have a work phone that is for work calls and work calls alone.

'While people are a lot more understanding about these things than they used to be, if you are a freelance you cannot afford to be making an important call with a crying child in the background or whatever it might be. You are being paid to do a good job, and that's what customers expect or they will just go somewhere else,' she continues.

Why do it?

Freelancing is, in many respects, as much an attitude to working as a way of working. When you are freelance it is you against the world but also you are the world, in that it is your career, you can choose who you work for and how and when you work and you call the shots – it is all about results and delivery. Yes, it can be a precarious and uncertain way to make a living, and not having a safety net can take some getting used to, but with that uncertainty also comes freedom, the freedom to take charge of your destiny, to have autonomy and control over your working day. It is probably not for the faint hearted or shy and retiring wallflowers but, if you can make it work for you, it can also be one of the quickest and easiest ways to turn around your career, as well as being an immensely satisfying and liberating way to live your life.

Key points

- Freelancing is an attitude to life and work as much as a way of working and is not something that everyone will be cut out for
- Most freelancers, at least at first, don't change what they're doing, they just change how they're doing it, and for whom, with networking and using contacts key
- Be prepared to go out and promote yourself, network, open up new income streams and markets and keep pushing all the time
- It's a good idea to have a financial buffer in place to tide you over until the cheques come in and to ride out the unexpected
- Keep on top of your financial affairs and credit control and don't ignore tax

CONCLUSION

The 9–5, Monday to Friday, clock-in, clock-out workplace is unlikely to disappear anytime soon. But, much as the arrival of the open-plan office from the 1970s onwards profoundly changed the way we worked and communicated, so it is possible to see the inexorable rise of the internet and mobile communications as, equally profoundly, changing where, how and for whom we work.

It is also possible to see the current recession as, if anything, accelerating this longer-term evolution, an evolution that is increasingly playing into the hands of career changers, or those of us who want to take greater control of our destiny, who want more from life than just one job in one place at one time.

The future will be agile

Let me explain. Even before the recession kicked in, the idea of coming into the same office every day, to the same desk and working with the same colleagues year in, year out was being questioned. We've all heard of hot-desking, where employers save space by having employees share workstations with others. This is still popular but what employers are increasingly talking about now is 'agility' in the workplace, no, not backflipping your way down to the coffee machine, but having workers who work in ever more flexible and collaborative ways.

So you might get teams coming together for specific projects and then breaking up, and more globalised working where teams or individuals work together for years yet never physically meet because they are on different continents. There may also be more 'knowledge-based' working, where it's not so much whether your bum is physically there on the seat in the office that matters, but the results you deliver.

In this scenario, it shouldn't matter if you've knocked off at 2pm to get back in time to pick up the kids from school because it's a given with your boss that you will pick up any outstanding work later on from your remote, probably laptop-based, workstation at home.

This is exactly the sort of future cutting-edge employers such as Microsoft already see, although it's arguable of course that, as providers of much of this sort of remote, wireless technology, it's in their interest to do so. Last year Microsoft published a range of crystal ball 'future work' scenarios, one of which, called 'freelance planet', argued that the workplace could in time become dominated by networks of largely freelance workers who would simply move around from employer to employer on a project-by-project basis.

Similarly, Jonathan Winter, founder of workplace consultancy Career Innovation, has argued in the *Guardian* that things such as people's internet reputation, or NetRep, will become much more important. Workers will increasingly become rated online for how they have worked, in a similar way to how buyers and sellers are currently rated for reliability and professionalism on sites such as eBay. We are already seeing organisations, such as the social enterprise Slivers of Time **www.sliversoftime.com**, which allows workers to 'sell' hours of their time to multiple employers, try to capitalise on this desire for greater flexibility and control in how and where we work.

Employers may even, in time, argues Winter, need to look at developing completely new models of employment, including possibly offering some sort of halfway house between employment and self-employment, so giving people the freedom to pursue multiple 'portfolio' careers and be more in charge of what they are doing, how and for whom, yet under the umbrella of a single, large employer.

As workplace 'futurologist' Ian Pearson also predicts:

'Companies will probably be smaller but backed up by a much wider network of people working on a freelance or consultant basis, perhaps on short-term contracts or simply on a project-by-project basis.'

Where the recession has come into play is that it has, inevitably, encouraged employers to look ever more closely at costs, so bringing to the fore the advantages of things such as video-conferencing rather than holding expensive face-to-face meetings. In some cases it has meant letting people work from home a few days a week to save on commuting or office space, going down to reduced hours and then working more intensively on the remaining days or considering whether it makes more financial sense to employ people on a freelance or contractual basis rather than on expensive permanent contracts.

At one point last year, for example, BT was encouraging staff to volunteer to work temporarily for other 'like-minded' companies in a bid to stave off redundancies. These trends are unlikely to reverse even when things pick up, argues Pearson.

'Offices will become much less places where you go to sit at a desk in front of a PC doing mundane jobs and more places where you simply go to meet other people, talk and make decisions,' he forecasts.

How this all benefits career changers is that this type of flexible, agile working lends itself more to people who are in control of their careers rather than those simply drifting passively from job to job. Clearly, freelancers and contractors could benefit from these trends if they come to pass.

But people who have simply thought about their career and what they want from life, thought about their skills and what they can offer, will almost inevitably also be more 'agile' in this workplace context. Similarly, the notion of having a portfolio or multiple career, of switching tack and changing direction regularly and of working into older age all become much more acceptable in this type of working environment. You are not so much what your title is or has been, but what you can deliver or bring to a workplace.

Take charge of your career, and your life

So, when we look back over this book, over the personal stories and the expert advice, what have we learned? The first thing is that changing your career can be a hugely rewarding, life-changing experience. Perhaps it's human nature, but not one of the career changers I spoke to had regretted the choices they had made and, indeed, they all relished the fact they had grabbed hold of their career with both hands and successfully moulded it much more into what they wanted.

But it is also abundantly clear that changing your career is not easy. You may have to give up your ambitions for material wealth and prosperity, at the very least temporarily and sometimes permanently. Your partner or family may have to play second fiddle for a while and they, even indirectly, will be required to change too. But what you can gain in return should probably more than make up for it. It also came through very clearly that there is no easy blueprint, no hard-and-fast, right-or-wrong answer to changing your career, whether it's switching to another industry or profession, gaining a new qualification, simply changing how or for whom you work or starting out in business as your own boss. Ultimately it's a case of what works, works.

However, the most important lesson, I would argue, and if you take away nothing else from this book please take away this, is that you can do it, that it is possible to achieve that *real* career you have always wanted, not the one you have somehow fallen into or which now has thrown you on the recession-fuelled redundancy bonfire. Yes, it may not happen overnight or all at once and, yes, it will probably take sacrifices and stubborn-mindedness to get there, but it can be done. There will always be a hundred reasons not to take that first step, to delay another year, to see out that project or just give that latest promotion a try.

Take that first step

Deep down, though, you know that's not the solution, so make that first 'what I want/don't want' list, hold that first setting-the-world-to-rights discussion or make that exploratory phone call or email and just see where it takes you. Reality TV celebrities love to witter on about 'their journey' but for once, in the context of career changing, it's a phrase with a ring of truth to it – career changing is almost always a journey; it may be a straight track from A to B or there may be branch lines, sidings, diversions or leaves on the line to negotiate along with the way. You may even end up at a completely different destination to where you thought you would be at the start. But without actually getting on with it and starting the process you will never know.

Finally, right back at the beginning of this book I wished you good luck. That still stands, of course. But when it comes to career changing, the words of legendary Hollywood producer Sam Goldwyn, when he said 'the harder I work, the luckier I get', pretty much sum it up.

When people see others who are passionate about their career and doing something every day that they love, they will often think or say 'How lucky you are'. It may well be that they just got lucky, but more often than not it is because they have worked bloody hard to get there, been absolutely focused and stuck with it, come what may.

So, yes, I wish you good luck in changing your career and reaching your destination. But more than that, I urge you to get out there and make your luck. You *can* do it.

USEFUL RESOURCES

Planning your career change

Good for general advice...
DirectGov
www.careersadvice.direct.gov.uk

Careers Scotland
www.careers-scotland.org.uk/home/home.asp

Monster
www.media.monster.com/uken/ebooks/ebook-careerchange.pdf

Good for job profiles...
Prospects
www.prospects.ac.uk

City & Guilds
www.cityandguilds.com/cps/rde/xchg/SID-5377A244-A1C389E7/cgonline/hs.xsl/18495.html

GradPlus
www.gradplus.com

Good for careers firms...
Association of Career Firms
www.acf-europe.org

International Coach Federation
www.coachfederation.org

Vocational retraining and adult learning

Good for general advice...
Directgov
www.direct.gov.uk/en/Education AndLearning/AdultLearning/index.htm

The Association of Colleges
www.aoc.co.uk

Lifelong Learning Networks
www.lifelonglearningnetworks.org.uk

The Qualifications and Curriculum Authority
www.qca.org.uk

National Institute of Adult Continuing Education
www.niace.org.uk

Connexions Direct
www.connexions-direct.com/index.cfm?pid=10

Scottish Credit and Qualifications Framework
www.scqf.org.uk

National Skills Academy
www.nationalskillsacademy.gov.uk

Learning and Skills Council
www.lsc.gov.uk/whatwedo/adultlearner

Train to Gain
www.traintogain.gov.uk

National Open Colleges Network
www.nocn.org.uk

The Alliance of Sector Skills Councils
www.sscalliance.org/

Good for foundation degrees...
Foundation Degree Forward
www.findfoundationdegree.co.uk

Good for access courses...
The Quality Assurance Agency for
Higher Education
www.accesstohe.ac.uk

Scottish Wider Access Programme
www.scottishwideraccess.org

Good for courses and providers...
City & Guilds
www.cityandguilds.com

learndirect
www.learndirect.co.uk
www.learndirectscotland.com

Workers Educational Association
(voluntary provider of adult
learning)
www.wea.org.uk

Higher education retraining/mature students

Good for general advice...
UCAS
**www.ucas.com/students/
maturestudents**

DirectGov
www.direct.gov.uk/maturestudents

Uniaid
www.uniaid.org.uk

The Open University
www.open.ac.uk

National Postgraduate Council
www.npc.org.uk

Good for careers advice...
C2 – The Graduate Careers Shop
(University of London Careers
Service)
www.c2careers.co.uk

Good for childcare advice...
The Daycare Trust
www.daycaretrust.org.uk

Good for students with disabilities...
Skill: the National Bureau for
Students with Disabilities
www.skill.org.uk

Access to Learning Fund
**www.direct.gov.uk/en/Education
AndLearning/UniversityAnd
HigherEducation/StudentFinance/
Extrahelp/DG_171615**

Student funding and finance

Good for general advice...
DirectGov
**www.direct.gov.uk/en/Education
AndLearning/UniversityAnd
HigherEducation/StudentFinance/
index.htm**

Student Finance England
**www.direct.gov.uk/en/Dl1/Director
ies/UsefulContactsByCategory/Edu
cationAndLearningContacts/DG_1
72310**

Student Finance Wales
www.studentfinancewales.co.uk

Student Finance Northern Ireland
www.studentfinanceni.co.uk

Student Awards Agency for
Scotland
www.student-support-saas.gov.uk

Individual Learning Accounts
Scotland
www.ilascotland.org.uk

Family Action
**www.family-action.org.uk/
section.aspx?id=1037**

Student Loans Company
www.slc.co.uk

Office for Fair Access
www.offa.org.uk

Learning & Skills Council
www.pcdl.lsc.gov.uk

National Union of Students
www.nus.org.uk/en/NUS-Extra/

Student Discounts
www.studentdiscounts.co.uk/

Research Councils UK
www.rcuk.ac.uk

Postgraduate Studentships
**www.postgraduatestudentships.
co.uk/**

Getting a job

Good for general advice...
Guardian Careers
www.careers.guardian.co.uk

Good for CVs...
Monster
**www.content.monster.co.uk/
section1921.asp**

Good for psychometric testing....
SHL
www.shldirect.com

Good for tackling ageism...
The Third Age and Employment
Network
www.taen.org.uk

The Employers Forum on Age
www.efa.org.uk

Starting out in business

Good for general advice...
BusinessLink
www.businesslink.gov.uk

Federation of Small Businesses
www.fsb.org.uk

Forum of Private Business
www.fpb.org

Confederation of British Industry
www.cbi.org.uk

British Chambers of Commerce
www.britishchambers.org.uk

Department for Business,
Enterprise and Regulatory Reform
www.berr.gov.uk

HMRC
www.hmrc.gov.uk

DirectGov
**www.direct.gov.uk/en/Pensionsand
retirementplanning/Working/
WorkingToSuitYou/DG_10027003**

Companies House
www.companieshouse.gov.uk

Institute of Chartered Accountants
in England and Wales
www.icaewfirms.co.uk

Association of Chartered Certified
Accountants
www.accaglobal.com

Chartered Institute of
Managament Accountants
www.cimaglobal.com

Institute of Chartered Accountants
of Scotland
www.icas.org.uk/directory

Startups
www.startups.co.uk
Newbusiness.co.uk
www.newbusiness.co.uk

Scottish Family Business
Association
www.sfba.co.uk

British Business Angels Association
www.bbaa.org.uk

British Venture Capital Association
www.bvca.co.uk

*Good for women and ethnic minorities in
business...*
Women in Business Network
www.wibn.co.uk

Prowess
www.prowess.org.uk

Opportunity Now
www.opportunitynow.org.uk

Women's Enterprise Ambassador
Network
**www.womensenterprisetaskforce.
co.uk/ambassadors.html**

Association of Scottish
Businesswomen
www.scottishbusinesswomen.com

Women in Business
www.womeninbusinessni.com

Ethnic Minority Business Task
Force
www.embtf.org.uk

Make Your Mark
www.enterpriseuk.org

DiversityNow
www.diversitynow.net

Good for older business owners...
Prime
www.primeinitiative.co.uk

Good for disabled business owners...
Employers Forum on Disability
www.efd.org.uk

Ready to Start
www.readytostart.org.uk

Business Ability network
www.businessability.co.uk

AbilityNet
www.abilitynet.org.uk

Franchising

Good for general advice...
British Franchise Association
www.thebfa.org

Whichfranchise
www.whichfranchise.com

Start-ups
**www.startups.co.uk/667884290914
5602420/start-a-franchise.html**

The Franchise Magazine
www.thefranchisemagazine.net

Freelancing

Good for general advice...
The Professional Contractors Group
www.pcg.co.uk/cms/index.php

Freelance.co.uk
**www.freelanceuk.com/become/is_
freelancing_for_me.shtml**

ACKNOWLEDGEMENTS

My thanks go to each and every case study who spared me their valuable time to pass on knowledge, experiences and advice. Their stories were truly inspirational.

Journalists too rarely acknowledge them, but there were also many press and PR people who greatly assisted in the researching of this book. In particular I would like to thank Carolyn Walker and Jennie Hudson at Blue Rubicon, Gay Turner at GTPR and Nicola Hunt at NHPR for their efforts in tracking down and sourcing so many of the people I needed to speak to.

My editor at Guardian Books, Helen Brooks, deserves many thanks for her patience, wise counsel and constructive comments and, of course, for agreeing in the first place that this was a book that needed to be written at this time. Similarly, my appreciation goes out to Vanessa Neuling for her invaluable copy-editing improvements.

Finally, for all her valuable advice and proofreading, and simply for being the wonderful person she is, to my wife Eliza – thank you.